W9-BHD-965

FLORIDA STATE
UNIVERSITY LIBRARIES

FEB 3 1994

TALLAHASSEE, FLORIDA

Africa's Ecology

Africa's Ecology

*Sustaining the Biological
and Environmental
Diversity of a Continent*

by
Valentine Udoh James

McFarland & Company, Inc., Publishers
Jefferson, North Carolina, and London

HC
800
Z65
J348
1993

British Library Cataloguing-in-Publication data are available

Library of Congress Cataloguing-in-Publication Data

James, Valentine Udoh, 1952–
    Africa's ecology : sustaining the biological and environmental
diversity of a continent / by Valentine Udoh James.
        p.   cm.
    Includes bibliographical references and index.
    ISBN 0-89950-859-6 (lib. bdg. : 50# alk. paper)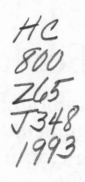
    1. Natural resources – Africa – Management.   2. Africa –
Environmental conditions.   3. Sustainable development – Africa.
4. Biological diversity conservation – Africa.   I. Title.
HC800.Z65J348   1993
333.7'096 – dc20   92-56654
                                                                              CIP

©1993 James Udoh Valentine. All rights reserved

Manufactured in the United States of America

McFarland & Company, Inc., Publishers
    Box 611, Jefferson, North Carolina 28640

To my father, Mr. Samuel James Inyang,
who instilled in me the spirit of
endurance, tenacity, and perseverance

Acknowledgments

In order to write a book of this type which required extensive travel from my academic home, the University of Virginia, personal and family sacrifices took place. My family's support was paramount in the data collection in Africa. The period of time away from Melanie, Marshall, and Jonathan was painful, but the reward of having completed this book makes it worth all the trouble.

I must rightfully place Melanie's effort in encouraging me and assisting with this work as the most crucial. As always, she listened and made suggestions and above all gave me the emotional support that is indispensable in coping with the pressures of being a scholar and an educator.

Many thanks to Dr. Christine Schonewald-Cox for her continued support and encouragement. Many times, our telephone conversations began and ended with subject matter related to this book. Her expertise in park management and conservation issues proved insightful and germane to ideas raised in this book.

A couple of years ago, I joined the faculty of Urban and Environmental Planning at the University of Virginia's School of Architecture. This book began because professors William Harris and David Phillips, both on the faculty at UVA, made my transition to the University of Virginia smooth and comfortable for me. They answered my innumerable questions without feeling disturbed and gave me several ideas on how to balance research with the teaching load at UVA. To them I give my highest gratitude. Special thanks also to my UVA graduate and undergraduate students for providing the excellent stimulating classroom experience which enabled integration of teaching, research, and writing.

The sources of inspiration for writing are varied. For me the inspiration often crystallized during and after long conversations and intellectual arguments with colleagues and friends. I have made many friends in Africa, and most of them would like to remain anonymous. To them I owe a deep sense of appreciation, and I will always look forward to the stimulating dialogues when I visit Africa.

— *Valentine Udoh James, January 1993*

Table of Contents

Acknowledgments   *vii*

Illustrations
  Figures   *xi*
  Tables   *xvi*

Abbreviations   *xix*

Preface   *xxi*

Introduction: Sustaining Africa's Diversity   *1*

Part I : The Status of
the African Environment

1 Africa's Parks and Reserves   *21*

2 Housing Conditions in Rural Africa:
   A Case Study of Ikot-Ekpene, Nigeria   *53*

3 Issues of Tourism Development in Africa   *72*

4 Agriculture: Commercial and Subsistence   *94*

5 The African Forest   *126*

6 The Savannas of Africa   *152*

7 The Desert of Africa   *170*

8 Impact on Water and Soil Resources   *183*

Part II : International and Domestic
Policies for Developing Africa's Resources

9 Past, Present, and Future Activities:
   Efforts and Consequences   *213*

10 Women's Contribution to the Preservation
     of Africa's Resources   235
11 Conclusions and Recommendations
     for Planning and Management   259

     Appendix: Survey Instrument   273
     Bibliography   279
     Index   287

Illustrations

FIGURES

0.1:   Pastoralism in Lagos-Badagry, Nigeria, 1991.   2
0.2:   Mulch prepared for fertilizing the soil, Lagos, Nigeria, 1991.   2
0.3:   Vegetable production in Lagos, Nigeria, 1991.   3
0.4:   Row planting in Lagos, Nigeria, 1991.   3
0.5:   Hole dug to store water for agriculture.   4
0.6:   Small-scale farming. Farmer watering his crops, Lagos,
       Nigeria, 1991.   4
0.7:   Typical traditional house in the southeastern region
       of Nigeria, 1991.   5
0.8:   Clearing the bush for human shelter, Ikot-Ekpene,
       Nigeria, 1991.   7
0.9:   Construction site for a modern house, Ikot-Ekpene,
       Nigeria, 1991.   7
0.10: Traffic congestion, Lagos, Nigeria, 1991.   13
0.11: Flooding during the rainy season resulting in traffic
       hazards, Lagos, Nigeria, 1991.   13
1.1:   Some African biosphere reserves.   22
1.2:   The parks and reserves of Kenya. Source: Williams, 1967.   28
1.3:   The parks and reserves of Tanzania. Source: Williams, 1967.   29
1.4:   The parks and reserves of Uganda. Source: Williams, 1967.   30
1.5:   An elephant at "Marine World/Africa USA," Vallejo,
       California, 1987.   37
1.6:   Giraffes at "Marine World/Africa USA," Vallejo, California,
       1987.   38
1.7:   Quarry facing erosion problems, Onitsha, Nigeria, 1989.   39
1.8:   Erosion conquering a quarry site, Onitsha, Nigeria, 1989.   39
1.9:   Vicarage of St. Thomas Anglican Church, Badagry,
       Nigeria, 1989.   41

xi

1.10:   Vicarage of St. Thomas Anglican Church and Nigerian
        tourists, Badagry, Nigeria, 1989.   41

1.11:   An American tourist inspecting the first two-story
        building in Badagry, Nigeria, 1989.   42

1.12:   Young cultural dancers, Ikot-Ekpene, Nigeria, 1989.   42

1.13:   Traditional houses, Badagry Beach, Nigeria, 1989.   43

1.14:   Masqueraders, Ikot-Ekpene, Nigeria, 1989.   44

1.15:   Parrots at a local zoo, Port-Harcourt, Nigeria, 1989.   44

1.16:   A leopard at a local zoo, Port-Harcourt, Nigeria, 1989.   45

1.17:   Nigerian couple enjoying a Sunday afternoon, Lagos
        Bar Beach, 1989.   45

1.18:   Nigerian children posing for tourist photos while at play,
        Badagry, Nigeria, 1989.   46

1.19:   Foreign tourist enjoying the beach, Lekki Beach, Nigeria, 1991. 46

1.20:   Fish farm and tourist centre, Ikot-Obong, Nigeria, 1991.   47

1.21:   Vultures in natural habitat, Eket, Nigeria, 1991.   48

1.22:   Mary Slessor's burial site, Itu, Nigeria, 1991.   48

1.23:   Murtala Mohammed Airport, Ikeja, Nigeria, 1991.   49

1.24:   Lagos Port, Nigeria, 1991.   49

1.25:   Lagos Island business center, Nigeria, 1991.   50

2.1:   Map of study area in Nigeria.   55

2.2:   Road network map of Ikot-Ekpene.   56

2.3:   Oil palm production farm.   57

2.4:   Clearing land for housing.   57

2.5:   Road leading to settlements.   58

2.6:   A property owner in his garden.   59

2.7:   Property owner describing the different fruits and crops in
        his compound.   60

2.8:   Traditional house.   61

2.9:   Property owner weaving the roof of his home.   62

2.10:   Children watching their skillful father weaving the
        palm fronds.   62

2.11:   Informal building to the left.   63

2.12:   Finished cinder blocks, ready for building and remodeling.   65

2.13:   Blocks are used for constructing a wall around a compound.   65

2.14:   Completed modern building.   66

2.15:   Village building.   66

3.1:   Privately managed transportation depot, Benin City,
        Nigeria, 1991.   74

3.2: Travelers emerging from transportation depot restaurant, Benin City, Nigeria, 1991. 74

3.3: A proud owner/driver of a canoe, 1991. 75

3.4: A foreign passenger being taken across the "Cross River" in Itu, Akwa Ibom state, 1991. 75

3.5: Itu dock for embarkment and disembarkment of passengers, 1991. 76

3.6: Bar Beach, Lagos, Nigeria, 1991. 76

3.7: Foreign tourists at Lekki Beach, Victoria Island, Nigeria, 1991. 77

3.8: Local citizens spending their weekend at Lekki Beach, Nigeria, 1991. 77

3.9: Local citizens preparing barbecue for sale to visitors at Lekki Beach, Nigeria, 1991. 78

3.10: Religious activities at Lekki Beach, Nigeria, 1991. 78

3.11: Traditional wood carvings for sale to visitors, Lekki Beach, Nigeria, 1991. 79

3.12: Transportation taxi for visitors at Lekki Beach, Nigeria, 1991. 79

3.13: Metropolitan Hotel, Calabar, Nigeria, 1991. 80

3.14: Qwa River Hotel, Eket, Nigeria, 1991. 81

3.15: Mobil Pegasus Club, Eket, Nigeria, 1991, housing for Mobil Oil Company guests. 81

3.16: Aesthetically pleasing Mobil Pegasus compound. 82

3.17: Tourist Plaza, Calabar, Nigeria, 1991. 82

3.18: Cultural Center, Lagos, Nigeria, 1991. 83

3.19: Slave Port, Badagry, Nigeria, 1991. 83

3.20: Rural nature expedition, Ikot Obong, Nigeria, 1991. 84

3.21: Local children at Badagry Beach, Nigeria, act as guides for tourists, 1991. 91

4.1: Population growth rates. 99

4.2: Erosion destroying an access road and damaging surrounding land, Ikot-Ekpene, Nigeria, 1991. 107

4.3: Subsistence farmlands threatened by erosion due to road construction, Ikot-Ekpene, Nigeria, 1991. 108

4.4: Clearance of forest by humans causing erosion in Ikot-Obong, Nigeria, 1991. 108

4.5: Typical soil profile. 109

4.6: The formation process of sheet and gully erosion. 110

4.7: Bush fallow (shifting cultivation) of plantain, banana, cocoyams, and oil palm, Ikot-Ekpene, Nigeria, 1991. 114

4.8:   Rudimentary sedentary agriculture (shifting cultivation) in which tree crops and goats are raised, Ikeja, Nigeria, 1991.   *114*

4.9:   Compound farming, intensive subsistence agriculture (shifting agriculture), Eket, Nigeria, 1991.   *115*

4.10: Compound farming, Ikeja, Nigeria, 1991.   *115*

4.11: Flood-land agriculture, maize, Itu, Nigeria, 1991.   *116*

4.12: Real commodity prices.   *119*

4.13: Subsistence farmers conducting daily business, Itu, Nigeria, 1991.   *123*

4.14: Community subsistence farmlands in the background, Itu, Nigeria, 1991.   *123*

5.1:   The forest in Akwa Ibom state, Nigeria, 1991.   *127*

5.2:   The impact of bridge construction on the forest, Itu, Nigeria, 1991.   *127*

5.3:   Unpaved roads in the forest cause environmental problems, Ikot-Obong, Nigeria, 1991.   *128*

5.4:   The establishment of rural business necessitates forest clearance, Ikot-Ekpene, Nigeria, 1991.   *128*

5.5:   Village center, Ikot-Ekpene, Nigeria, 1991.   *129*

5.6:   Village elementary school, Ikot-Ekpene, Nigeria, 1991.   *129*

5.7:   Forest burning and clearance for industries and roads, Ogbomosho, Nigeria, 1991.   *132*

5.8:   Cultivated habitat, Lagos-Badagry Road, Nigeria, 1991.   *132*

5.9:   Deforestation in Africa.   *134*

5.10: Nigeria's net trade in forest products (sawnwood + panel + pulp + paper).   *138*

5.11: A study of the public's awareness of soil, water, and natural resource problems in Nigeria.   *139*

5.12: Fishing industry is threatened by offshore exploration, Eket, Nigeria, 1991.   *145*

5.13: Urbanization threatens quality of water and fish, Eket, Nigeria, 1991.   *145*

5.14: The Nigeria environmental problem.   *146*

6.1:   Schematic diagram of savanna formation.   *153*

6.2:   Savanna vegetation, western Nigeria, 1991.   *154*

6.3:   Burning in a savanna region of western Nigeria, 1991.   *154*

6.4:   The biogeographical map of Africa.   *156*

6.5:   Africa's natural vegetation.   *157*

6.6:   Cattle grazing in western Nigeria, guinea savanna woodland.   *159*

7.1:   Africa's vegetation zones.   *171*

8.1: Rivers and lakes of Africa. *194*

8.2: Major dams of Africa. *195*

8.3: Project impact matrix. *197*

8.4: Bridge linking villages to water source, Calabar River, Nigeria, 1991. *202*

8.5: Modern water supply facility, Ikot-Ekpene, Nigeria, 1991. *204*

8.6: Drums of water for domestic use, Ikot-Ekpene, Nigeria, 1991. *204*

8.7: Tank containing water for sale, Orile, Iganmu, Nigeria, 1991. *205*

8.8: Well water in an urban area, Orile, Iganmu, Nigeria, 1991. *206*

8.9: Young boys and girls fetching water from neighbors, Ikot-Ekpene, Nigeria, 1991. *207*

8.10: Schematic flow diagram of environmental impact assessment. *208*

9.1: Residents of Orile, Iganmu, Nigeria, display a snake killed. *215*

9.2: The rivers provide fish for inhabitants of Ibuno, Nigeria, 1991. *215*

9.3: The division of Africa, 1885. *218*

10.1: Young girls returning home with buckets of water, Uyo, Nigeria, 1991. *236*

10.2: Woman farmer going to her farm, Ikot-Ekpene, Nigeria, 1991. *236*

10.3: Young mother and child, Eket, Nigeria, 1991. *237*

10.4: Women traders, Lagos, Nigeria, 1991. *237*

10.5: Young hawker of goods, Orile, Nigeria, 1991. *238*

10.6: Club manager with "middle-class" friends, Eket, Nigeria, 1991. *238*

10.7: Females in total school enrollment (1988, %). *239*

10.8: Young Nigerian secondary-school students, Uyo, Nigeria, 1991. *240*

10.9: Women in agriculture (% share of economically active women, 1980). *241*

10.10: Nigerian women, educator and nurse, with a male engineer, Benin City, Nigeria, 1991. *251*

10.11: Nigerian woman enjoys the calmness of Lekki Beach, Nigeria, 1991. *251*

11.1: Shanty development, Lagos suburb, Nigeria, 1989. *261*

11.2: Shanty housing and business establishments, Lagos suburb, Nigeria, 1989. *261*

11.3:   Scattered public housing, Lagos, Nigeria, 1991.   262
11.4:   Poorly planned housing development, Lagos, Nigeria, 1991.   262
11.5:   Modern public high-rise building, Victoria Island,
        Nigeria, 1991.   263

TABLES

0.1:   Projects with Environmental Components Approved in
       Fiscal 1990   15
0.2:   Expenditures by Bank Environmental Units in Fiscal 1990   16
1.1:   Percentage of Land Area in Park Land   25
1.2:   The National Parks and Game Reserves of East Africa   27
1.3:   Estimates of Forest Areas and Deforestation Rates
       in the Tropics   32
1.4:   African Countries with the Highest Numbers of Species
       for Selected Organisms   36
2.1:   Comparison of Ratings of Housing Attributes in Ikot-Ekpene   69
3.1:   Growth of Tourist Arrivals in Zambia   89
3.2:   Tourist Arrivals in Zambia   90
3.3:   Comparative Data on International Tourism in
       Selected Developing Countries, 1970   91
3.4:   Tourism Financing by the International Finance Corporation   92
3.5:   Commitments for Tourism Projects under World Bank
       Loans to Development Finance Companies   92
4.1:   Agriculture and Food Situations of African Countries   96
4.2:   Africa: Environment and Development Indicators
       (per capita)   100
4.3:   Urbanization in African Countries   104
4.4:   Food Aid Requirements, 1991   106
4.5:   Prevailing Systems of Agriculture on Small Farms,
       Main Regions of Use, Major Crops and Animal Species,
       and Food Sources for Animals in Africa   112
4.6:   Shifting Cultivation in Some African Countries   117
4.7:   Relationships between Livestock Production and Crop
       Production in Africa   121
4.8:   Pastoral and Agro-pastoral Communities in Tropical Africa   122
5.1:   Wildlife Habitat Loss in Africa South of the Sahara   131
5.2:   Household Energy Consumption   135
5.3:   Household Energy Consumption for Selected Countries
       (1980)   136

5.4:	Health and Nutrition	140
5.5:	Nigerian Population Census Figures	143
5.6:	Awareness of the Seriousness of Ecological Problems of Soil, Water, and Natural Resources in Nigeria	149
5.7:	Adequacy and Appropriateness of Ecological Services for Soil, Water, and Natural Resources in Nigeria	150
6.1:	Development of International Tourist Arrivals and Receipts in Africa (1980–89)	167
6.2:	International Tourism Receipts and Exports (1984 and 1988) in Africa	168
8.1:	Population Growth and Projections of African Countries	185
8.2:	Water Resources of African Countries	186
8.3:	1980 Expected Levels of Service (Populations in Thousands and %)	188
8.4:	Decade Targets for Urban Water Supply and Sanitation	190
8.5:	Decade Targets for Rural Water Supply and Sanitation	191
8.6:	African Scholars' Ranking of Water Supply Constraints	192
8.7:	World Bank Lending in Rural Water Supply and Sanitation: Total Lending and Percentage of Project Lending, 1974–85	193
8.8:	Assessment Parameters	198
9.1:	Structure of Manufacturing	224
9.2:	Manufacturing Earnings and Output	226
9.3:	Growth of Consumption and Investment	228
9.4:	U.S. Biodiversity Investments per 1000 Hectares in Africa in 1989	232
10.1:	African Women in Development	246
10.2a:	Forests, Protected Areas, and Water	248
10.2b:	Forests, Protected Areas, and Water	249
10.3:	Elephant Numbers: Regions and Selected Countries	257
11.1:	African Countries by Region	270

Abbreviations

ADC	Andean Development Corporation
ADRA	Adventist Development and Relief Agency International
AED	Academy for Educational Development, International Division
AsDB	Asian Development Bank
ASEAN	Association of Southeast Asian Nations
AWF	African Wildlife Foundation
CARIFTA	Caribbean Free Trade Association
CITES	Convention on International Trade in Endangered Species
DAC	Development Assistance Committee (of OECD)
ECA	Economic Commission for Africa
ECE	Economic Commission for Europe
ECLA	Economic Commission for Latin America
ECOWAS	Economic Community of West African States
EDF	European Development Fund
EEC	European Economic Community
EFTA	European Free Trade Association
ESCAP	Economic and Social Commission for Asia and the Pacific
FAO	United Nations Food and Agricultural Organization
GATT	General Agreement on Tariffs and Trade
GDP	gross domestic product
GNP	gross national product
IBRD	International Bank for Reconstruction and Development (World Bank)
ICSU	International Council of Scientific Unions
IDA	International Development Association

IDB   Inter-American Development Bank
IFAD   International Fund and Agricultural Development
IFC   International Finance Corporation
IIEP   International Institute for Educational Planning
IITA   International Institute of Tropical Agriculture
ILO   International Labor Organization
IMF   International Monetary Fund
ITTO   International Tropical Timber Organization
IUCN   International Union for the Conservation of Nature and
            Natural Resources
LAFTA   Latin American Free Trade Association
MAB   Man and the Biosphere Program
NAN   News Agency of Nigeria
NRCT   Natural Resources Conservation Trust
ODA   Official Development Assistance
OECD   Organization for Economic Co-operation and
            Development
OPEC   Organization of Petroleum Exporting Countries
PVO   Private Voluntary Organization
SCOPE   Scientific Committee on Problems of the Environment
SEGC   Station D'etude Des Gorillas et Chimpanzees
UNCTAD   United Nations Conference on Trade and Development
UNDP   United Nations Development Programme
UNEP   United Nations Environmental Programme
UNESCO   United Nations Education, Scientific, and Cultural
            Organization
UNHCR   Office of the United Nations High Commissioner for
            Refugees
UNICEF   United Nations Children's Education Fund
UNIDO   United Nations Industrial Development Organization
UNITAR   United Nations Institute for Training and Research
UNPAAERD   United Nations Program of Action for African
            Economic Recovery and Development
WCED   World Commission on Environment and Development
WFP   World Food Program
WHO   World Health Organization
WRI   World Resources Institute
WWF   World Wildlife Fund

Preface

> Over the last few decades large numbers of people in the
> Western industrialized nations have become conscious of an ap-
> proaching global ecological crisis. One manifestation of this
> developing awareness has been a growing interest in the en-
> vironmental problems of Africa, where human and animal life,
> soils and vegetation seem to be vulnerable as never before. The
> Western media, especially television with its use of stark and
> compelling images, have helped to focus public attention, thus
> linking Africa's predicament to the mainstream of European and
> North American concerns [MacGregor 1989:201].

This book concerns itself with the environmental and ecological problems of Africa and follows in the footsteps of work that has already been
done to highlight the problems of the "Garden of Eden" — Africa. While the
purpose of this book is academic in perspective, the author endeavors to
incorporate an applied perspective into some of the chapters.

For decades, the rest of the world has envisaged Africa as a continent
which provides spectacular wildlife, sceneries, and experiences to those
who visit it. Conservationists and environmentalists have for several years
thought that in order to protect the wildlife of Africa and its environment,
only technical issues needed to be seriously considered.

The social and cultural aspects of Africa, however, play significant
roles in the survival of wildlife in the continent and should be recognized
when preservation and conservation strategies are being considered in the
development of resources.

Many of the problems discussed in this book could be resolved by
recognizing that environmental management problems in Africa are technical as well as institutional and organizational in nature. This book
stresses the significant role of and need for proper and adequate institutions and organizations in remedying the decline of the African environment.

Introduction: Sustaining Africa's Diversity

In the wake of global recession, Africa finds itself in a very difficult situation because the prices of the agricultural commodities and the prices of the minerals useful to the industrialized world have plummeted. Market forces have made economic development an odious task. Alongside the global recession is the fact that the populations of major African urban centers are increasing at alarming rates due to increased birth rate and rural-urban migration (James 1991 a,b). The rural environments are also showing signs of decline. These have a negative impact on natural resources (ecological systems, flora and fauna). There is an immediate need for the basic necessities of life—food, shelter, clothing, and energy. In the past, when population was sparse in Africa, the hunter-gatherer societies lived in harmony with the environment. But with the emergence of large communities, it has been necessary to establish agricultural lands, which means clearing land for slash-and-burn cultivation or shifting cultivation. These efforts have rendered many parts of the savannas and forests hopeless because of the deforestation and desertification that have emerged.

Growing crops for cash as well as subsistence consumption has caused a decline in the environmental quality of Africa (Figures 0.1–0.6).

Shelter problems in the developing countries seem to be increasing year after year. Many African governments have not been able to meet housing demands, and the private sector has not been able to provide enough housing for the public (James 1989). Hence, in many parts of Africa, traditional housing is still predominant in the rural areas (Figure 0.7). Traditional houses are built of raw materials which can be found locally. Again, problems arise because there is an increasing number of people who are dependent on the raw materials such as palm fronds for roofing the huts. The demand for these resources has exceeded their carrying capacity, and forest regeneration cannot keep pace with the demand.

The problem of environmental degradation in Africa, as in many other places in the world, poses an enormous threat to economic, industrial,

1

Figure 0.1: Pastoralism in Lagos-Badagry, Nigeria, 1991.

Figure 0.2: Mulch prepared for fertilizing the soil, Lagos, Nigeria, 1991.

Figure 0.3: Vegetable production in Lagos, Nigeria, 1991.

Figure 0.4: Row planting in Lagos, Nigeria, 1991.

Figure 0.5: Hole dug to store water for agriculture.

Figure 0.6: Small-scale farming. Farmer watering his crops, Lagos, Nigeria, 1991.

Figure 0.7: Typical traditional house in the southeastern region of Nigeria, 1991.

and social development. The discussions in this book present the reader with the argument that immediate and sound environmental management practices are fundamental to Africa's successful development in all spheres of economic, social, agricultural, and industrial endeavors.

The environmental issues presented in this book cover six broad problem areas: (1) the destruction of wildlife; (2) the declining quality and quantity of natural habitats; (3) pollution in urban and rural areas of Africa; (4) contamination of fresh water; (5) land degradation; and (6) human shelter.

Natural resource depletion in Africa is occurring at an alarming rate and has to be checked at all costs. Of 56 tropical countries that have been reported as suffering from severe deforestation problems, 28 are African (James 1991a). Africa's environmental problems occur as a result of many overlapping problems. Consequently, a systems approach is necessary to curb the problem. James (1991b) contends that the environmental problems in the emerging nations of the world are partially due to population pressures, the use of inappropriate Western technologies, low environmental consciousness among the government officials, and the growing African debt crisis.

It is clear to the international community that less-developed countries cannot embark on the preservation and conservation of their renewable natural resources alone. The assistance of advanced nations, such as the United States, is very important. Hence, there is a need to translate international goals into African goals. With some encouragement these goals could be transmitted from the national level to the local farmers who play the most pivotal role in the processes that may maintain or reduce biological diversity and preserve the natural environment.

Agricultural projects, just as every development project in Africa that incorporates modern techniques, have merits and demerits that must be evaluated. In an attempt to meet agricultural demands, African farmers are using fertilizers and chemical-based pesticides. Unfortunately, the fertilizers and pesticides contaminate the air, water, and food.

In developed countries, environmental groups exert pressure on industries and governments to ban the use of materials that harm people and the environment. The legislature responds to the will of the people and powerful interest groups that lobby for environmental protection. In many developing nations this type of mechanism is virtually absent, and chemical-based substances are still being imported by developing countries for agricultural purposes. Although these substances increase food production, they cause health problems which in the long run tax the limited health services and damage the environment of Third World countries.

In the last two decades, agricultural production in Africa has not kept pace with the exponential increase in population. In order to reverse this trend many African countries embarked on a "green revolution." The green revolution was meant to intensify and extensify farming systems, and it is responsible for the increased use of chemically based pesticides, herbicides, and fungicides.

Multinationals engaged in the production of insecticides should take into consideration the impact of the chemicals on the environment of Third World countries. Also, powerful synthetic pesticides should be used with great care, planning, and monitoring. Cultural, mechanical, and biological methods should be fully explored before embarking on the use of chemically based substances.

Figures 0.8 and 0.9 show the process of clearing the bush and cutting down trees in order to build modern housing. Clearing, as shown in the pictures, occurs in the rain forest region of Nigeria. The forest regions of Africa are declining at a very rapid pace. The palm trees that used to be on the piece of land shown in the illustrations have been felled to make room for a modern, Western-style, five-bedroom building. In Africa, the forests are being cleared in order to make room for settlement, agriculture, and other infrastructures.

Africa's population is growing rapidly, and alongside of this phenomenon is the change in taste of young, affluent Africans. Middle-

Figure 0.8: Clearing the bush for human shelter, Ikot-Ekpene, Nigeria, 1991.

Figure 0.9: Construction site for a modern house, Ikot-Ekpene, Nigeria, 1991.

class Nigerians have acquired Western tastes because they do not only want to improve their standard of living, but also because the African economy is now intricately linked with Western economy. The question that confronts those concerned with Africa's future is whether the environment has to suffer as a result of development and modernization.

Certainly the answer is no. Hence, the reader will find in the chapters that follow a detailed accounting of species loss and ecological calamity and strategies for future action in conservation and preservation.

Thirty years ago, the environmental problems in Africa were negligible. The demand on Africa's natural resources was not as much, and Africa's population did not exceed the carrying capacity of its resources. In the eighties and nineties, however, Africa's population has increased enormously. For instance, the United Nations in 1991 estimated that Nigeria's population will double (from 100 million to 200 million) in twenty years. Such an increase in population is bound to bring tremendous environmental and ecological problems to the country if proper planning is not embarked upon as quickly as possible (Radio Nigeria 1991).

In Africa bush burning is problematic. It has been reported that in many northern states of Nigeria, traditional rulers have expressed concern over the alarming rate at which bush burning is carried out (Radio Nigeria 1991). Deforestation is occurring at a very rapid pace in Africa. This is of utmost concern to the governments and international communities and organizations, especially the World Bank and the United Nations.

Since in this book an attempt is made to establish cause-and-effect relationships in environmental problems and to examine the socioeconomic impact of environmental degradation, it is deemed appropriate to highlight the wide range of parameters or factors which exacerbate environmental degradation in Africa. Certainly these factors include, but are not limited to, economic depression, unsustainable use of resources, and inadequate institutional capability to deal with environmental problems.

It is generally accepted that one of the most important factors that contribute to environmental problems in Africa is the lack of economic diversity (James 1991a). African countries currently owe international private lending institutions and foreign governments hundreds of billions of dollars. The governments of the African countries seem to have more commitment to economic development than to protecting the environment.

African countries like many other developing countries have not been able to make much progress in paying back their loans. Some have had to reschedule their loans because they could not pay the interest. Because developing countries are confronted with the overwhelming problems of overpopulation, poverty, and debt, it is almost impossible for them to enforce their environmental ordinances or laws to stop forest slash-and-burn practices for farming, grazing, lumbering, and nonrenewable resource extraction. One such case occurs in the Rivers state and Akwa Ibom state of Nigeria where oil companies do not obey environmental laws and the federal government does very little to ensure the enforcement of the environmental laws. Ayeni (1991:750) contends that the Nigerian environment has been seriously degraded as a result of industrialization:

> Apart from the environmental hazards of soil erosion due largely to over-grazing, bush-burning and indiscriminate tree felling for domestic cooking, industrial hazards, due to pollution of the environment are long over-due for prompt government attention. Tales of paralysed social and economic lives due to oil spillage are as old as the history of oil exploration in Nigeria. In Bendel, Rivers, Cross River, and Akwa Ibom which are mainly oil producing states, farmers often suffer irreparable damages after every oil pipe blowout while fishermen live in perpetual dread of the oil slick. In Iko village in Akwa Ibom State, the plight of villagers was amplified by a representative who said: "The discovery of oil in our village has caused great damage; our water has been polluted and rendered undrinkable while fishing, our main occupation and source of income is no more." Some of them perpetually complain that the oil companies "took over their farmlands and paid compensation only for the crops on them and not for the land acquired." However, sources from some oil industries claim that oil producing areas are adequately catered for.

The foreign oil companies are desperately needed by the African government due to the former's ability to provide the needed revenue for the government. Because African countries are in debt to foreign banks and governments, all efforts are made to increase the exploitation of natural resources and agricultural lands. The net result is that under such intensified and extensified production, marginal lands are developed and the countries' soils are degraded, environmental pollution emanates, and of course the long-term ramifications far outweigh the short-term economic gains. Côte d'Ivoire, Ghana, Senegal, Nigeria, Ethiopia, and Kenya are examples of countries where debt and need for export earning have exacerbated deforestation and environmental degradation. Africa's environmental crisis is best summarized in the September 1991 issue of *West Africa* which submits:

> Virtually the whole of Africa now has deforestation problems, says the latest UN report on the continent's environmental features. "Deforestation is continuing at such a pace that on average, only 9 trees are planted for every 100 cut down. In some countries fuelwood supplies will soon be exhausted unless massive replanting is undertaken," the report says.... A worrying picture of environmental degradation on the continent emerges from these statistics. (i) Africa loses over 3.8m hectares of forest every year, less than South America and Asia. Africa's reforestation rate (9.2 per cent) is better than South America's but far worse

than Asia's. (ii) By 1980, Africa was losing some 2.3m hectares of open woodland a year (out of world losses of 3.8m hectares). This rate probably increased during the 1980s. (iii) By the early 1980s, Africa had 37 per cent of the world's drylands (hyper-arid, or desert; semi arid and arid), and the rate of desertification appears to be accelerating. The worst affected regions center on the Sahara, Kalahari and Namib deserts, and touch much of North Africa, West and Southwest Africa, stretching east to include Uganda, Kenya and Somalia. (iii) By 1989, half the African governments responding to a questionnaire from the UN Sudan-Sahelian Office said drought and desertification had become significantly worse since 1986 in terms of falling groundwater levels, drying up of surface water, rangeland degradation, deterioration of rainfed and irrigated cropland, and deforestation. (iv) At current trends, soil erosion could lower agricultural output in Africa by 25 per cent over the 1975–2000 period. Higher population density and pressure on land use has cut the average fallow period for cultivated land from 20–25 years to 5–10 years. (v) Most Africans depend on wood (and charcoal) for household fuel. With fuelwood deficit estimated at about 72 m cubic meters in 1980, Africa's needs could double by year 2000 [Editorial, *West Africa* 1991a:1462].

Western market forces and policies force African governments to sell their forest and agricultural products and other natural resources at cheap prices. African countries, like other developing countries of South America, Central America, and Asia are exploiting their natural resources without careful environmental consideration. In order to rescue the failing economies, African governments are exploiting their resources. They do not have any leverage to negotiate with multinational corporations because they are heavily indebted to foreign banks and governments. This argument is supported by a September (1991:1462) issue of *West Africa* which notes:

> Africa lost revenue totalling $50bn in export earnings between 1986 and 1990 due to falling prices of export commodities.... The report, which points out that the continent's over reliance on the export of raw material puts it at a disadvantage when the price of commodities falls, says nine out of ten African countries depend on primary commodities for 70 per cent or more of their exports. "The basic nature of most African economies has remained virtually unchanged for the last 30 years. During the 1980s 25 out of 38 African countries for which data exist actually increased their dependency on commodities or saw little significant change. Only six African countries – Gabon, Ghana, Mauritius, Morocco, Sierra Leone and Tunisia – have significantly reduced their dependence," the report says. Between 1985 and 1989 African cocoa producers, according to the report, lost over $3bn, despite a 26 per cent jump in output as prices, in real terms, fell to their lowest levels ever. The report urges that producers should cooperate and regulate supply so as to avoid the gluts that lead to sudden dramatic price falls. "Joint research and promotional efforts could lead to new and expanded market opportunities," it says. Meanwhile, according to the World Bank, Africa's share of primary

commodity exports excluding oil fell from 7 per cent to below 4 per cent between 1970 and 1985. The fall was particularly acute in cocoa and coffee, where the continent's market share shrank by 33 and 13 per cent respectively over the same period. Prices during the decade varied between commodity groups. Metal prices, generally, increased during the UNPAAERD period, in nominal and real terms, though they failed to reach the levels prevailing in the 1970s.

In many African countries, there is widespread indiscriminate use of land and water resources. Because the carrying capacity of land has been exceeded in certain parts of the continent, soil erosion is very common. Satellite imagery and ground research seem to suggest that about 15 percent of Africa can support large-scale farming of the type that is carried out in North America and Europe. The expanding population puts tremendous pressure on the prime agricultural land by exceeding its carrying capacity. When carrying capacity is exceeded, the yield from the land declines and farmers must find other ways of supporting themselves. Hence the number of people in poverty increases.

As the reader will find in a later chapter, ecological systems play significant roles in regulating weather patterns. For instance, it is well known that the tropical forests of Africa play a substantial role in the atmospheric chemistry of the continent. The destruction of the forests definitely means an increase in the carbon dioxide and carbon monoxide concentrations in the atmosphere.

The destruction of Africa's rain forests has made it impossible for the atmosphere to break down the carbon monoxide and methane present in the environment. Thus, it is not surprising that the problem of acid rain is growing in some parts of West Africa. The resulting acid rain increases the acid content of the soil and makes it difficult for agricultural production to flourish as it used to in Africa.

Africa's species diversity has declined tremendously over the past four decades without the careful cataloguing of the different flora (plant) and fauna (animal) species in the continent. Humanity stands to lose enormously because the world community has not been able to identify and investigate the potential pharmaceutical benefits that could be derived from the plant and animal life forms. Potential industrial products, energy sources, biological control agents, drugs, and, of course, foods are gradually being destroyed.

The issue of land degradation in Africa has been identified by international agencies and by some African governments as being one of the major problems of the twenty-first century because of the economic ramifications (World Bank 1990a). Another problem that poses significant threat to economic progress in Africa is water pollution. Along with this problem is the issue of the depletion of fresh-water resources. It should be recognized by African governments that Africa has one of the greatest potentials of hydroelectric power in the world. A rough estimate of about 4,200 billion m3/yr of fresh water flows out of Africa's rivers to the ocean. By implementing basic harvesting methods, such water could be diverted for domestic use and for irrigation purposes. However, caution must be applied because of the negative impact of water diversion and irrigation.

In some parts of Nigeria a rough estimate of the price of a bucket of pipe-borne water is fifty cents, which is 9 naira, and a tanker of water is about twenty dollars (360 naira). This is expensive for the average Nigerian who earns an estimated average monthly salary of 450 naira (1991 estimates).

In order to remedy the problem of water supply and pollution, some African governments have established water-supply projects, but it must be emphasized that not everyone will benefit from such projects. As noted in a later chapter, past development projects in Africa have been focused toward satisfying the needs of the urban dwellers. Hence, unless policies address rural issues as well, many rural dwellers might continue to be without an adequate, clean water supply.

The World Bank in its efforts to address the economic and environmental problems in Africa and other developing countries is attempting to replace traditional sectoral strategies with an integrated approach to water resource management. This effort involves a systems approach to managing the agricultural, energy, industrial, and municipal uses of water. This type of strategy is currently in operation in North Africa and could prove beneficial if initiated in the rest of sub–Sahara Africa.

✓ Industrialization, rural-urban immigration, and growing urban populations bring tremendous pollution problems to Africa's urban centers. Air quality problems in African cities such as Accra (Ghana), Lagos (Nigeria), and Nairobi (Kenya), are growing at alarming rates and need to be addressed urgently and adequately. Ghana, Nigeria, and Kenya are at the infancy of establishing ambient air-quality standards, although leaded gasoline is still being used by the ever-increasing number of motorists in major cities, which means that hazardous pollutants are still being emitted into the atmosphere. The congestion in the streets poses more than environmental hazards. On a typical day during the rainy season, as shown in Figure 0.10, a minor motor accident may result in major traffic congestion.

The major thoroughfares are sometimes flooded during the rainy season. The haphazard planning of the towns and the poor construction of the roads also pose significant environmental problems (Figure 0.11).

There is an urgent need to include environmental management issues with economic development strategies and policies of Africa. The World Bank has already started this process by playing a leadership role and

Figure 0.10: Traffic congestion, Lagos, Nigeria, 1991.

Figure 0.11: Flooding during the rainy season resulting in traffic hazards, Lagos, Nigeria, 1991.

Africa's Ecology

setting a good example. A recent issue of *West Africa* (1991b:1602) notes
that the World Bank has given environmental issues in developing nations
high priority:

> The 1992 World Bank report will be dedicated to the theme of environ-
> ment and development. According to the bank's 1991 annual report, the
> momentum of addressing environmental problems has been accelerated
> by the forthcoming United Nations Conference on Environment and
> Development, to be held in Brazil next year. "National governments and
> international organizations have begun preparatory work on environ-
> mental priorities and policy proposals that will contribute to an Earth
> Charter and an environmental agenda for the 21st century," the report
> says. The report notes that there is some evidence that the burning of
> fossil fuels, deforestation, some agricultural practices, and other human
> activities will raise global temperatures through a "greenhouse effect." It
> adds that there remains, however, a considerable uncertainty about the
> magnitude and consequences of such an effect [Editorial].

Table 0.1 shows approved World Bank projects in Africa in 1990. As
the reader will observe in the third column, these projects have environmental components which are meant to preserve and conserve the environment. Table 0.2 shows the expenditures by the World Bank environmental units in fiscal 1990. A total amount of $2,419,000 was spent by the
bank's environmental unit in Africa.

Environmental management and economic development problems
must be tackled at the same time. The main purpose of economic development is to provide a higher standard of living to everyone, but it should
be realized that such development goals must not be achieved by destroying the environment. There is no doubt that some modification of the environment will be necessary in order to achieve a desired economic benefit,
but such modifications have to be environmentally and economically
sound. The construction of infrastructures such as highways, power-
generating plants, dams, irrigation canals, and public housing projects in
urban and rural areas can upset ecological systems by bringing in an imbalance that can be detrimental to a developing society. The negative
impacts are not only limited to human health, but tertiary impacts could
be felt in the sociocultural arena of a developing society. Planners and
decision makers involved with development projects in Africa must take
into account the impact of all the different phases of a project on the ecological and socioeconomic systems. The policy makers must be able to
delineate the choices available to the governments, and along with cost/
benefit analysis, environmental impact assessment must be conducted
before projects begin.

This book is designed primarily as a resource book and text book to
acquaint its readers (students, scholars, and policy makers) with what is

Table 0.1: Projects with Environmental
Components Approved in Fiscal 1990

Country	Project	Environmental Components
Burkina Faso	Urban II	Develop a solid waste management system and drainage improvements.
Burundi	Transport Sector	Provide technical assistance for developing institutional capacity to review and evaluate the potential environmental impacts of road works (such as risks of erosion, drainage problems, and compaction of earth roads) and to design appropriate remedies if needed; incorporate safeguards in bidding documents and contracts to minimize potential environmental damage caused by road works.
Cameroon	Agricultural Extension Training	Develop techniques to protect catchments and conserve soil; support adaptive research to develop pest- and disease-resistant crop varieties.
Guinea	Urban II	Rehabilitate urban infrastructure, such as paved roads and storm water drainage, to minimize dust pollution and limit flooding; coordinate with ongoing environmental action plan to develop coherent policies and national programs in various areas, including urban environment.
Kenya	Coffee Improvement II	Install full water recirculation and pollution control systems in factories, which would entail separating coffee, pulp and water, disposing of pulp, and recirculating process water.
Niger	National Agricultural Research	Carry out applied research to develop improved land, water, crop, livestock, forestry management practices.
Nigeria	Agricultural Development Projects	Help to develop state environmental action plans.
Senegal	Agricultural Services	Improve cultural practices and herd management, through soil conservation, water harvesting, control planting, zero tilling, composting, alley-cropping, and agroforestry.
Somalia	Farahaane Irrigation Rehabilitation	Develop and rehabilitate irrigation ways; carry out studies on integrated pest management and land tenure; improve land tilling.

Source: World Bank, 1990, pp. 89–95.

Africa's Ecology

Table 0.2: Expenditures by Bank
Environmental Units in Fiscal 1990

Regional division
(thousands of dollars)

	Environment Department	Africa	Asia	Europe, Middle East, and North Africa	Latin America and the Caribbean	Total
Bank funded						
Salary budget	1,692	444	627	601	498	3,862
Nonsalary budget	1,518	318	542	648	113	3,139
Research committee	109	---	---	---	---	109
Environmental Assessment Fund	---	1,088	700	588	185	2,561
Subtotal	3,319	1,850	1,869	1,837	796	9,671
Non-Bank funded (a.)						
France	---	---	---	5	---	5
Japan	---	---	103	---	---	---
Norway	442	569	304	140	122	1,576
Sweden	---	---	---	45	---	45
United States	---	---	---	---	---	59
UNDP	183	---	---	28	---	28
Subtotal	625	569	407	218	122	1,713
Total	3,944	2,419	2,276	2,055	918	11,384

--- = Not applicable or negligible.

(a.) Includes where appropriate seconded staff.

Source: World Bank, 1990, p. 97.

happening at the present time to Africa's resources and what could happen given the present economic situation in Africa. Also included in the discussion are some country-by-country accounts of environmental problems. Since the World Bank and the United Nations play significant roles in development projects in Africa, several of the chapters include discussions of efforts of these two international bodies and efforts by several Western countries in sustaining the ecological and environmental diversity of Africa.

The most significant and noteworthy aspect of this book is the discussion of the conservation, preservation, management, and sustainability of Africa's resources. These resources have been seriously mismanaged in the past, and this book argues for proper management techniques, sound environmental policies, and enforcement strategies.

Part I
The Status of the African Environment

1. Africa's Parks and Reserves

The continent of Africa contains an abundance of wildlife which is rivaled only by that of South America. The endemism is spectacular in most cases. The riches in wildlife and natural resources of this most central of all the continents are threatened by the ever-growing population and natural catastrophes. With the creation of national parks and several other protected areas such as the Ziama, Monts Nimba, Bia, Tai, Omo, Dja, Impassa-Makokou, Luki, Odzala, Basse-Lobaye, Yangambi, Volcans, and Dimonika, Africa's wealth will remain for the world's benefit and for future generations. The establishment of these reserves in Africa is an attempt by the governments of the countries involved and international organizations to address the problems of deforestation, air pollution, global warming, and desertification (Figure 1.1.).

Western nations with experience, scientific knowledge, and financial resources can play a large and active role in the efforts to save the African diverse ecological habitats before they are destroyed as a result of expanding population and development. Biological diversity needs permanent protection, and in this chapter I examine Africa's protected lands and make some observations and suggestions that are meant to inspire even more and better efforts.

Mismanagement or inadequate management often results from not defining the conservation and preservation efforts properly. This argument is supported by McNeely et al. (1990:37):

> In seeking ways to conserve biological resources, it is necessary to have a clear understanding of the major threats to biological resources on the ground and in the water. Solutions depend above all on how the problem is defined, and it appears that the *problems facing the conservation of biological diversity have tended to be defined in ways that do not lead to acceptable solutions.*
>
> When the problems are defined in terms of insufficient protected areas, excess poaching, poor law enforcement, land encroachment, and illegal trade, possible responses include establishing more protected areas, improving standards of managing species and protected areas, and enacting international legislation controlling trade in endangered species. All of

21

Figure 1.1: Some African biosphere reserves.

these measures are necessary. But they respond to only part of the problem. Biological diversity will be conserved only partially by protected areas, wildlife management and international conservation legislation.

Even though the attention in the 1970s shifted to oil and the habits of conspicuous consumption expanded globally, visits to parks rose steadily. In the mid–1980s, the environment became media headlines and turned vogue again. Amidst themes of recycling, improving air quality, global warming, and protection of biological resources, environmental plans have regained momentum. This can create renewed efforts for the development of parks, and to that hope, it is helpful to consider where we are today and how we got here so that plans for future conservation strategies may be comprehensive, long range, and generally better.

The focus here is on the continent of Africa and its efforts to protect the natural wealth that it has, much of which is endemic to the continent, one country, or even a single park. These protected lands and resources are essential and integral aspects of a sustainable planet. The idea of linking parks with sustainability is not a new concept. Since the establishment of parks and reserves, human beings have endeavored to simultaneously have parks while attempting to develop their resources. Sustaining the development has not always been easy.

It is important to examine what goes on in African national parks, game reserves, and biosphere reserves. Activities within the boundaries of lands with these labels vary according to the label itself and the local interpretation of it. There are conflicts and struggles in the management of the parks. The examination of these struggles and conflicts is essential to proper management and resolution of problems. Benefits will be detailed to inspire purpose, and strategies will be suggested from successful operation and authorities in the field of national parks and reserves.

Boundaries for Protected Parks

The industrialized world's perspective for national parks was founded at Yellowstone, the first national park in the world. In the industrialized and wealthy nations, many parks were established to preserve scenic vistas and wildlife as national treasures to be held in the public trust in perpetuity. Economic success made it easy to take a piece of the country out of development permanently and fund it for recreational and scientific purposes.

The success of the Western parks is transferable to the developing nations of Africa today but not without modification to adapt to African culture and economies. The idea of extending America's expertise to a distant foreign land is echoed by Eddy (1987) when he notes: "Our wish is to preserve some remnant of the wild, of the rapidly vanishing natural world. And we [Westerners] have projected that wish onto distant African nations without regard for the realities." It must be stated that such desire is bound to be confronted with some resistance from the indigenous African people. Owen (1962) notes that "conservation is completely alien to most Africans." Many Africans recently have been migrating to urban areas, but most of the continent is still rural. Conservation was a way of life, not an occasional thought about recycling or sending a contribution to World Wildlife Fund, as it is to Westerners. Traditional African customs demand that land should be held by communities, and the community and village elders play significant roles in the land-management and tenure procedures.

Although there are intrinsic and extrinsic cultural differences between

African and Western land-use practices, conservation practices can be transferred to African countries from the industrial world. Since urbanization has a tendency to gain momentum once the process is begun, it is imperative that African countries take the issue of preservation and conservation seriously. The idea of setting land aside for conservation purposes is slowly becoming a reality. For instance, the rediscovery of western lowland gorillas in Southeastern Nigeria has prompted the government to consider creating the Boshe-Okawango National Park in order to protect the gorillas. It is estimated that in 1987, six or seven of these gorillas were killed, and the rate of destruction of these magnificent animals far exceeds the reproduction rate.

So far one can claim that the conservation concept is gradually growing in Africa. One only needs to examine the success of many East African countries to appreciate the efforts being made there, although the challenge of continuing to work on conservation strategy is still evolving.

In order to establish park boundaries, many sacrifices need to be made. Political, financial, and social commitment must be there in order to have a successful boundary. National park boundaries cannot control natural phenomena, such as migration of animals and debris, nor can they hold back pollution. As a political demarcation it is one that is easily and frequently penetrated by undesirable elements, including some humans. Trespassers can only be held back by expensive, sometimes military, efforts.

With all of this in mind it might be thought that only the wealthy industrialized nations could afford national parks or reserves, but statistics prove this to be wrong. Affluence of a nation is not the most significant factor in the establishment of national parks, and Africa is strongly represented in global national park figures. As indicated in Table 1.1 many African countries have set aside a significant portion of their land for parks. The idea of conservation and preservation is growing in Africa as a result of education, government involvement, and foreign encouragement. The main problem confronting African nations is the sustainable maintenance and management of the parks, and some African parks are already showing the strains of economic problems.

Despite economic concerns, many African countries are continuing to designate large portions of their land for protective purposes. For instance, Rwanda has designated approximately 16 percent of its land resources to the establishment of national parks. Rwanda's Akagera and Volcanoe are part of the system of national parks in that country. Tanzania has about 25 percent of its land reserved for parks.

An examination of the literature on protected areas indicates that there is no accepted worldwide definition or interpretation of protected areas. The definitions and interpretations vary from region to region,

Table 1.1: Percentage of Land Area in Park Land

1. New Zealand	8.00%	7. South Africa	4.23 %
2. Botswana	7.87%	8. Chad	4.13 %
3. Zambia	7.87%	9. Ghana	3.91 %
4. Benin	6.89%	10. Uganda	3.57 %
5. Singapore	4.68%		
6. Japan	4.38%	18. U.S.A.	1.758%

Source: Wilkinson, 1978.

although a researcher can rely on world conferences, which have provided specific criteria and a general framework for protective land definitions. The most common definitions for national parks, reserves, and the myriad other terms come from the International Union for Conservation of Nature and Natural Resources (IUCN). Three major categories are commonly used in discussion: national park, reserve, and strict nature reserve. But the IUCN recognizes eight distinct classes of protected areas:

1. Scientific reserve/strict nature reserve.
2. National park.
3. Natural monument/natural landmark.
4. Managed nature reserve/wildlife sanctuary.
5. Protected landscapes.
6. Resource reserve.
7. Natural biotic area/anthropological reserve.
8. Multiple-use management area/managed resource area [McNeely et al. 1990].

The IUCN recommends that areas defined as national parks should be a minimum size and that vigorous enforcement of laws and regulations related to the protection of national parks be carried out. More detailed information on the guidelines given by IUCN follows:

1. Legal Protection: The area must have statutory legal protection (within the laws of the host nation) establishing it as a permanently protected area.
2. Effective Protection: This protection must be funded to provide for staff to prevent exploitation.
3. Size: Expecting cases of unique biotic phenomena, the area must be a minimum of 1,000 continuous hectares with distinct use zones.
4. Exploitation: Alteration of the land for agricultural use, resource extraction, etc., as well as hunting and fishing activities, is to be prohibited, except for cultural reasons.

5. Management activities: Support facilities for tourism and scientific use are to be encouraged [Wilkinson 1978].

There are five significant purposes for the establishment of reserves around the world: (1) the preservation of the naturally occurring vegetation (most often trees); (2) the reforestation of some destroyed lands (making them once again productive); (3) forestry efforts to raise new species (providing some economic return or soil protection; (4) the protection of wildlife habitats; and (5) guarding the land for their future use (Wilkinson 1978).

Reserves are especially important because they act as a stage between preservation and unchecked harvesting made by local people on unprotected lands. In Africa where wood is the major source of energy supply, reserves enable the local citizens to practice a controlled type of firewood collection, grazing, and even agricultural production by establishing an acceptable and environmentally sound protection level.

In order to exclude any use of a reserve, an extreme concept of the national park theme of minimum use is sometimes used. African governments have attempted to protect their natural resources by developing serious conservation goals, but definitional and political realities in the country have made such efforts difficult. For example, in 1975 an internal realignment of state boundaries in Nigeria confused the state's previous park and reserve efforts. Now the lands are under a national government and may be redefined (Ojo 1978).

As was stated previously, many countries in Africa have set aside lands for parks. It is a fact that East African countries such as Kenya, Tanzania, and Uganda have set aside substantial portions of land for parks and wildlife reserves. Fromm (1983) claims that Tanzania has set aside one-quarter of its land for parks and wild land reserves. By 1984, the Republic of South Africa had about 11 national parks and was already making plans to set aside more land. Some well-known parks in South Africa are Kruger, Tsitsikama Coastal, Tsitsikama Forest, Augrabies Falls, Bontebok, Karoo, Addo Elephant, Mountain Zebra, Golden Gate Highlands, Kalahari Gemsbok, and Langebaan national parks. South Africa has a long history of preservation and conservation which started in 1895 with the establishment of Hluhluwe and Umfolozi game reserves (Brynard, A.M. 1984, foreword in Bannister et al. 1984).

In Kenya, Tanzania, and Uganda there are several parks and reserves that have been established to protect and preserve wildlife. Table 1.2 gives a list of some national parks, game reserves, and other protected areas in East Africa. Figures 1.2, 1.3, and 1.4 pinpoint the location of these parks and reserves in their respective countries.

Table 1.2: The National Parks and Game Reserves of East Africa

Kenya
1. Aberdare National Park
2. Amboseli National Park
3. Dodori National Reserve
4. Ferguson's Gulf, Lake Turkana (Rudolf)
5. Fort Jesus National Park
6. Gedi National Park
7. Lake Baringo
8. Lake Bogoria National Reserve
9. Lake Magadi
10. Lake Naivasha and Hell's Gate
11. Lake Nakuru National Park
12. Lambwe Valley Game Reserve
13. Losai National Reserve
14. Kakamega Forest
15. Kisite Mpunguti Marine National Park
16. Kongelai Escarpment
17. Malindi and Watamu Marine National Parks
18. Marsabit National Reserve
19. Masai Mara National Reserve
20. Meru National Park
21. Mida Creek
22. Mount Elgon National Park
23. Mount Kenya National Park
24. Mwea National Reserve
25. Nairobi National Park
26. Ngai Ndethya National Reserve
27. Ol Doinyo Sabuk National Park
28. Olorgesailie National Park
29. Saiwa Swamp National Park
30. Samburu-Buffalo Springs-Shaba National Reserves
31. Shimba Hills National Reserve
32. Sokoke-Arabuku Forest
33. The Tana River Reserves
34. Tsavo National Park

Tanzania
1. Arusha National Park
2. Biharamulo Game Reserve
3. Eastern Usambara Mountains
4. Gombe Stream Game Reserve
5. Katavi Plain Game Reserve
6. Kilimanjaro National Park
7. Lake Manyara National Park
8. Mikumi National Park
9. Mkomazi Game Reserve
10. Ngorongoro Crater Conservation Area
11. Poroto Mountains
12. Ruaha National Park
13. Rukwa Valley
14. Selous Game Reserve
15. Serengeti National Park
16. Tarangire National Park
17. Uluguru Mountains

Uganda
1. Ajai Game Reserve
2. Aswa Lolim Game Reserve
3. Bokora Corridor Game Reserve
4. Budongo Forest
5. Bwamba Forest
6. Bwindi Impenetrable Forest Gorilla Sanctuary
7. Entebbe Animal and Bird Sanctuary
8. Impenetrable Kayonza Forest
9. Jinja Animal and Bird Sanctuary
10. Kabalega Falls National Park
11. Karuma and Bugundu Game Reserves
12. Katonga Game Reserve
13. Katwa Bird Sanctuary
14. Kazinga Animal Sanctuary
15. Kibale Forest Corridor Game Reserve
16. Kidepo Valley National Park
17. Kigezi Game Reserve
18. Kigezi Mountain Gorilla Game Reserve
19. Kitangata Game Reserve
20. Kyamburu Game Reserve
21. Lake Mburo Game Reserve
22. Malaba Sanctuary
23. Matheniko Plains Game Reserve
24. Mpanga Forest
25. Nkosi Island Sitatunga Sanctuary
26. Pian Upe Game Reserve
27. Rwenzori National Park
28. Toro Game Reserve
29. West Nile White Rhinoceros Sanctuaries
30. Zoka Forest Elephant Sanctuary

Source: Adapted from Williams, 1967, pp. 5–6.

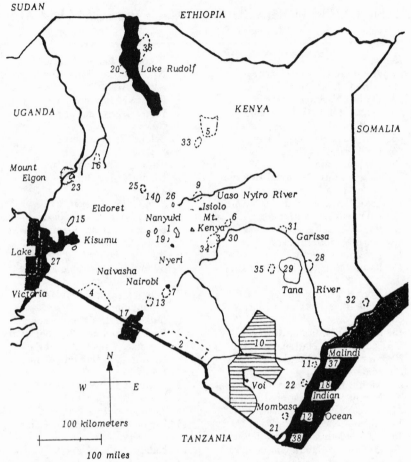

CA=Camping Area   GR=Game Reserve   NP=National Park   NR=Nature Reserve

1. Aberdare NP	14. Lake Baringo	28. Arwake GR
2. Amboseli NP	15. Kakamega Forest	29. Boni GR
3. Mt. Kenya NP	16. Kongelai Escarpment	30. Kora GR
4. Masai-Mara GR	17. Lake Magadi	31. Rahole GR
5. Marsabit NR	18. Mida Creek	32. Dodori NR
6. Meru NP	19. Lake Naivasha	33. Losai NR
7. Nairobi NP	20. Ferguson's Gulf	34. Mwea NR
8. Lake Nakuru NP	21. Shimba Hills	35. Ngai Ndethya NR
9. Samburu-Buffalo	22. Sokoke-Arabuku Forest	36. Sibiloi NR
Springs-Shaba GR	23. Mt. Elgon NP	37. Malindi and Watamu
10. Tsavo NP	24. Ol Doinyo Sabuk NP	Marine NPs
11. Gedi NP	25. Saiwa Swamp NP	38. Kisite Mpungut
12. Fort Jesus NP	26. Lake Bogoria NR	Marine NP
13. Olorgesailie NP	27. Lambwe Valley GR	

Source: Adapted from Williams, 1967.

Figure 1.2: The parks and reserves of Kenya.

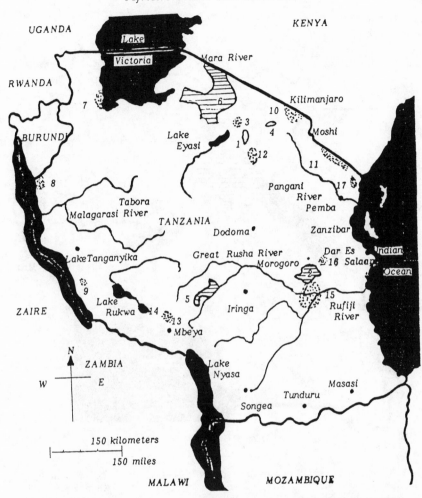

CA=Camping Area   GR=Game Reserve   NP=National Park   NR=Nature Reserve
1. Lake Manyara NP   7. Biharamolo GR   13. Poroto Mountains
2. Mikumi NP   8. Gombe Stream GR   14. Rukwa Valley
3. Ngorongoro CA   9. Katavi Plain GR   15. Selous GR
4. Arusha NP   10. Kilimanjaro NP   16. Uluguru Mountains
5. Ruaha NP   11. Mkomazi GR   17. Eastern Usambara
6. Serengeti NP   12. Tarangire NP   Mountains

Source: Adapted from Williams, 1967.

Figure 1.3: The parks and reserves of Tanzania.

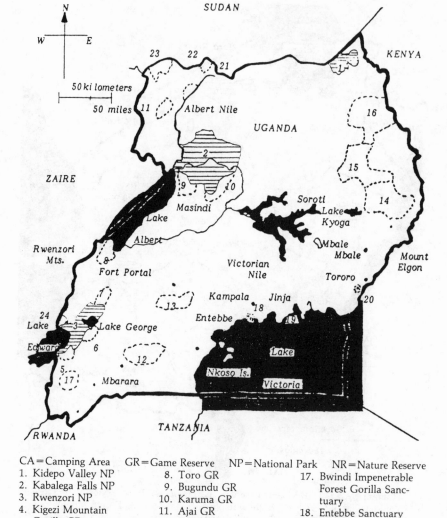

CA=Camping Area   GR=Game Reserve   NP=National Park   NR=Nature Reserve

1. Kidepo Valley NP
2. Kabalega Falls NP
3. Rwenzori NP
4. Kigezi Mountain
   Gorilla GR
5. Kigezi GR
6. Kyambura GR
7. Kibale Forest
   Corridor GR

8. Toro GR
9. Bugundu GR
10. Karuma GR
11. Ajai GR
12. Lake Mburo GR
13. Katonga GR
14. Pian Upe GR
15. Bokora Corridor GR
16. Matheniko Plains GR

17. Bwindi Impenetrable
    Forest Gorilla Sanc-
    tuary
18. Entebbe Sanctuary
19. Jinja Sanctuary
20. Malaba Sanctuary
21. Dufile Sanctuary
22. Otze Forest Sanctuary
23. Mount Kei Sanctuary

Source: Adapted from Williams, 1967.

Figure 1.4: The parks and reserves of Uganda.

Human Interests versus Environmental Conservation Interests

Environmental perturbations induced by natural and human-development endeavors spoil the perfect ideals of protective intents. Aside from the destructive capabilities of human activities, natural threats sometimes undermine park and reserve goals. These threats include forest fires, droughts, floods, and diseases. The deforestation and habitat deterioration that resulted from elephant overpopulation in the 1960s in a Ugandan national park (Machlis et al. 1985) is a good example of inter-woven events that prevent preservation.

In many African countries, it is very common to find human set-tlements at the edges of parks. This condition creates an immediate conflict between wildlife and humans. The concept of boundaries is inundated with many problems which make the management of parks a very difficult issue. In describing the case of Nigerian parks, Ojo notes that "in a country with a varied and complex system of land tenure, it is necessary to under-take detailed studies of how to superimpose modern land-holding practices on existing ones without creating unnecessary social and legal friction" (Ojo 1978:291).

A redefinition of land use anywhere at any time is going to cause some conflicts. No one is willing to concede without some compensation for other provision, and current inhabitants must be moved or informed of new restrictions. Nigeria has a policy of restricting people from using public reserves, but the policy has been ignored because of lack of public support and police power to enforce laws.

A frequent conflict is brought about by food availability. Many cases of illegal hunting have been witnessed, such as the "cropping" of animals by locals at the Chirisa Safari Area in Zimbabwe (Shelton 1983). The crea-tion of parks in Africa has made it difficult for Africans who are basically hunters and subsistence farmers to continue their traditional way of life. They are not able to hunt the animals as they used to in the past.

It should be pointed out that the goal of protecting the land has not been fully met as local residents of rural areas continue to push the land to provide food, cotton for clothing, and shelter. This situation is repeated across the African continent. Limited and sometimes scarce supplies of water and fertile lands need to be protected, but the protection status limits the availability of resources for human sustenance.

Many Africans who live close to areas where parks are located see the creation of parks and reserves as taking away their livelihood and their way of life. Forest reserves in Africa such as the Apoba Forest Reserve in Nigeria have competing users. A small number of indigenous people use resources of the reserves for subsistence, but international organizations

Table 1.3: Estimates of Forest Areas
and Deforestation Rates in the Tropics

Country	Closed Forest area (1,000 ha)	Percent deforested per year
Tropical Africa		
Côte d'Ivoire	4,458	6.5
Nigeria	5,950	5.0
Rwanda	120	2.7
Burundi	26	2.7
Benin	47	2.6
Guinea-Bissau	660	2.6
Liberia	2,000	2.3
Guinea	2,050	1.8
Kenya	1,105	1.7
Madagascar	10,300	1.5
Angola	2,900	1.5
Uganda	765	1.3
Zambia	3,010	1.3
Ghana	1,718	1.3
Mozambique	935	1.1
Sierra Leone	740	0.8
Tanzania	1,440	0.7
Togo	304	0.7
Sudan	650	0.6
Chad	500	0.4
Cameroon	17,920	0.4
Ethiopia	4,350	0.2
Somalia	1,540	0.2
Equatorial Guinea	1,295	0.2
Zaire	105,750	0.2
Central African Republic	3,590	0.1
Gabon	20,500	0.1
Congo	21,340	0.1
Zimbabwe	200	(a)
Namibia		(a)
Botswana		(a)
Mali		(a)
Burkina Faso		(a)
Niger		(a)
Senegal	220	(a)
Malawi	186	(a)
Gambia	65	(a)
Totals	216,634	0.61

Source: Cited in McNeely et al., 1990, p. 45.
(a) not available, some of these areas are very small.

would like the parks to remain as they are, preserved in perpetuity. A large number of people would like to see the reserves serve some economic purposes. Table 1.3 shows the tropical forests and the rate of deforestation in African countries.

Unlike Western nations, African governments give very little financial assistance to parks because of lack of capital. Protected areas compete with agricultural and resource development, urban infrastructure, health, and education for money (James 1991a). The Luangwa Valley of Zambia provides an excellent example. This land was previously thought to be useless due to tsetse flies and seasonal floods. The development of agriculture has increased tremendously as populations expand. Even though more than two-thirds of the land is officially designated as park and wildlife reserves, agricultural investment in the remaining one-third of the valley was 400 times greater than wildlife protection spending. It is recognized that agricultural development provides food that would otherwise be captured from the wildlife lands, but the protection of the land seems to be too low a priority (McNeely et al. 1990). Human interests often prevail in the long run, and wildlife suffers as a result of such perspectives.

Park boundaries do not mean anything to wildlife. During their seasonal migration and daily wandering for food and water, wild animals are known to cross the boundaries set by humans and destroy farmlands and domesticated animals. Growing population means less and less park land. This results in the wildlife exceeding the carrying capacity of the land on which it exists.

Trees are harvested for several reasons in Africa, and in the past undesirable species were poisoned to allow for more desirable trees to grow. While this practice is within the confines of a reserve's definition, the land where such harvesting occurs perhaps needs national park status. In 1980, logging began in many African countries. Increasing use by local urban populations brought about suggestions for more facilities for visitors. The lands, still rich in vegetative variety, do not qualify for IUCN national park status as the resources are still extensively tapped (Oguntola 1980). As long as parks exist and more land is set aside as reserve, conflict will continue on how land should be used. New park plans should be established to minimize the problems of park management and nature preserve establishment.

Protected Lands

Parks and reserves, as discussed previously, are not isolated places. They are intricately linked with the local communities. Although one of the fundamental functions of parks and reserves is to sustain species or ecosystems (protecting biological diversity), a number of side effects are also potentially very positive and can help to add justification for their establishment. The development of parks and reserves for tourism has been receiving considerable attention and is particularly important to African parks, where growth opportunities are desperately needed. Countries such as Kenya, Tanzania, Malawi, and Zambia are benefiting from the growth of tourism, and Zaire and South Africa have enjoyed increases in the number of tourists visiting the parks and forest reserves. Ecological impacts upon surrounding lands are often unachievable without parks or reserves, so they too cannot be overlooked as sustainable development is considered. Protected lands have immense benefits that cannot be priced.

Africa has a very long history of people coexisting in harmony with the forest. This coexistence is eloquently articulated by Talbot (1912) who was one of the first British who set foot in Oban in the remote southeastern part of Nigeria. He observed that even in 1902 and before, the people of Oban seemed to have devised a sophisticated way of living with their wildlife. The large animals — leopards, elephants, gorillas, large reptiles (crocodiles), and a host of others — provided meat for the people.

Biological and Ecological Diversity Protection

It seems that the major goal of African parks as well as reserves is to keep humans from destroying the plants and animals that are of most value to us. Usually these are the big plants and animals. Mason (1962:111) points out:

> The maintenance of the genetic diversity of organisms genetically related to ethnologically and economically important plants and animals is fundamental to the further development of the resources. . . . To allow the permanent depletion of the natural diversity . . . is a symptom of a decline in culture. To maintain it or to increase it lays the foundation upon which a culture may advance.

The urgent and rapid growth in research to seek cures for diseases makes African plants and animals economically significant as a medicine or as the carrier of genes that can enhance another species survival or productivity. Monkeys and other animals are already being used as guinea pigs in laboratories for testing new drugs and for experimenting with the impacts of germs on animals. Regardless of personal philosophies regarding animal rights, the reality is that medical research has been using chimpanzees for a long time and will probably continue to do so well into the future. In this regard of their importance, funding their protection guarantees their perpetuity. In many instances, these gene storehouses have benefited the world at large (James 1991a). Therefore, they should be considered treasures for all, and those who benefit from the use of the plants and animals should be encouraged to contribute financially for their conservation. It is a fact that the industrialized countries benefit a great deal more from these plants and animals than the developing countries. Africa's contribution to mankind can increase significantly if and when innovations and progressive ways are achieved in preserving and conserving the biological diversity of Africa. Many lands are still available in Africa for parks. A major barrier to their establishment has been the unavailability of start-up funds and continued economic justifications. Debates have been going on in Africa in recent times about reparation of Africa due to the damage brought about by colonialism. One could argue that such reparation of Africa by former "colonial masters" could be paid in the form of research and development. Such efforts could be geared toward helping Africa to sustain the diversity of its environment, ecology, and biological species.

It should be understood that the small plants and animals are also important because of the linkages that exist in the food chain and food web. The wild plants of Africa are useful in many parts of the world. Timberlake (1985) contends that Africa is home to many animals and plants that have global significance. Table 1.4 indicates the richness of African countries in species diversity.

A large number of species in one place gives the world a natural laboratory which can be useful for research, recreation, improvement of the aesthetic quality of man's environment, and more important, an outside classroom for the study of plant and animal species of the world. As the reader will see in a later chapter, parks serve the useful purpose of being the standards against which one can judge a deteriorating environment.

Africa is unique because it has many species of plants and animals that are beneficial and can be of great importance to the world. Some of these species are found only in Africa (see Figures 1.5 and 1.6). African animals are being exported overseas to provide excellent recreational experiences to millions of people in the developed world.

In Africa and many other countries of the developing world, the lack of funds makes the establishment and maintenance of parks or reserves very difficult. The world recession has made it very difficult for governments of Third World nations to continue to subsidize public parks and reserves. Funding from nongovernmental organizations (NGO) has declined while the pressure to use the parks for other purposes and poaching has been on the increase.

It is time the world realized that the wildlife of Africa has a cultural

Table 1.4: African Countries with the Highest
Numbers of Species for Selected Organisms

Mammals		Birds		Amphibians	
1. Zaire	409	Zaire	1086	Zaire	216
2. Uganda	311	Kenya	1046	Cameroon	190
3. Tanzania	310	Uganda	973	Madagascar	144
4. Kenya	308	Tanzania	969	Tanzania	127
5. Cameroon	297	Cameroon	849	Nigeria	96
6. S. Africa	279	Ethiopia	827	S. Africa	93
7. Angola	275	Nigeria	824	Congo	88
8. Nigeria	274	Zambia	728	Angola Gabon	86
9. Sudan	266	S. Africa	725	Cote d'Ivoire	80
10. Ethiopia	256	Ghana	721	Kenya	79

Reptiles		Swallowtail Butterflies (1)		Angio-sperms (2) Estimate	
1. S. Africa	281	Zaire	48	S. Africa	21,000
2. Zaire	280	Cameroon	39	Zaire	10,000
3. Madagascar	269	Congo	37–38	Madagascar	10,000
4. Tanzania	244	Tanzania	34	Tanzania	10,000
5. Angola	217	Uganda		Cameroon	9,000
		(W. Africa)	31–32		
6. Cameroon	183	Kenya	30	Gabon	7,900
7. Namibia Somalia	166	Angola	27	Kenya	6,750
8. Mozambique	159	Gabon	25–31	Ethiopia	6,200
9. Nigeria	147	C.A.R.	24–29	Mozambique	5,000
10. Uganda	143	Zambia	23	Uganda	4,500

Source: McNeely et al., 1990, p. 90.

and scientific value that is priceless. The value of Africa's wildlife far exceeds the agricultural and livestock value of Africa. If properly managed, Africa's wildlife could bring in prosperity to Africa in perpetuity. For instance, the animals could be cropped for food to alleviate the hunger problem, although Mathews (1962) argues that the park lands of Africa are being put to their best use when they remain as parks. The income that countries such as Kenya, Tanzania, and Zambia receive from tourism would probably not be equaled if their park lands were put to other uses.

African parks certainly have their economic justification, and it appears that some African nations are beginning to view their parks as productive lands. West African countries such as Ghana, Nigeria, and Côte d'Ivoire (formerly Ivory Coast) have expressed sincere enthusiasm about maintaining their natural areas (Dzisah 1991).

Maintaining large tracts of land in their natural forms without

Figure 1.5: An elephant at "Marine World/Africa USA," Vallejo, California, 1987.

significantly changing them has many benefits. One of the major benefits is that it helps to control erosion problems (Figures 1.7 and 1.8).

All development efforts disrupt the natural order of the environment. This is a fact because entropy increases with development. Hence, careful and deliberate planning must precede all such projects. In Africa many ecological disasters have emanated as a result of the conversion of land from the natural state to plantation for the production of crops. Such endeavors have grave ecological problems. For instance, in the Hanang Plains located in the southeast of Arusha in Tanzania, wheat production created erosion problems and led to the destruction of cultural diversity of the Barbaig pastoralist (Timberlake 1985).

Figure 1.6: Giraffes at "Marine World/Africa USA," Vallejo, California, 1987.

The preservation of land as parks and reserves restricts runoff to a natural rate and thus guarantees a reliable water supply. Since more than 70 percent of Africans still live in rural areas, it is necessary to maintain parks because such an endeavor will improve the surrounding environment of the protected lands.

National parks such as the Yellowstone and Yosemite in the United States are spectacular sights. In Kenya one is bound to appreciate the beauty of Mount Kenya, Amboseli, Aberdare, Tsavo, Mount Elgon Meru, and Lake Nakuru national parks. In their natural and untouched forms these lands offer the world scenic vistas and wildlife viewing opportunities and the quality of recreational experience that last a lifetime. These parks

Figure 1.7: Quarry facing erosion problems, Onitsha, Nigeria, 1989.

Figure 1.8: Erosion conquering a quarry site, Onitsha, Nigeria, 1989.

have been centers of attraction for decades, and their economic impact has ramifications that bring about development along the edges of the parks.

There is a growing awareness in the Western industrialized countries of the significance of African parks and reserves. As will be noticed in a later chapter, the number of foreign visitors to Africa's national parks has increased in recent years. Travel to parks and reserves in Kenya, Tanzania, and South Africa has increased to see the aesthetically beautiful places these countries have to offer. When visitors spend their money in African countries, they link the continent with the rest of the world economically. The local people who live close to the parks benefit as a result of tourism and also have the infrastructures in their communities improved by the governments so as to keep the tourists coming. Employment is created locally for the inhabitants.

The Revenues and Problems

Africa's rich cultural heritage and its wildlife have been attracting visitors from all over the world, and some countries have shown a remarkable increase in revenue due to tourism. It has been reported that tourism revenue in Ghana increased from $19.5 million in 1985 to $72.0 million in 1989. As a matter of fact, Ghana has been showing a steady increase between those years. In 1986 it recorded $26.6 million; in 1987 it went up to $36.4 million; and in 1988 it was $55.3 million (Ephson 1991). Estimates of visitors to Ghana show arrival figures to be 85,000 in 1985 and 113,800 in 1988. Although Ghana has been experiencing conflict between human interests and the protection of its wildlife, it is doing all it can to maintain an ecological balance in the country. As recently as June 1991, two men were killed at Baare in the upper east region of Ghana (Editorial, *West Africa* 1991c).

Nigeria is taking tourism very seriously. It is encouraging both rural and urban tourism that is environmentally sensitive. Development of natural resources is the key to the attraction of Nigeria to tourists. Historic places such as the vicarage of the St. Thomas Anglican Church built in 1842 are also very popular. Figures 1.9 and 1.10 show the entire building. It is said to be the first two-story building in Nigeria as indicated in Figure 1.11.

In an attempt to encourage the tourism industry in countries such as Nigeria, the Economic Community of West African States (ECOWAS) has taken an active role in advising member countries on strategies that will enable private individuals to invest in West Africa. Cooperation in trade, finance, and industry is being enhanced by the governments, and incentives

Figure 1.9: Vicarage of St. Thomas Anglican Church, Badagry, Nigeria, 1989.

Figure 1.10: Vicarage of St. Thomas Anglican Church and Nigerian tourists, Badagry, Nigeria, 1989.

Figure 1.11: An American tourist inspecting the first two-story building in Badagry, Nigeria, 1989.

Figure 1.12: Young cultural dancers, Ikot-Ekpene, Nigeria, 1989.

are being provided to local communities to accentuate their cultural heritage. Thus visitors who travel to Africa to see the wildlife may also have the opportunity to examine the culture. Figure 1.12 shows a group of young men and women who belong to a dancing group in Ikot-Ekpene, Nigeria.

Figure 1.13 shows the traditional homes at the beach in Badagry (Nigeria). Foreign visitors have the opportunity of interacting with the locals and witnessing a different lifestyle. The local inhabitants depend on the foreign and domestic tourism that supports their community. Figure 1.14 shows the masqueraders who entertain tourists and perform other traditional rituals. Tourists have many recreational opportunities available to them in the cities and the rural communities. For instance, there are zoos in Nigeria so that urban dwellers and city visitors have the opportunity to enjoy the wildlife of the country (Figures 1.15 and 1.16).

The beach provides excellent opportunities for tourists. Badagry Beach provides a serene environment for tourists to get away from urban life. In Figures 1.17, 1.18, and 1.19 one appreciates the quality of the experience that tourists can have from travel to the beach in Nigeria. In the rural areas, the government of Nigeria is taking very bold steps in boosting tourism. Roads are being constructed to places such as the famous Yankari Game Reserve in one of the northern states, to the warm spring in Ikogosi in Ondo State, and to the world famous Obudu Cattle Ranch which is one

Figure 1.13: Traditional houses, Badagry Beach, Nigeria, 1989.

Figure 1.14: Masqueraders, Ikot-Ekpene, Nigeria, 1989.

Figure 1.15: Parrots at a local zoo, Port-Harcourt, Nigeria, 1989.

Figure 1.16: A leopard at a local zoo, Port-Harcourt, Nigeria, 1989.

Figure 1.17: Nigerian couple enjoying a Sunday afternoon, Lagos Bar Beach, 1989.

Figure 1.18: Nigerian children posing for tourist photos while at play, Badagry, Nigeria, 1989.

Figure 1.19: Foreign tourist enjoying the beach, Lekki Beach, Nigeria, 1991.

Figure 1.20: Fish farm and tourist centre, Ikot-Obong, Nigeria, 1991.

of the few places in Nigeria where efforts have been made to protect the forests and wildlife. Figure 1.20 shows a genuine attempt by the Akwa Ibom state of Nigeria to make rural tourism a success in the state. In Akwa Ibom state there are many attempts to protect wildlife, and birds such as the vultures shown in Figure 1.21 are now being protected by local laws.

Other things of interest are significant historical personalities and events. Western tourists who travel to Akwa Ibom state of Nigeria can learn about Mary Slessor who was a missionary in Itu. She educated the local inhabitants and spread Christianity. Her burial site is now part of a national park (Figure 1.22).

One of the problems confronting tourism in Africa is transportation. Air travel to Africa is still plagued with problems. Some of the airports do not have facilities comparable to those available at airports in Western industrialized countries, but some countries like Nigeria, Kenya, South Africa, and Tanzania have made great efforts to build more modern airports (Figure 1.23). Travel by sea is also possible (Figure 1.24). Tourists who wish to enjoy the beauty of the African parks can reach the major sea ports of Africa and then travel by domestic airlines or drive to the sites, although road conditions are poor. Surprisingly, Western tourists may find that the skyline in many major African cities is much the same as those in the industrialized countries. The skylines of Abidjan, Lagos, and Accra, for example, look like Western skylines (Figure 1.25).

Figure 1.21: Vultures in natural habitat, Eket, Nigeria, 1991.

Figure 1.22: Mary Slessor's burial site, Itu, Nigeria, 1991.

Figure 1.23: Murtala Mohammed Airport, Ikeja, Nigeria, 1991.

Figure 1.24: Lagos Port, Nigeria, 1991.

Figure 1.25: Lagos Island business center, Nigeria, 1991.

However, it should be pointed out that increased tourism does bring about some environmental degradation. Mini-vans that travel the parks degrade the vegetation, and contact between animals and people could mean taming the natural behavior of the animals to suit man's desires. It is the role of planners and park administrators to solve the problems and bring about sustainability in all developmental agendas in Africa. The primary role of an environmental planner is to maximize the use of a resource and minimize the depletion.

The conflict discussed in this chapter points out the fact that tourism in Africa needs to be organized and that parks have to be properly planned and managed. Hotels, airports, and other supporting infrastructures that make tourism possible and enhance economic development compete for land and money that could be used for social programs.

Planners have often shied away from addressing the negative impact of tourism adequately. Opponents of tourism in developing countries have often argued that tourism fosters a dependency syndrome because the major airlines, hotels, and managerial jobs are controlled by foreign interests. In this case tourism in Africa is perceived as a multinational interest. It is also argued that tourism in Africa is a Western cultural imposition and that park creation and the development emanating as a result of the imposition are not for the benefit of the local people (James 1991a).

Planners have to be innovative in designing parks and establishing reserves since such developments impinge upon many aspects of the host-country infrastructure. There have been instances in some African countries like Côte d'Ivoire, Cameroon, Kenya, and Tanzania where new infrastructures had to be built and land-use patterns have been changed. It should be pointed out that if the new roads are not properly constructed, erosion and other ecological problems may arise. The wildlife which attracted people in the first place may actually be destroyed by the humans who come to see it. Remoteness is beneficial to the protection of the parks because the numbers of visitors will not exceed the carrying capacity of the land.

Parks offer great economic opportunities internationally and domestically to African nations. There is prosperity in the proper management of the parks and wildlife reserves. The objective of planners must be to plan parks to fit with the goals and aspirations of local communities. The best parks are those that have the support and blessings of the indigenous people of the host country.

Planning for Park Systems

The debate surrounding whether or not park systems should be supported and encouraged in Africa suggests that a comprehensive plan for the system is necessary. It seems that a cohesive master plan will take into consideration the short-range, middle-range, and long-range goals of the park system in order to make it successful. Comprehensive plans for parks have the quality of enhancing sustainable development that will incorporate social, economic, and environmental benefits.

Kenya is a good example. Shelton (1983) in his article "Parks and Sustainable Development" contends that in Amboseli National Park in Kenya the needs of the Masai have been met while at the same time the ecological system has been sustained. Masai received monetary compensation from revenue brought in as a result of tourism. They use park facilities for their ceremonies and important gatherings, and piped water is delivered to Masai lands. On the other hand, the park provides a safe environment for the wildlife such as the rhino, and visitors to the park are able to view the animals. The planning that was established at Amboseli ensures the provision of a buffer zone. The need for a continuous watchful eye on reserves in Africa is emphasized in an article by Morell (1985:6–7) in which she states the following:

> The desire among many Masai to "settle down" has been encouraged by the creation of the Masai Mara Game Reserve. The Mara was set aside by British colonial settlers in the 1930s. At that time, land bordering the

park was given to the nomadic Masai, who wanted nothing to do with European ways. In 1961, the reserve was taken over by the Narok County Council—the county in which the majority of the Masai people live. All profits from the park's tourism were then funneled through the council to the Masai. The reserve produced jobs for many tribesmen as park rangers, hotel employees and guides. "This park is the primary industry in Narok," pointed out the Senior Warden, John Naiguran, himself a Masai. "It is the first place that our young people think of when they want a job."

Conservationists on the outside view this relationship with misgivings. "It is like the wolves watching the sheep," scoffed one. "The Masai have never accorded the wildlife any special rights," said another. "They are only interested in the money the animals can make for them. If the park brings them less money than some other scheme, like wheat farming, then the Masai will pressure the council to abandon it."

Indeed, there are problems in the reserve: Poaching of black rhino has reduced the population from 28 to 8 animals; uncontrolled tourism has left a confusing maze of roads crisscrossing the land; corruption and inefficiency in the park's management have reduced the monies going to the Narok Council; agricultural projects on the borders of the park have pushed the nomadic Masai to its very edge and Masai cattle are often seen grazing within the park's boundaries. Furthermore, there is a lack of a clearly defined line of authority, making it difficult, sometimes, to know who is responsible for what.

Obviously the management practices in the parks and wildlife reserves in Africa need improvement. An overall plan that recognizes human needs as well as the need to protect the parks and reserves ought to be put in place. This step will bring about the much-needed balance that is required in many of Africa's parks and reserves.

It is impossible to distribute a country's wealth equitably among its people. When areas become protected zones, the people that experience the loss should be compensated because the benefits of the protection are for the good of all. Hence, the protection of natural areas in Africa will continue to need foreign assistance.

2. Housing Conditions in Rural Africa: A Case Study of Ikot-Ekpene, Nigeria

Introduction

Human beings have always attempted to improve their standards of living by improving their living environment. Providing decent and adequate shelter in many rural parts of Africa is a complex problem. The housing types in rural and urban Africa depict the societal strata of economic level. In all of Africa, scattered programs have been established to increase the production of shelter with permanent building materials, but the programs have only been beneficial to a few government and working-class people. A greater proportion of people in Africa rely on themselves for their housing needs. There appear to be four groups of participants in the housing aspect of Africa: private owners, entrepreneur owners, government (federal, state, and local), and renters. The shelter issue is becoming more and more complex with the growing population and the dwindling economic bases of rural areas of Africa.

Aims and Objectives

The aim of this study was to investigate the housing conditions of a growing rural town in Nigeria. The study explored the changing housing conditions based on the following aspects: (1) traditional housing; (2) modern homes; (3) informal settlements; (4) affordability of homes; (5) government and private entrepreneur involvement in housing; (6) housing demand and supply; and (7) infrastructure to support houses.

Data Collection

The techniques used in gathering the information for this study included field research, interviews, and investigation of secondary data sources. The field research involved the survey of housing types in the town of Ikot-Ekpene. The housing types were documented photographically. Face-to-face interviews with randomly selected residents of the town proved to be very valuable in the study. Other people selected for this study were contractors, developers, builders, and government officials.

The Setting

Akwa Ibom state is a small state of about 8.412 sq. km and is located in the southeastern corner of Nigeria. Ikot-Ekpene is located in this state which was created by the federal government of Nigeria in September of 1987. Ikot-Ekpene's local government area is one of ten in the state. The town is located between Aba (Imo state) and Uyo (Akwa Ibom state).

Figure 2.1 shows the location of Ikot-Ekpene with respect to the surrounding towns in the country. Figure 2.2 shows the villages that make up the town. The villages are Ifuho, Ikot Obong Edong, Nkap, Utu Ikpe, Uruk Uso, Abiakpo Ikot Essien, and Ikot-Ekpene.

Ikot-Ekpene's physical environment can be described as flat, low-lying land. Climatically, the town enjoys two seasons: rainy and dry. The wet season begins in April and ends in early October, and the dry season begins in mid–October and ends in early April. The heavy rainfall of about 2,500–3,000 mm per year and warm temperatures maintain green foliage year round. Most of the forests, as can be seen in Figures 2.3 and 2.4, have been cleared or are being cleared for agriculture, human settlement, and roads.

Despite the clearance of the forests for human purposes, Ikot-Ekpene and its other local government areas are responsible for most of the country's palm produce.

The creation of the state has brought many changes to Ikot-Ekpene. For example, more job opportunities are available in the state capital of Uyo. Many people from the surrounding towns, including Ikot-Ekpene, now have employment opportunities in Uyo. The state governor's decision not to provide additional housing units in Uyo to accommodate the government officials encourages commuting from places such as Ikot-Ekpene to Uyo. Hence, workers maintain their homes in Ikot-Ekpene which contributes to the economic base of the town.

The population density in Ikot-Ekpene is 646.37 persons per square

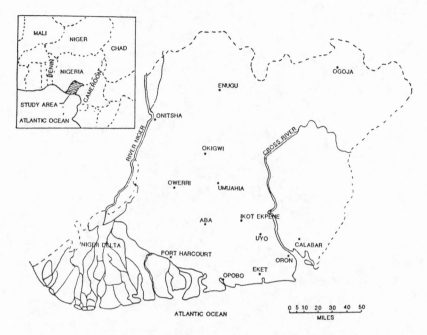

Figure 2.1: Map of study area in Nigeria.

kilometer. The local language is Annang, although there may be slight differences in pronunciation of some words as one goes from one village to another. The Annang, according to the 1963 and more recent 1992 census, occupy an area which has a dense population by comparison with other areas south of the Sahara.

The 1992 census estimates the population of Ikot-Ekpene to be slightly less than 19,000 people. The civil war of 1966–69 devastated the town since this is part of the region where heavy fighting occurred. Several thousand people died during the war, and the development of the town was set back. Nonetheless, there has been tremendous progress since the war. The inhabitants have been able to slowly bring back some much-needed vitality and vibrance to the development process of the town. Their efforts need encouragement and incentives by the state and federal governments.

The overall economic condition of Nigeria is not good at the present time. The country's past reliance on oil has made development difficult. Oil prices have been fluctuating, and development programs have suffered. The inability to diversify the industrial base has also compounded the problem.

Nowhere else is this floundering economic situation more visible than in the rural areas where unemployment has increased. For a society that depends on its labor-intensive work force, the growing number of people

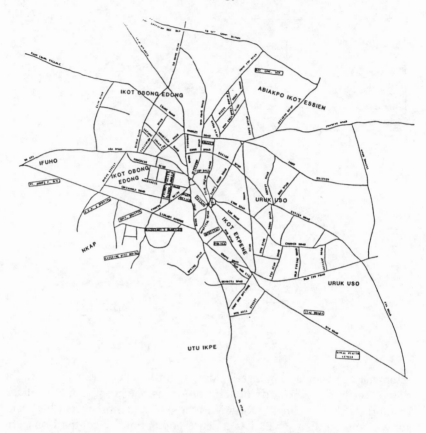

Figure 2.2: Road network map of Ikot-Ekpene.

that are unemployed is not a good sign for stability. The unemployment
in both rural and urban areas has resulted in the exacerbation of the slum
conditions in the country.

Young graduates from high schools and universities have serious
difficulties in gaining employment. The unemployment in the rural and urban areas has made it difficult for people to build their own homes, and
squatter shelters are not uncommon. Urban areas become overcrowded
when young graduates move there from rural settings to join relatives.

With the increasing cost of building materials, the possibility of young
graduates being able to afford to build their own modern homes is very
slim. Although the cost of labor for construction is relatively low, an
average worker in Nigeria cannot afford to save enough money to employ
laborers and contractors to build a home. The average monthly income of
a university graduate of N400–500 naira (about twenty-four to thirty U.S.
dollars in 1992) is not enough to support such a person adequately.

Figure 2.3: Oil palm production farm.

Figure 2.4: Clearing land for housing.

Figure 2.5: Road leading to settlements.

Another problem that makes affordability of homes a problem is the rising cost of land. Competition for land use, transportation, and agriculture for example, has escalated the price of land. The new land-use reforms of the federal government in 1979 also hinder the possibility of young people being able to build their own modern homes. The bureaucratic arrangements for purchasing land are too cumbersome for many middle-income Nigerians and often discourage many potential builders.

Compound Land (Ikure)

The Ikot-Ekpene people traditionally live in large compounds which are headed by one older man who is married to more than one wife. The wives and their respective children live in huts or separate wings of a house. Thus, in a traditional compound, one is bound to find several dwellings (bungalows or huts).

The land-owning rights are controlled by the nuclear family. In some cases, some subsistence agriculture is done in the compound. Plots are made available to local residents on a lease basis by the local government for agricultural purposes (Figures 2.6 and 2.7).

Population and economic pressure are changing the way people use

Figure 2.6: A property owner in his garden.

their land for the construction of houses. The latest trend is for apartment and rooming houses to be constructed on family land.

Traditional Houses

By definition, traditional homes are built of mud, with thatched or a combination of mud, bamboo, and zinc roofing. Traditional houses have been in existence since humans first set foot in Nigeria. As people's needs have changed, so have the traditional homes evolved. Although these houses differ structurally (architecturally) from one part of the country to another, they are basically constructed out of local raw materials which are relatively inexpensive. Often, traditional homes are constructed from scratch by the family members and intended residents.

These houses are constructed of mud and bamboo sticks for the walls and palm fronds and grasses for the roof thatching. Figure 2.8 shows an example of a traditional house in Ikot-Ekpene. This traditional house was constructed about twenty years ago and has undergone several renovations. The owner maintains the house by replacing the thatched roof with new palm fronds. This type of house is usually very cool in the dry season and inexpensive to renovate since the owner usually does the necessary work personally.

Figure 2.7: Property owner describing the different fruits and crops in his compound.

In many rural parts of Nigeria, the creation of new states has brought about a sense of need for development in terms of the provision of job opportunities, construction and maintenance of infrastructures, improvement of educational systems at primary, secondary, and post-secondary levels, and the improvement of housing standards. Most owners of traditional houses work very hard keeping their dwellings habitable, but development brought about as a result of modernity is diminishing and reducing the raw materials which are used to build this type of house. This

Figure 2.8: Traditional house.

seems to be the trend in the whole country. The designs of traditional dwellings and their arrangements in compounds and along streets depict the social atmosphere in the town. As has been pointed out, the characteristic materials for the construction of traditional houses are clay and thatch, which are found locally and are cheap. However, in the last decade, the destruction of the forest has made it difficult to find bamboo trees in the wild, and clay is now being sold for profit. This new phenomenon makes it more difficult to build traditional houses than in the past. The owners of traditional houses take great pride in the maintenance of their houses. Children and young people learn the art of constructing houses by watching their parents do the work and by participating in the process of construction (Figures 2.9 and 2.10).

Before the discovery of oil in Nigeria, life in the rural as well as urban areas was simple and the cost of living was affordable to a majority of Nigerians. Building a traditional home was very inexpensive. But in recent times, the costs of local materials for the construction of homes have escalated. The traditional homes have evolved in terms of design, objectives, and goals in order to accommodate the prevailing economic and environmental conditions and the availability of local and imported raw materials. The raw materials for construction are gathered by the potential resident with assistance from his or her relatives and neighbors. In the past (about twenty to thirty years ago) the plots on which traditional houses

Figure 2.9: Property owner weaving the roof of his home.

Figure 2.10: Children watching their skillful father weaving the palm fronds.

Figure 2.11: Informal building to the left.

were constructed were usually large; but with the growing population and the fact that siblings share the property, the plots have become smaller.

Informal Settlement

A type of settlement which does not fit traditional or modern settlement categories is the informal construction. Ikot-Ekpene has some informal dwellings in which the owners use both local materials (traditional and discarded or purchased modern materials). The use of mud and bamboo poles is combined with galvanized iron sheets and cement (Figure 2.11). This type of dwelling is usually built on family property. Levin (1981:132) contends that for this type of dwelling the following observations hold true:

a) The use of iron sheets for roofing and cement blocks for floors, the construction of foundations, etc., requiring skills which the builder-owner often does not have.

b) The builder-owner (head of household) is a full-time employee or self-employed and does not have time to do all the work himself.

c) Assistance from family relatives and friends cannot be relied upon, as they usually live in rural areas and cannot come to the town to help with the building.

d) Traditional building materials often become scarce in the immediate vicinity of squatter areas and the builder-owner must purchase them from dealers.

e) For reasons of prestige, the builder-owner usually prefers to build with industrially produced materials.

It is important to mention that when the owner of an informal building is financially capable of finishing the building, the complete work is carried out. It usually is not a very complicated task since the whole building is not torn down. Only the walls of cement are brought down and then replaced with cinder blocks.

Modern Houses

Ikot-Ekpene, like many other rural communities in Nigeria, is experiencing some form of development, growth, and urbanization. This change is reflected in the gradual decrease in the number of traditional houses and transformation of existing traditional homes. The change is necessary due to the following:

1. Growth in population and the need for proper and adequate housing.
2. More than 60 percent of the population of Ikot-Ekpene could be classified as underemployed.
3. The traditional homes are substandard in terms of provision of pipe-borne water, electricity, and indoor plumbing.
4. The federal and local government policies foster the idea of the change or modernization of the traditional homes.
5. Bank policies on loans seem to reinforce the idea of modern houses, especially if the house is to be rented out to tenants (Adedibu 1981).

Modernizing the existing traditional homes is a very slow process, since renovation usually includes rebuilding sections of the house with cement blocks, plastering the walls, and fencing the property. This exercise is usually very expensive and usually undertaken only by private individuals who are able to obtain bank loans. Adedibu's (1981) research on the indigenous house amplifies the fact that modernization seems to be appropriate for planning purposes. This is because new housing fulfills the set goals and objectives of public policy, which is to improve the standard of living in the community (Figures 2.12, 2.13, and 2.14).

There are basically two kinds of modern housing in Ikot-Ekpene: (1) Government building (Figure 2.15); and (2) Private housing.

Figure 2.12: Finished cinder blocks, ready for building and remodeling.

Figure 2.13: Blocks are used for constructing a wall around a compound.

Figure 2.14: Completed modern building.

Figure 2.15: Village building.

Ikot-Ekpene Local Government Role in Housing

In the last ten to fifteen years, there has been an increase in the demand for modern housing in Ikot-Ekpene. The complexity of the housing problems which need urgent and immediate attention can be made clear when one examines the issues of provisions, maintenance, and service of housing.

The creation of Akwa Ibom state has elevated the status of Ikot-Ekpene with regard to its role in the overall development of the state. Its proximity to the state capital (Uyo) makes it an ideal place to live and commute to Uyo. It will continue to absorb populations of people seeking to live in a less expensive town while working in the state capital. The growing trade and government institutions have also led to an increase in the demand for housing.

The government workers, such as senior staff officials, doctors, educators, and lawyers, have their homes subsidized. They are offered cheap modern housing in neighborhoods far away from the traditional homes. Barnes (1982) notes that government subsidized housing is a legacy of the colonial governments that provided their expatriate administrators housing with modern amenities in order to retain them. This type of government policy tends to meet the housing needs of the elite group and is limited by construction cost. The local government is involved in the provision of lesser quality homes to junior government officials such as police and civil servants. Their housing has the appearance of dormitories, containing mostly rooms and flats. In order to facilitate transportation for the employees, the local government has a public transportation system that is currently being run in an adequate manner. However, more buses need to be purchased to keep the program efficient. The maintenance of the transportation system must be a high priority in order to encourage the decentralization of development in the state.

The government is not involved in the provision of housing for the poor in Ikot-Ekpene. It is very expensive either to rent a house from private individuals or to build one. The high construction costs make the purchase or renting of houses almost impossible for the average worker in Ikot-Ekpene or elsewhere in Nigeria. Public housing provided by the government is very limited, and the stock of available houses is not sufficient for the growing population.

Private Ownership of Housing

In Ikot-Ekpene, about 99 percent of the housing is owned by private individuals. The new constructions are predominantly modern housing types. As mentioned earlier, the owner, family members (relatives of owner), and a contractor who hires the laborers are all involved in the building of the houses. Individuals are often personally involved in the construction of their homes and supervise various stages of construction.

Barnes (1982), in her study of public and private housing in some parts of Africa, identified three types of private housing, "authorized, customary, and spontaneous." The authorized housing, by definition, is the type that has the approval of local and/or state government authorities, such as the town planning department.

In Ikot-Ekpene, this approval involves the local government planning headquarters located in the state capital of Uyo. An architectural plan must be submitted for approval, and the planning office in Uyo examines the housing plan in order to see whether or not it meets the established specifications and regulations. The approved or unapproved plan is then returned to the architect who subsequently communicates the outcome of the decision to the owner of the intended building.

If the plan is unapproved for certain reasons, the architect is expected to make the modifications necessary for the plan to be approved. The process of approval involves bureaucratic maneuvering which costs about 800 naira (N1600). This is equivalent to approximately eighty U.S. dollars but constitutes the average earnings of a worker for a two- or three-month period. Needless to say, this would become a substantial investment and could be restrictive to many who wish to build suitable personal housing.

The introduction of a new land-reform decree in Nigeria in 1979 nationalized the unused land in the country. This has led to the eradication of the "customary housing" practice in which housing could be constructed on property purchased from a group, family, chief, or traditional owner.

Spontaneous housing is another type of housing which can be found in Ikot-Ekpene. These homes are unauthorized and usually squatter-like in appearance. They are usually erected by unemployed, homeless, or uninformed individuals, who put up structures on public or government land or on relatives' land or personal property without proper permission or approval for construction. The town planning officials in Ikot-Ekpene are trying to make sure that such buildings are not put up, and indeed, there are few such buildings in Ikot-Ekpene. The lack of manpower to enforce land-use laws and regulations makes planning work difficult and sometimes frustrating.

Survey of Housing Conditions

In order to fully comprehend the housing issues in Ikot-Ekpene, one has to take an in-depth look at the public's attitudes toward traditional

Table 2.1: Comparison of Ratings of Housing Attributes in Ikot-Ekpene

Housing Attributes	Property Owners (landlords)		Small Contractors		Government Officials (Planners & Policy Makers)		Tenants (Residents)	
	N1	P1	N2	P2	N3	P3	N4	P4
1. Supply (adequate)	20	40	10	30	10	20	50	20
2. Demand (high)	20	90	10	90	10	100	50	75
3. Availability to finance to potential owners	20	30	10	20	10	50	50	6
4. Government's role is good in:								
(a) regulating	20	20	10	30	10	90	50	50
(b) subsidizing	20	5	10	10	10	50	50	5
(c) stimulating	20	10	10	10	10	40	50	0
(d) servicing	20	5	10	10	10	50	50	0
(e) providing	20	5	10	0	10	20	50	5
5. Addition to the housing supply is high	20	40	10	10	10	30	50	20
6. Pattern of housing production is "private"	20	90	10	90	10	30	50	90
7. The housing choice is determined by income	20	100	10	100	10	100	50	100
8. The traditional housing environment promotes								
(a) unsanitary conditions	20	50	10	70	10	70	50	40
(b) unsafe conditions	20	50	10	40	10	50	50	30
9. The modern houses eliminate slums	20	90	10	100	10	100	50	70
10. The poor infrastructure, such as roads, water supply hinders modernization of housing conditions	20	90	10	100	10	100	50	70
11. Traditional homes have an important role to play in the development of the town	20	60	10	40	10	40	50	80

N = Sample Size; P = Percentage

housing, modern housing, affordability of homes, government policies, housing demand and supply, and infrastructure to support houses. Those that were surveyed consisted of property owners (landlords), small contractors, government officials (planners and policy makers) and tenants (renters) as indicated in Table 2.1.

The supply, demand, and finance of housing are important components of development. In order to ensure that the citizens of Akwa Ibom state have decent housing, rural housing conditions are being examined and evaluated by the government officials. A few residents of the state participated in government-sponsored seminars in 1987 on how to provide low-cost housing through new technology. Their viewpoints and desires have been incorporated into a statewide housing plan. It is impossible to predict whether or not this plan will be implemented. In 1987, the author of this book conducted a survey to investigate people's perception of the housing problem in Ikot-Ekpene. The result is shown in Table 2.1.

In investigating the aspect of the housing supply, all groups of people surveyed indicated that the housing supply was insufficient for the town, while demand was significantly high. New home construction is an important indication of development and economic progress of a town. The availability of financing to construct homes is also an important factor for home construction. Hence, the third concern addressed in Table 2.1 is whether financing was available to potential owners. Of all groups, only government officials indicated a fifty-person favorability. The other groups showed a very low indication that finance was available through either private banks or government financial establishments.

Item four examines the government's role in the provision of housing with respect to regulation, subsidizing, stimulating, servicing, and providing housing. The results of the survey showed that the ratings by the property owners, small contractors, and tenants of the government roles in these issues were insufficient and poor.

Item five shows that the rate at which additional houses were being built was not keeping up with the rate of growth of the population as assessed by the four groups of people surveyed. In order to cope with the growing population and to improve the quality of life of citizens, private individuals are involved in building new homes for personal occupancy or for renting to others.

Item six shows that the predominant pattern of housing production is private. These houses usually take an average of six years to complete, depending on the owners' ability to make the money for construction available to contractors. One of the problems confronting potential renters is that a majority of them cannot afford modern housing. This argument is substantiated by results presented in item seven. Only the wealthy and the small middle class in Ikot-Ekpene can afford to rent the apartments.

An examination of the housing environment is an important aspect of the study. The advantages of modern houses are that they have both outdoor and indoor plumbing and electricity and are both safe and sanitary. Sanitary conditions are lacking in traditional houses since they do not have these amenities unless the houses are modernized (renovated). Items 8a and 8b confirm that the overall impression is that traditional houses on the average promote unsanitary and unsafe environments, while item nine shows that investment in modern housing eliminates slums. Poor housing conditions are exacerbated by the poor infrastructure condition as shown by item ten.

Overall, traditional housing has an important role to play in the development of the town, since unemployment is still a major problem and a majority of the people can only afford to live in traditional houses. No one region or country has yet been able to solve its housing problem because of the growing population and the cost of providing public housing, but it is hoped that with good national policy, the federal, state, and local housing authorities will address the housing problem more adequately. Family planning and good sanitary programs must be integral parts of Ikot-Ekpene's housing policy strategy.

3. Issues of Tourism Development in Africa

In Chapter 1, mention was made of the attractiveness of the wildlife of Africa to tourists. It is important at this juncture to elaborate on the significance of tourism to the African economy, its impact on the host countries, and the future of tourism in the continent. In Chapter 2 we examined the housing conditions in Ikot-Ekpene in Nigeria. This town is famous for its wood carvings and raffia industry. It, too, like most rural communities in Africa, offers unique experiences to tourists. The housing conditions are important from the stand point of how tourism impacts the African landscape and how foreign visitors perceive them. This chapter examines some of the tourism issues of Africa.

The economic and industrial transformation of African countries has been very slow, and in some cases progress has not taken place at all. These situations occur in countries that are well endowed with natural resources (both renewable and nonrenewable) and countries with limited natural resources. The objective of many African governments is to speed up the economic transformation in order to enable their countries to participate fully in the new world economic order.

One area that has not been fully tapped is the tourism industry. It is an area of economic development that can yield developing nations tremendous revenue if properly planned and managed. The potential of tourism in these countries is enormous and should be harnessed properly and sensibly.

Before elaborating on the planning and management aspects of tourism, it should be pointed out that the term "tourism" has several interpretations depending on whether it is examined in the light of its positive impacts or its negative impacts. For the purposes of the discussion in this chapter, tourism will be defined as the temporary movement of people from their homes and places of work to other places (destinations) for recreational purposes. In Africa both domestic tourism and international tourism occur.

Domestic tourism is a phenomenon that occurs in Africa in a way that is often misunderstood by many researchers. It is not a new phenomenon in Africa; rather it is much more pronounced in recent times because of the impact Western tourism and the high profile that African big game has received in recent times. Africans traditionally travel to their places of origin within the same country. This travel always occurs during major holiday periods and usually involves attendance of major festivities. Domestic tourism occurs in rural as well as urban areas. Travel to the rural area usually begins with a well-organized individual or group trip. Departure from an urban area is initiated by making arrangements for public transportation a day or two before the desired date of travel. This is because of limited public transportation in Africa (Figures 3.1 and 3.2).

Upon arrival in the rural parts of some African countries, there may be a need to travel over a body of water in order to reach a remote part of the country. Traveling in southeastern Nigeria sometimes entails such a journey. In the Niger delta of Nigeria, Itu, Oban, and Calabar travel often includes journeys by ferry, boat and canoe. The canoes are rented for short distances. As can be seen in Figures 3.3, 3.4, and 3.5, in Itu passengers travel by canoe to get from one part of town to another. Building bridges costs exorbitant amounts of money, and unless they are absolutely necessary, reliance upon locally built canoes is encouraged and will continue in many parts of Africa.

International tourism is a growing phenomenon in Africa. Tourists who travel to Africa can enjoy both the urban and the rural settings of this beautiful continent. Historically, the most developed parts of Africa are the cities and towns along the coastal areas. Hence, international tourists and Westernized Africans who live close to the beaches of most of the cities and towns take advantage of the recreational opportunities offered by rivers and oceans that wash the shores of the countries. Lagos has two beaches, Bar Beach and Lekki Beach, that are popular places for visitors, especially on weekends (Figures 3.6, 3.7, and 3.8).

Most of the activities that go on at the beach are a mixture of Western and African culture styles. It is a common occurrence to find people riding horses, merry-go-rounds, and swings. Refreshments are sold, and African style barbecue is sold to visitors. Visitors can also witness traditional African cultures at the beach, such as the religious practices which attempt to blend traditional African religion with European style religion. Visitors can also buy ebony wood carvings and raffia bags and baskets. Numerous taxis are available for transportation to and from the beach (Figures 3.9, 3.10, 3.11, and 3.12).

The tourism industry in Africa both benefits and suffers from the fact that development has changed the landscape of the urban centers, but it should be emphasized that opportunities are created for the continuous

Figure 3.1: Privately managed transportation depot, Benin City, Nigeria, 1991.

Figure 3.2: Travelers emerging from transportation depot restaurant, Benin City, Nigeria, 1991.

Figure 3.3: A proud owner/driver of a canoe, 1991.

Figure 3.4: A foreign passenger being taken across the "Cross River" in Itu, Akwa Ibom state, 1991.

Figure 3.5: Itu dock for embarkment and disembarkment of passengers, 1991.

Figure 3.6: Bar Beach, Lagos, Nigeria, 1991.

Figure 3.7: Foreign tourists at Lekki Beach, Victoria Island, Nigeria, 1991.

Figure 3.8: Local citizens spending their weekend at Lekki Beach, Nigeria, 1991.

Figure 3.9: Local citizens preparing barbecue for sale to visitors at Lekki Beach, Nigeria, 1991.

Figure 3.10: Religious activities at Lekki Beach, Nigeria, 1991.

Figure 3.11: Traditional wood carvings for sale to visitors, Lekki Beach, Nigeria, 1991.

Figure 3.12: Transportation taxi for visitors at Lekki Beach, Nigeria, 1991.

growth of the industry. Ghana has benefited from the industry in several ways.

In Ghana the tourist industry has met with a great deal of success. The government at all levels has taken a vivid interest by promulgating programs in the urban and rural areas in order to boost the industry. Tourism has created job opportunities for several thousand people. In 1991 the industry employed about 170,000 people, and that number is expected to increase by more than 80 percent by 1995 (Ephson 1992).

Other African countries such as Nigeria also have a lot to offer tourists. In the urban environment, tourists can find excellent accommodation at hotels that provide modern Western convenience.

Tourist centers are available in major metropolitan centers across the country. The tourist centers provide information about the country's cultural and natural resources which should be of interest to visitors. Tourism in Africa embraces the urban as well as rural environment and by so doing offers the visitor a true picture of what the African ecological system entails (Figures 3.13 through 3.20).

Reasons for Tourism Development

The world community must take the issue of tourism development in Africa and other parts of the Third World seriously. Many countries in

Figure 3.13: Metropolitan Hotel, Calabar, Nigeria, 1991.

Figure 3.14: Qwa River Hotel, Eket, Nigeria, 1991.

Figure 3.15: Mobil Pegasus Club, Eket, Nigeria, 1991, housing for Mobil Oil Company guests.

Figure 3.16: Aesthetically pleasing Mobil Pegasus compound.

Figure 3.17: Tourist Plaza, Calabar, Nigeria, 1991.

Figure 3.18: Cultural Center, Lagos, Nigeria, 1991.

Figure 3.19: Slave Port, Badagry, Nigeria, 1991.

Figure 3.20: Rural nature expedition, Ikot-Obong, Nigeria, 1991.

Africa are willing to develop this aspect of their economy provided their interest is taken into account when foreign entrepreneurs engage in the development of the tourism industry. Tourism in Africa could lead to numerous benefits and indirectly encourage the development of secondary and tertiary development:

1. Tourism development enhances in-situ and ex-situ conservation.
2. It fosters the idea of global ownership of natural resources — especially the endangered species — and thus focuses attention on the protection and preservation of the species.
3. International tourism encourages international collaboration on research for the benefit of the world community.
4. Successful development of the tourism industry encourages innovative ideas in terms of wildlife protection.
5. It leads to the education of visitors and hosts with regard to the importance of ecological principles surrounding natural systems.
6. Foreign exchange and revenue become available to local citizens.
7. It brings to light the actual worth of the natural resources.
8. It reverses the environmental degradation due to poaching.
9. It could cause habitat destruction to be properly checked and controlled.
10. It could bring about international friendship — cultural exchange.
11. It leads to the possibility of infrastructure construction which will have a ripple effect in the economic situations of host countries.

12. Strategic planning of tourism can negate the impact that the lack of coordinated planning can have on local communities.

13. Tourists can be informed about the norms of other countries.

14. It could lead to investment by wealthy tourists who are genuinely interested in improving the lives of the citizens of the host country. Appropriate investments include the transfer of appropriate technology using local raw materials and labor. The initial stages of tourism development should be labor intensive which could gradually move toward automation in the future.

15. The world tourism industry is growing at a rate of approximately 6 percent annually. Africa needs to receive a share of this market.

16. There is a clear indication from many studies that the growing awareness in the Western societies of the richness of Africa will continue to increase people's curiosity about the continent [IUCN 1985].

17. As Africans and African governments continue to demand a role in world affairs many people of African descent living in the diaspora will become interested in the continent of their ancestry.

The role of Africans in the conservation of the world's most precise wildlife reserves will continue to grow.

Constraints Which Make Tourism Development Difficult

Despite the desire of many countries of Africa to increase tourism activities, there are many obstacles which make it difficult for them to speed up the tourism growth.

1) *Capital:* In order to elevate tourism to an international level which will compete for a reasonable share of the world tourism industry, African countries must invest a high percentage of their earnings into tourism. Some East African countries such as Kenya and Tanzania are attempting to do so and have had some success. But capital is scarce, and investment in tourism, although growing, still needs more encouragement.

2) *Media* (marketing and promotion of tourist products): In order to attract more users of the resources available in the tourism industry in African countries, advertisement must be done at the national and international arenas. Such promotion is expensive, but the economic rewards are enormous. Other non–African countries such as Jamaica, Bermuda, and other Caribbean nations have succeeded enormously in advertising. The rewards have been steady growth in the industry and employment opportunities for the citizens of these countries.

3) *Services:* The lack of expertise in technical and managerial services hinders the industry.

4) *Accessibility:* Infrastructures in accessibility are critical. Transpor-

tation is poor to some exotic sites which could be economically significant to tourism.

5) *Domestic politics:* Domestic civil wars are constantly being fought in Africa. A country at peace is more of a draw to tourists.

6) *International politics:* These occur due to wars and lead to embargoes.

7) *Population explosion:* Overpopulation in Africa has led to the destruction of natural habits of ecological importance for the tourism industry.

8) *Agricultural programs:* The lack of agricultural programs or an effective agenda hinders development. Sound agricultural agendas preserve natural resources from unplanned development.

9) *Infrastructures:* The lack of infrastructure to support the tourism industry could discourage potential visitors.

10) *Accommodations:* Facilities and accommodations should provide minimum safety and sanitary standards. The availability of world-class hotels is a good incentive for attracting tourists to both urban and rural areas of Africa. Not all African countries have facilities of the type that can rival those in Europe and South America. However, in Nigeria the Eko Hotel and the Sheraton Hotel are both excellent.

11) *Communication:* Telephone and telex facilities are important aspects of the tourism industry. For instance, foreign tourists would like to be able to reach their families overseas immediately in case of an emergency.

12) *Economic base:* The lack of a diversified economic base of host countries limits the ability of African countries to take full advantage of tourism.

Theoretical Viewpoints of Tourism Development

In writing about tourism potential in Ghana, Ephson (1992:971) makes the following assessment about the problems the tourism industry is encountering in that country:

> Ghana's tourism potential is constrained by a number of factors, some being the lack of an effective international marketing strategy, the lack of good hotel accommodation and services outside the capital, Accra and lack of direct flight to and from the North American continent. Uncompetitive high visa fees and bureaucratic immigration requirements are also limiting facts.

It should be emphasized that all the aforementioned constraints discourage well-meaning tourists who are willing to bring in the much-needed foreign exchange to African countries.

Distorted development looms all across the African landscape from the Mediterranean to the northern borders of South Africa and from the west coast to the east coast of the continent. One can point to the source of this distortion as being the scramble for Africa which occurred in the 1800s and the colonial administrations that followed. Tourism in Africa has suffered because the scramble for Africa resulted in a lack of a comprehensive plan to harness the national resources properly.

In all aspects of African life, one notices the struggle that the continent faces in its efforts to find permanent solutions to its economic problems and environmental decline.

It could be argued that tourism's past performance in Africa gives one little indication that it could be part of a package that would solve Africa's problems. The framework of this argument emerges from the standpoint of political economy which emphasizes that the encouragement of tourism in Africa only exacerbates the problem of "dependency." This phenomenon (dependency) is looked at by the supporters of this school of thought as a continuation of colonialism (Yansane 1980).

A quick examination of the tourist industry in the Third World could help to elucidate the dependency viewpoint. At the present time in many African nations that are involved in the tourism industry, the major carriers that convey tourists from the industrialized countries to the host countries are foreign owned. African countries that have their own carriers actually have little business (patronage) with foreign nationals. These foreign nationals feel safer traveling with Western airlines. Thus the revenue that could have gone to the host countries does not. Another problem with the carriers is that they are expensive to finance and maintain (James 1991a). For instance, Nigerian Airlines has been having great difficulties making payments on its 747 fleet. Some East African countries once formed a consortium that went into the business of running an airline that served the East African countries. The idea was to increase the tourist business in East Africa and also to retain some of the money that went to the multinational corporations that owned the foreign airlines. The project failed for a number of reasons which included the lack of managerial skills and financial woes. The airlines depend on foreign companies for spare parts and maintenance, and thus dependency continues.

Another area of criticism of the tourism business in Africa as well as other Third World countries has been the management of support facilities of the tourist industry, such as hotels and local transportation. It is argued that many of the hotel chains, such as Sheraton, which one can find in the capital cities of Third World countries are foreign owned and operated. Hence most of the top management personnel are foreign. What this amounts to, it is argued by proponents of the political economy paradigm, is that remittances to foreign banks are carried out. This does not allow the host countries to develop the necessary economic base that could have a multiplier effect on the host country's economy.

Other areas of criticism of tourism are the problems of environmental degradation and social and cultural decay. It is argued that in some places of the Third World environment, tourism has accelerated the pace at which the landscape is changing, including the destruction of vegetation. It is contended that prime areas are exposed to vehicles; making access to areas with wildlife leads to the destruction of the habitat (Mathieson and Wall 1986).

Negative sociocultural impacts are many, but only a few will be discussed in this chapter. In many places where tourism has been attempted in the Third World, prostitution has been on the increase. Botswana, Lesotho, Tanzania, and Kenya are a few countries where this has been the case. The emulation of foreign lifestyles by host-country citizens can sometimes be problematic. Often, it is the negative values of foreigners that last longer with people of the host country (Greenwood, 1977; Peters, 1979). Nonetheless, many good values are also learned from foreign visitors. Such values include good conservation practices, preservation, education, and eco-development.

It should be emphasized that there are problems with tourism because the planning phase of tourism is not properly and adequately undertaken. Standards and codes of conduct must be stipulated so that both the foreign visitors and the host country can benefit from their contact.

Planning Tourism in Africa

Like every business venture, there are costs and benefits associated with tourism. Every developing country interested in developing its tourism potential must be ready to make the trade offs that are necessary in order to enjoy the benefits of the tourism industry. The idea is to maximize the benefits of tourism while minimizing the negative impacts. This can only be achieved through careful planning. The planning should be long range and sensitive to the ecological system, and planners should bear in mind that the most successful tourism projects are those which respect the natural laws (first and second laws of thermodynamics).

Essence of Planning for Tourism

Every African country is blessed with unique natural and cultural resources, although the diversity of these resources is declining. It is the rapid decline of the resources that is the basis for planning for preservation and conservation. The key to any successful tourism planning program in Africa is its positive economic, social, and environmental impacts on African societies. As long as tourism development brings improvements in the transportation network, hotel accommodations, catering businesses, and recreation, the economy of the host country will improve and local citizens will have employment. One country that has experienced growth in the tourist industry is Zambia. Table 3.1 shows the growth of tourist arrivals in Zambia. In Table 3.2, one observes that between 1970 and 1981, Zambia's share of the tourism industry improved, but there was a slight decline between 1981 and 1985. Nonetheless, the overall assessment of the tourist industry continues to be favorable for this country.

The economic benefits of tourism should not be concentrated in one area of a country. The attempt is to ensure that there is a distribution of the tourism revenue so that an even development occurs throughout a country. By so doing, a majority of the inhabitants of the host country can understand and appreciate the significance of preserving a heritage of sound ecological wealth (flora and fauna). In order to continue to benefit from tourism, all efforts must be made to understand the nature of the main attractiveness of African resources to tourists. For instance, the wildlife of East African countries is continually under study in order to understand the impact of tourism on the animals. Such study also keeps track of the wildlife population as a result of human encroachment and poaching. Tourists want to experience a quality vacation, and countries that depend on tourists for their foreign exchange must ensure such an excellent experience at a cost to visitors.

Knowledge of the volume and the intensity of use of a resource by tourists is of great importance in planning for tourism. When a resource is overused by tourists, there is a tendency for the deterioration of the resource to result. Planning should embrace the understanding of the maximum use the resource can withstand. Limits must be set for numbers of tourists allowed at parks. Sometimes it might even be necessary to close

Table 3.1: Growth of Tourist Arrivals in Zambia

(average annual change: % per annum)			
Region	1970–80	1975–82	1979–84	–1985
Zambia	6.4	12.7	19.1	22.7
Africa	9.4	3.8	4.0	5.0
World	5.7	3.8	2.3	4.1

Source: Husbands, 1989.

Table 3.2: Tourist Arrivals in Zambia

Year	From Africa Number	Share	From Europe Number	Share	Rest of World Number	Share	Total
1970	37,269	79.3	7,526	16.0	2,177	4.7	46,970
1975	26,884	52.0	13,252	25.6	11,544	22.4	51,680
1978	35,129	65.9	12,568	23.6	5,630	11.5	53,680
1979	31,022	57.6	15,179	28.2	7,684	14.2	53,327
1980	64,816	74.6	14,918	17.2	7,197	8.2	86,931
1981	111,251	77.3	22,683	15.5	10,615	7.2	149,649
1982	83,696	70.6	24,688	20.5	10,263	8.6	118,627
1983	93,745	76.8	16,699	16.1	8,607	7.1	122,051
1984	99,789	77.3	19,392	15.0	8,926	7.7	129,197
1985	72,466	72.7	19,092	19.1	8,276	8.3	99,834

Percentage of year's total.

Source: Husbands, 1989.

down the use of the resource for a while. Lake Chad, for example, on which the Arugungu festival is held annually, is said to be overused. The number of fish in the lake has declined drastically, and the lake itself is shrinking. East African parks are suffering due to automobile exhaust; the tour buses destroy the ecology of the parks. More profit can be made by maintaining the quality of the parks and limiting the number of vans in the parks so as to allow the vegetation a period to rejuvenate.

It is also crucial to ensure that after the tourism industry has been established profits recirculate at the destination and are not routed to another area. Many African governments are now attempting to ensure local participation, and they are engaging the local citizens in the process of development (Figure 3.21).

Development schemes for tourism are being embarked upon by governments in Africa. These programs identify regions where potential for tourism exists and then educate local citizens and entrepreneurs on how to take advantage of the opportunities that exist in their region. For instance, the Ghanian government established the Tourism Development Scheme for the Central Region of Ghana (TODSCER). Tourists who visit the area are given tours of the region's historical and ecological sites, and local private companies are involved in the business of tour packages and the general operation of the project (Ephson 1992).

The Ghanian plan includes a visit to the site where slave trade was conducted, a visit to the three world heritage monuments in Ghana, a showing of the famous Kente apparel, a visit to the Kakum Nature

Figure 3.21: Local children at Badagry Beach, Nigeria, act as guides for tourists, 1991.

Table 3.3: Comparative Data on International Tourism in Selected Developing Countries, 1970

	Estimated Foreign Visitor Arrivals	Growth of Foreign Visitor Arrivals Index 1969 (1965-100)	Average Length of Stay of Foreign Visitors (Nights)	Gross Foreign Tourism Receipts ($ million)	Average Daily Foreign Tourist Expend. ($)	Gross Tourism Receipts Compared to Merchandise Exports ($)
East Africa						
Ethiopia	53	– –	4.0	6	28.0	4.9
Kenya	344	– –	8.8	52	16.8	24.0
Tanzania	63	– –	9.0	14	24.8	5.6
Uganda	80	– –	9.7	19	24.0	7.7
West Africa						
Ivory Coast	42	– –	4.0	5	30.0	1.5
Senegal	40	– –	3.5	4	25.0	2.6

Source: World Bank, 1972.

Table 3.4: Tourism Financing
by the International Finance Corporation

Country/ Project	Original Amount of IFC Commitment or Approval ($ Thousand)	By Original Commitment or Approval	Investment held by IFC as of December 31, 1971 ($ Thousand) Equity	Loan	Total	Comments
Kenya/ Hotel Properties	3,204	1967/68	561	1,550	2,111	Part-financing of 200-room hotel in capital city, some game lodges and 100-room beach hotel.
Tunisia/ Cie. Financiere et Touristique	9,905	1969	1,905	6,891	8,786	Tourism development and holding company.
Kenya & Uganda/ Tourism (K) Promotion (U) Services	2,420 1,180	1971	− −	3,600	3,600	Financing of six (6) hotels and lodges comprising 950 beds and 138-vehicle touring service.
Lts.	16,709		2,466	12,041	14,497	

Source: World Bank, 1972.

Table 3.5: Commitments for Tourism Projects Under
World Bank Loans to Development Finance Companies

Country	Name of Company	# of Projects	Bank Funds Committed by DECs as of December 31, 1971 ($ Thousand)
Tunisia	Societe Nationale d'Investissement	32	14,510
Morocco	Credit Immobilier et Hotelier	22	8,131
Morocco	Banque Nationale de Development Economique	22	7,871
Total		76	30,512

Source: World Bank, 1972.

Reserve, and a tour of the famous Virgin Beach of Bremu Akyinim. This plan is a successful one.

Conclusion

There is no doubt that tourism development in Africa can be a part of the general economic strategy. A deliberate and well-thought-out plan needs to be designed for each country based on its potential and limitations. Certainly the technical and managerial expertise for managing tourism is still at its infancy in many African countries, but this should not be a handicap. Appropriate assistance must be sought from Western countries who have successfully operated programs related to tourism. As shown in Table 3.3, some African countries such as Kenya, Tanzania, and Uganda have gained from the tourist industry, but their success was due in part to foreign assistance and the dedication and courage the citizens of these countries had to improve their economies.

Although assistance from international organizations, foreign governments, and the World Bank has been difficult to obtain for the purposes of tourism development, African governments have been supported for the preservation and conservation of their natural resources. Assistance has also been given to African governments to develop their tourism industries based on their potential as illustrated in Tables 3.4 and 3.5. It is hoped that the assistance will continue in the future for a true partnership between foreign governments, agencies, and African governments to develop tourism in Africa. Economic success in the tourism industry in Africa will translate to much-needed employment opportunities for millions of Africans.

4. Agriculture: Commercial and Subsistence

Introduction

In the last two decades there has been a plethora of literature on the agricultural crisis in Africa. Journal articles and books have lamented the poor agricultural conditions of the continent of Africa. The causes of these problems have been very well documented as well as the linkages of the causes and effects of agricultural decline. In this chapter, an attempt is made to review the current agriculture situations of the continent and to examine the reasons for the failure of agriculture in the continent. The various dimensions of agricultural productivity will also be examined.

The environmental, social, economic, and political aspects of agriculture are of great importance in analyzing Africa's difficulties in producing food for the growing population. First, this perspective is important because the issue of environmental decline affects the food production precisely because food supply in Africa depends upon the regenerative ability of just a few inches of topsoil spread across the bedrock. The future of agriculture in Africa is rooted in the ability to preserve the quality of its soils. Sustaining the integrity of the soil should be carried out in a manner that is ecologically, economically, and socially viable in a comprehensive long-term agenda. Continuous cropping leads to the decrease of soil fertility. The second reason for examining agricultural production in Africa from an interdisciplinary manner is that social ramifications in Africa have played significant roles in the current situation in agricultural production. The third angle is because political upheaval has determined production levels in certain parts of Africa. The fourth reason is that economic situations in Africa have determined the types of technology and investment that are put into agricultural sectors of the African countries.

A quick glance at Table 4.1 shows the reader Africa's condition in terms of its ability to feed itself given the world's recession. Food production in Africa has not kept pace with the demand for staple food by the

94

ever increasing population. Thousands of metric tons of food aid have continued to go to many African nations in order to relieve the plight of many of the thousands of people who suffer from malnutrition and others who cannot afford food or those who are caught in the problems of drought and civil war.

Africa's Food Supply

A number of factors have contributed to the decline in food production in Africa. The most significant cause for the decline is the neglect of the agricultural sector which provides food for the urban population. The emphasis of many African nations in the past twenty-five years has been on the development of the urban areas in which only 20 percent of the people live. The majority of Africans still reside in the rural areas and depend heavily on the subsistence agriculture that they practice.

The governments of many African nations have not paid enough attention to the development of rural agriculture, but the focus on agriculture is currently being taken seriously. Social and political upheaval in many parts of Africa, such as Angola, Chad, Ethiopia, Somalia, and the Sudan, has interrupted agricultural production and has decimated the land.

Industrialization in some African countries has not been truly diversified. Most countries have merely depended on the extraction of natural resources. For instance, Algeria has concentrated on the development of the energy-producing industry. Angola has depended on the production of diamonds since the 1970s, and the industry has been experiencing financial difficulties ever since. Oil and iron-ore production has been plagued by financial difficulties because of fluctuating world prices.

Another example of neglect of the agriculture sector is Guinea, where bauxite mining was the major development. The problem is that this particular mining sector only employs about 6 percent of the total active population. Although the mining industry which enjoyed the investment of Canadian, French, and British interest has flourished, Guinea has not been able to adequately diversify its economy in order to provide employment to a majority of its citizens. The government has also engaged in the extraction of gold and diamond, but these operations are subject to widespread smuggling and corruption. Inability to recognize the importance of agriculture and limiting and regulating environmental degradation due to the mining of minerals poses a grave problem to the country. Thirty percent of Guinea's GDP is represented by the agricultural sector which provides about 4 percent of the total export earnings of the country and represents a significant part of the Guinean economy. Neglecting the

Table 4.1: Agriculture and Food Situations of African Countries

Low & middle income economies	Value added in agriculture (millions of current dollars 1970	– 1989	Cereal imports (thousands of metric tons) 1974	– 1989
1. Algeria+	492	6,187	1,816	7,461
2. Angola	– –	– –	149	248
3. Benin	121	729	7	104
4. Botswana+	28	75	21	77
5. Burkina Faso	121	871	99	120
6. Burundi	159	535	7	6
7. Cameroon+	364	2,978	81	345
8. CAR	6	442	7	28
9. Chad	142	364	37	37
10. Congo, Peo. Rep.+	49	311	34	82
11. Côte d'Ivoire	462	3,295	172	693
12. Egypt, Arab R.	1,942	5,858	3,877	8,543
13. Ethiopia	931	2,254	118	690
14. Gabon+	60	353	24	50
15. Ghana+	1,030	2,570	177	244
16. Guinea+	– –	812	63	183
17. Kenya	484	2,208	15	119
18. Lesotho	23	83*	48	140
19. Liberia	91	– –	42	158
20. Libya	93	– –	612	1,515
21. Madagascar+	243	717	114	103
22. Malawi	119	498	17	86
23. Mali+	207	1,048	281	89
24. Morocco+	789	3,679	891	1,329
25. Mauritania	58	339	115	207
26. Mozambique	– –	704	62	400
27. Namibia	– –	187	– –	0
28. Niger+	420	744	155	105
29. Nigeria	5,080	8,874	389	240
30. Rwanda+	135	799	3	10
31. Senegal	208	1,028	341	515
32. Sierra Leone	108	409	72	145
33. Somalia	167	705	42	186
34. South Africa	1,362	4,635	127	296
35. Sri Lanka	545	1,648	951	1,177
36. Sudan	757	– –	125	556
37. Tanzania	473	1,795	431	83
38. Togo+	85	446	6	111
39. Tunisia	245	1,235	307	1,655
40. Uganda	929	2,986	36	16
41. Yemen, Rep.+	– –	– –	306	1,378
42. Zaire	805	2,846	343	323
43. Zambia	191	617	93	123
44. Zimbabwe	214	664	56	52

*Other years.   +Value=purchaser.

Table 4.1: (cont.)

Food aid in cereals (thousands of metric tons)		Fertilizer consumption (hundreds of grams of plant nutrient per hectare of arable land=100)		Average index of food production 1979–81
74/75	88/89	70/71	87/88	87–89
54	39	163	320	97
0	79	33	29	84
9	16	36	49	114
5	33	15	7	68
28	49	3	57	115
6	6	5	20	98
4	6	34	71	96
1	0	12	4	90
20	15	7	17	101
2	2	114	25	98
4	19	74	90	96
610	1,427	1,312	3,505	109
54	573	4	39	89
– –	– –	– –	46	81
33	46	13	38	109
49	42	19	6	90
2	112	238	421	101
14	34	10	125	80
3	28	63	94	95
– –	– –	62	416	109
7	76	61	21	93
0	217	52	203	85
107	62	31	59	97
75	238	117	376	120
48	70	11	55	88
34	424	22	21	83
– –	– –	– –	– –	95
73	83	1	8	86
7	0	2	94	96
19	2	3	20	77
27	53	17	40	106
10	38	17	3	89
111	73	29	40	97
– –	– –	422	541	90
271	272	555	1,094	87
46	198	28	40	87
148	76	31	92	90
11	11	3	76	89
59	284	76	222	96
– –	17	14	2	87
33	85	– –	63	– –
1	55	8	9	94
5	66	73	183	97
0	10	446	505	90

Source: Adapted from World Bank, 1991, pp. 210–11.

agricultural sector could prove to be catastrophic both domestically and for foreign exchange purposes.

One freelance writer, Okereke (1991:32) in describing the situation in Nigeria notes:

> A direct result of the near-collapse of the oil-dominated Nigerian economy is the need for the nation to return to the land. The land, until the advent of the petro-dollar and the oil boom of the 1970s, was the backbone of the national economy. Realization has come that the land is potentially a resource of almost boundless limits and potentials provided, of course, that it is well managed and treated with the respect it deserves. But to reap from it all that it is willing and capable of yielding for the survival of the teeming Nigerian population, there is the need to invest in the land.
>
> To invest in the land is to develop the rural areas of the nation which constitute some 70 per cent of the total land area and wherein up to 80 per cent of the population reside and make their living and contribution to the development of the economy.
>
> For the avoidance of doubt, the need for rural development is hardly new, for even before the recent urban population explosion there had been a national call to stem the rural-urban flow both to check unbridled urban growth and to prevent rural depopulation with its consequent effect on the rural function of agricultural production. What was lacking until lately was the political will to commit resources to address the issue.
>
> Rural development consists mainly of providing infrastructure to remove tedium from rural economic activities and to enhance commercial interaction between the rural and urban dwellers, and within the rural communities themselves. In addition, there is the need for social amenities and essential services for which the allure of cities has been overpowering, entirely irresistible in some instances, and sometimes an outright means of survival.

An examination of Table 4.2 shows the data relating the African environment to development indicators. The data in the third column shows high population figures. Table 4.3 indicates the rate of growth in urbanization which directly affects food production. This rise in urbanization has led to African nations importing food from abroad in order to supplement the domestic food supply. However, there are countries in Africa that have been hard struck by economic problems and are heavily indebted to foreign banks. Some also have food supply problems because of the ravages of war. For these countries, the Food and Agricultural Organization (FAO) contends that there is a need for immediate assistance:

> "Unless there is a massive acceleration of the flow of food aid to the affected populations, we are going to see widespread deaths from starvation between now and the next harvest at the end of the year," claims FAO Director-General, Mr. Edouard Sauma. In a statement issued from Rome on June 18, the FAO notes that Africa needs 5.7 m tons of emer-

gency food aid and that, as yet, only 3.4 m tons have been pledged by donor countries and organizations (sic).

The FAO identifies Ethiopia, Sudan, Mozambique, Somalia, Liberia and Angola as the countries most affected by the problem, but warns that Burkina Faso, Chad, Côte d'Ivoire, Ghana, Madagascar, Malawi, Mauritania, Niger, Sierra Leone and Uganda are all likely to be affected by harvest shortfalls or in need of help to feed refugee problems [Editorial, *West Africa:* 1029.]

Table 4.4 indicates the food aid requirements for 1991 for eight African countries. The situation has worsened in 1992 and it is argued that unless the economic conditions change, it will continue to decline.

In order to appreciate Africa's food crisis, compare the population growth rates of Africa with those of Latin America and Asia (Figure 4.1).

During the seventeenth ministerial session of the World Food Council

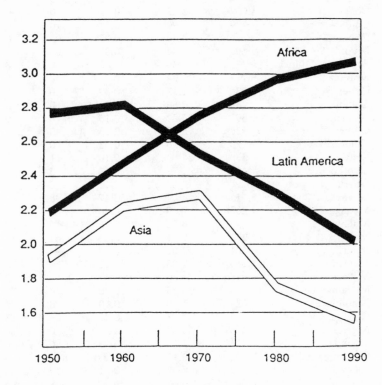

Source: UN *Africa Recovery,* September 1991, p. 36.

Figure 4.1: Population Growth Rates (annual % change).

Table 4.2: Africa: Environment
and Development Indicators (per capita)

Country	GNP 1990 ($)	Population 1990 (mn)	Cultivated 1990 (ha)	% Total land arid	% Total land semi-arid
1. Algeria	2,058	24.96	0.30	92	3
2. Angola	609	10.02	0.38	4	6
3. Benin	362	4.63	0.40	0	1
4. Botswana	2,049	1.30	1.06	62	38
5. Burkina Faso	328	8.99	0.40	1	15
6. Burundi	211	5.47	0.24	0	0
7. Cameroon	941	11.83	0.59	0	1
8. Cape Verde	894	0.37	0.11	100	0
9. Central Afr. Rep.	393	3.03	0.66	0	0
10. Chad	189	5.67	0.56	87	7
11. Comoros	482	0.55	0.18	0	0
12. Congo	1,007	2.27	0.07	0	0
13. Côte d'Ivoire	729	11.99	0.31	0	0
14. Djibouti	n.a.	0.40	0.00	100	0
15. Egypt	603	52.42	0.05	100	0
16. Equatorial Guinea	325	0.35	0.65	0	0
17. Ethiopia	118	49.24	0.28	38	16
18. Gabon	3,234	1.17	0.39	0	0
19. Gambia	260	0.86	0.21	0	0
20. Ghana	392	15.02	0.16	0	0
21. Guinea	428	5.75	0.13	0	0
22. Guinea-Bissau	179	0.96	0.35	0	0
23. Kenya	368	24.03	0.10	71	14
24. Lesotho	470	1.77	0.18	15	13
25. Liberia	n.a.	2.57	0.14	0	0
26. Libya	5,315	4.54	0.47	98	1
27. Madagascar	233	12.00	0.26	5	0
28. Malawi	195	8.75	0.28	0	0
29. Mali	271	9.21	0.23	64	16
30. Mauritania	501	2.02	0.10	94	5
31. Mauritius	2,263	1.08	0.10	0	0
32. Morocco	948	25.06	0.37	54	10
33. Mozambique	77	15.65	0.20	8	0
34. Namibia	1,029	1.78	0.40	78	21
35. Niger	308	7.73	0.47	86	13
36. Nigeria	266	88.50	0.29	0	8
37. Rwanda	311	7.23	0.16	0	0
38. Sao Tome & Prin.	393	0.12	n.a.	n.a.	n.a.
39. Senegal	708	7.32	0.71	7	14
40. Seychelles	4,541	0.07	n.a.	n.a.	n.a.
41. Sierra Leone	237	4.15	0.43	0	0
42. Somalia	n.a.	7.49	0.14	93	7
43. Sudan	374	25.20	0.50	55	11
44. Swaziland	816	0.78	0.21	0	26

Table 4.2: (cont.)

Food prod. 1986–89	Water use 1990 (cu.m.)	Access to safe water (% of pop.)	Traditional fuel, 1989 (% energy use)	Ann. average deforestation rate % 1981–85	Total forest lost %
99	161	71	3	2.3	n.a.
85	43	35	55	0.2	45
114	26	54	86	1.7	59
68	98	53	n.a.	0.1	62
116	20	69	92	1.7	80
98	20	38	92	2.7	88
96	30	32	49	0.4	59
84	148	71	0	n.a.	n.a.
90	27	12	86	0.2	55
101	36	n.a.	92	0.6	80
121	15	n.a.	0	n.a.	n.a.
97	20	38	41	0.1	49
95	68	18	59	5.2	78
n.a.	28	47	0	n.a.	0
108	1,202	89	4	n.a.	n.a.
n.a.	11	n.a.	75	0.2	50
90	48	19	91	0.3	86
81	51	68	35	0.1	35
94	33	77	77	2.4	91
108	35	57	67	0.8	80
90	115	32	72	8.8	69
108	18	25	67	2.7	80
102	48	30	79	1.7	71
79	34	48	n.a.	n.a.	67
95	54	55	78	2.3	87
107	623	94	1	n.a.	n.a.
93	1,675	22	82	1.2	75
85	22	56	90	3.5	56
97	159	38	87	0.5	78
88	473	66	0	2.4	90
101	415	95	52	3.3	n.a
122	501	61	5	0.4	n.a.
84	53	24	89	0.8	57
92	77	n.a.	n.a.	0.2	n.a.
86	44	n.a.	73	2.6	80
98	44	48	62	2.7	76
78	23	64	88	2.2	80
85	n.a.	n.a.	n.a.	n.a.	n.a.
106	201	54	51	0.5	82
n.a.	n.a.	100	n.a.	n.a.	n.a.
90	99	42	76	0.3	88
97	167	37	85	0.1	67
88	1,089	21	81	1.1	74
99	414	53	n.a.	n.a.	56

Table 4.2: (cont.)

Country	GNP 1990 ($)	Population 1990 (mn)	Cultivated 1990 (ha)	% Total land arid	% Total land semi-arid
45. Tanzania	129	27.31	0.19	7	15
46. Togo	405	3.53	0.41	0	0
47. Tunisia	1,419	8.18	0.57	66	16
48. Uganda	276	18.79	0.36	0	5
49. Zaire	228	35.56	0.22	0	0
50. Zambia	418	8.45	0.62	0	2
51. Zimbabwe	644	9.70	0.29	8	41

Source: Adapted from UN Africa Recovery, No. 5, June 1992, p. 2.

(WFC) in Denmark in June of 1991, the declining food supply situation in the Third World was discussed. The poor food-supply conditions were linked with rising environmental degradation of the ecological system. In a previous meeting in Bangkok, WFC had stated the following as its priorities: (1) To eliminate starvation and death caused by famine; (2) to drastically reduce malnutrition and mortality among young children; (3) to have a substantial decline in chronic hunger; and (4) to eliminate major diseases associated with nutritional deficiency (West Africa 1991a).

The WFC has given assistance to many countries through its food aid and drought programs. Ethiopia received 108,000 tons of emergency food aid in 1991, at an estimated cost of $43.4 million.

The United Nations' Program of Action for African Economic Recovery and Development (UNPAAERD) was active in combatting the impacts of drought. Unfortunately, the deteriorating agricultural climate forced many countries to be more concerned about providing short-term solutions to complex problems. For instance, pressure to obtain foreign exchange has caused many African countries to concentrate on producing cash crops and minerals instead of food crops.

Conferences are being organized to address the food-supply problems in Africa and to raise the consciousness of international communities. In May of 1991, the Center for Applied Studies in International Negotiations (CASIN), based in Geneva, organized a conference which took place in Tanzania. The central idea was the discussion of "Africa's Agricultural Development in the 1990s." The participants examined the sustainability of African agriculture. Sustainability as an agronomic concept refers to the long-term use and management of land for crop production. Using the

Table 4.2: (cont.)

Food prod. 1986-89	Water use 1990 (cu.m.)	Access to safe water (% of pop.)	Traditional fuel, 1989 (% energy use)	Ann. average deforestation rate % 1981-85	Total forest lost %
89	36	56	90	0.3	40
89	40	71	43	0.7	65
96	325	68	15	1.7	n.a.
86	20	20	67	0.8	79
95	22	34	76	0.2	57
96	86	59	58	0.2	30
94	129	n.a.	25	0.4	56

land for sustainable agriculture requires proper application of appropriate technology, indigenous knowledge, research, and training.

Soils

The African soils are experiencing a tremendous amount of erosion. The current level of erosion in African countries could lower agricultural production by 25 percent over the 1975–2000 period (UN *Africa Recovery*, 1991).

Soil management in Africa should include adequate soil conservation and the application of scientific techniques to stop soil erosion. If erosion is not checked, its impact can be devastating environmentally, socially, and economically. The case of Ideota in Imo state of Nigeria has been very well documented. Wabara (1991) indicates that the problem of erosion has halted the rubber processing industry at Ideota local government area of Imo state. The state government benefits enormously from rubber production, and the loss of jobs has brought other social problems to the area. It is estimated that about 22 communities in Ideota have been devastated economically as a result of the grounding of rubber production. Besides the economic devastation of this community, the citizens of Ideota complain that the landscape of the community has been changed drastically as a result of erosion. The vegetation has obviously been impacted negatively, the fauna of the area has most likely suffered irreparable damage, and water pollution has occurred.

Wabara (1991:32) suggests that fear has been expressed by the

Table 4.3: Urbanization in African Countries

	Urban population as a % of total population		Average annual growth rate (%)	
	1965	1989	1965–80	1980–89
1. Algeria	38	51	3.9	4.9
2. Angola	13	28	6.4	5.8
3. Benin	13	37	8.9	5.2
4. Botswana	4	26	12.5	10.1
5. Burkina Faso	5	9	4.1	5.4
6. Burundi	2	5	6.9	5.6
7. Cameroon	16	40	7.6	6.1
8. Central A.R.	27	46	4.3	4.9
9. Chad	9	29	8.0	6.5
10. Congo, P.R.	32	40	3.5	4.8
11. Côte d'Ivoire	23	40	7.6	4.7
12. Egypt, A.R.	41	46	2.7	3.1
13. Ethiopia	8	13	4.9	5.3
14. Gabon	21	45	7.3	6.4
15. Ghana	26	33	3.2	4.2
16. Guinea	12	25	4.9	5.7
17. Kenya	9	23	8.1	8.2
18. Lesotho	6	20	7.5	7.1
19. Liberia	22	45	6.2	6.1
20. Libya	26	69	9.8	6.5
21. Madagascar	12	24	5.2	6.3
22. Malawi	5	12	7.4	6.3
23. Mali	13	19	4.4	3.6
24. Morocco	32	47	4.3	4.3
25. Mauritania	9	45	10.6	7.7
26. Mozambique	5	26	10.2	10.7
27. Namibia	17	27	4.6	5.3
28. Niger	7	19	7.2	7.7
29. Nigeria	17	35	5.7	6.2
30. Rwanda	3	7	7.5	8.1
31. Senegal	33	38	3.3	4.0
32. Sierra Leone	15	32	5.2	5.4
33. Somalia	20	36	5.2	5.5
34. South Africa	47	59	3.2	3.7
35. Sri Lanka	20	21	3.3	1.3
36. Sudan	13	22	5.9	3.9
37. Tanzania	5	31	11.3	10.8
38. Togo	11	25	6.6	6.9
39. Tunisia	40	54	4.0	2.9
40. Uganda	7	10	4.7	5.1
41. Yemen, Rep.	11	28	6.6	7.3
42. Zaire	26	39	4.6	4.6
43. Zambia	23	49	6.6	6.2
44. Zimbabwe	14	27	6.0	6.0

Source: Adapted from World Bank, 1991, pp. 264–65.

Table 4.3: (cont.)

| Population in capital city (%) | | Population in cities of 1 million or more in 1990 (%) | | | |
| Urban 1990 | Total 1990 | Urban | | Total | |
		1965	1990	1965	1990
23	10	16	22	4	10
61	17	49	61	6	17
12	4	– –	– –	– –	– –
38	10	– –	– –	– –	– –
51	5	– –	– –	– –	– –
82	4	– –	– –	– –	– –
16	6	– –	– –	– –	– –
51	24	– –	– –	– –	– –
43	13	– –	– –	– –	– –
68	28	– –	– –	– –	– –
44	18	30	45	7	18
37	17	53	52	22	24
29	4	27	30	2	4
57	26	– –	– –	– –	– –
22	7	27	22	7	7
89	23	47	88	5	23
26	6	41	27	4	6
17	4	– –	– –	– –	– –
57	26	– –	– –	– –	– –
– –	– –	55	65	14	45
23	6	– –	– –	– –	– –
31	4	– –	– –	– –	– –
41	8	– –	– –	– –	– –
9	4	39	36	12	17
83	39	– –	– –	– –	– –
38	10	68	38	3	10
30	8	– –	– –	– –	– –
39	8	– –	– –	– –	– –
19	7	23	24	4	8
54	4	– –	– –	– –	– –
52	20	40	53	13	20
52	17	– –	– –	– –	– –
31	11	– –	– –	– –	– –
11	6	40	30	19	18
17	4	– –	– –	– –	– –
35	8	30	35	4	8
21	7	38	18	2	6
55	14	– –	– –	– –	– –
37	20	35	37	14	20
38	4	– –	– –	– –	– –
11	3	– –	– –	– –	– –
25	10	17	25	5	10
24	12	– –	– –	– –	– –
31	9	– –	– –	– –	– –

Table 4.4: Food Aid Requirements, 1991

	Numbers of people in need of immediate assistance	Food aid required by total population at 1,500cal/500g cereal per capita per day	
	Millions	For one day	For one year
Angola	1.9	950mt	346,750mt
Ethiopia	9.0	4,500mt	1,642,500mt
Liberia	1.5	750mt	273,750mt
Malawi	1.8	900mt	328,500mt
Mozambique	2.0	1,000mt	365,000mt
Somalia	2.5	1,250mt	458,250mt
Sudan	7.9	3,950mt	1,441,750mt
Total	26.6	13,300mt	4,856,500mt

Source: West Africa, 1991, p. 1027.

chairman of the local government area as to the repercussions of uncontrolled erosion in Ideota. He states:

> According to Ananukwa, the Umuago-Urualla erosion is about 220 meters long, 132 meters wide and 128 meters deep. The zone, like others, has over the years claimed more than six kilometers of farmland, forced several families to flee from their ancestral homes and rendered roads to schools and other facilities inaccessible due to soil fragmentation.
>
> The chairman says that farm crops, economic trees, residential and industrial complexes, tourist resorts, historical buildings and other infrastructure like electricity poles, NITEL cables and water pipelines have also been damaged by surging floods. The consequence of these disruptions is the paralysis of vital socio-economic activities.
>
> It is feared, by some inhabitants of the areas involved, that unless something is done and in time too to check these distressing developments, many families may neither have any land for habitation nor would there be access roads in the near future.
>
> The secretary to the local government, Mr. O. Nwosu, says that between 1985 and 1988, three villages — Ezenwoke, Otuli and Umueze — embarked on the construction of a seven-kilometer drainage system measuring eight by six feet and carrying 26 culverts at the cost of N5.7 million, through self-help effort in order to grapple with the recurring problem. "But, today, the enormity of the issue has diminished all that," he says.

This calamity is not limited to Nigeria but seems to be a growing problem throughout Africa. Once the process of soil erosion begins, it appears to be compounded by human activities conducted at the site of the erosion.

Soil erosion is severe in many parts of Africa and renders the land unsuitable for agriculture and other development endeavors. Figures 4.2, 4.3, and 4.4 illustrate some of these problems. Of all the environmental problems caused by human activity in Africa, soil erosion seems to be the most devastating and pervasive. Not only does soil erosion damage the land where it occurs, but the area where the eroded material and soil are deposited is also damaged.

The degree of damage depends on the quantity of the soil and the type of material swept along with the soil.

Soil Formation

There are many soil types in Africa and their classification depends on the moisture content, texture, and color. The degree of soil moisture content in Africa is affected by their geographical location. To a great extent their acidity/alkalinity is an aspect of the parent material from which they are formed, evaporation in the region and other climatic factors. Over time, climate, land configuration, micro-organisms and plant life are

Figure 4.2: Erosion destroying an access road and damaging surrounding land, Ikot-Ekpene, Nigeria, 1991.

Figure 4.3: Subsistence farmlands threatened by erosion due to road construction, Ikot-Ekpene, Nigeria, 1991.

Figure 4.4: Clearance of forest by humans causing erosion in Ikot-Obong, Nigeria, 1991.

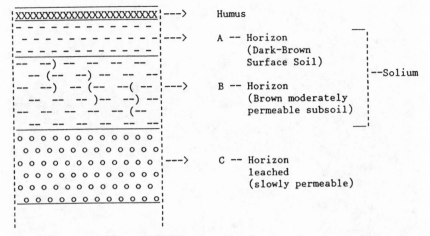

Figure 4.5: Typical soil profile.

also part of the soil formation factors. The climate is influential in the weathering activity, water content and the temperature of the soils. The soils of Africa, like all soils anywhere in the world, are dynamic. They are constantly changing as water enters and leaves and plants and animals live and die releasing the essential nutrients for the cycles of carbon, nitrogen, and phosphorous. The profiles of most soils are never exactly the same over time.

As shown in Figure 4.5, the A-horizon is the part of the soil that is exposed to constant changes due to weathering and the activities of the flora and the fauna. The layers of the soil do not change drastically unless erosion sets in. The maturity of the soil depends on how undisturbed it is by man and development. Thus a mature soil is able to maintain its rich integrity as a result of concentrated resistant material in its topsoil. This rich integrity is essential for plant growth. The B-horizon is rich in clay content, and over a long stretch of time the amount of clay builds up. The C-horizon constitutes the parent rock material and may be completely absent in some soil profiles.

Surface soil can be removed by erosion in a few years, and in some cases in a matter of hours the soil surface that took hundreds or thousands of years to form could be completely destroyed. The erosion process goes through increasingly damaging stages. Water drops detach soil particles, and when the soil is inundated with water, erosion flow ensues. Sheet erosion is commonly formed when more particles are picked up by the flowing water running down a slope of gentle or sharp gradient. Accelerated erosion is particularly troublesome in hilly and mountainous parts of Africa, where gullies are formed. In Figure 4.6, the creation of a man-made fish farm has resulted in sheet erosion and gullies.

Figure 4.6: The formation process of sheet and gully erosion.

In East Africa, especially near the Serengeti National Park, soil erosion due to slash-and-burn agriculture has resulted in the silting of streams in areas which could be classified as rain forest.

Erosion causes the loss of productivity of the soil. Eroded soils lose their ability to store water and are more vulnerable to drought conditions. Soils in Niger, Chad, Ethiopia, and Nigeria have suffered this fate.

The soils contain minerals essential to plants and animals. For example the forest elephants of the Central African Republic are known to feed on the soil of the reserve where they exist. Pesticides, fungicides, herbicides, fertilizers and other pollutants are carried as runoffs into streams, rivers, and lakes leading to the eutrophication of the lakes and destroying the fish and other fauna. Lake Chad is already experiencing some problems due to pollution. The deposition of silt is also a direct result of erosion which pollutes the rivers of Africa. Silt buildup affects navigation, reduces the river capacity — which could lead to flooding — and clogs the deltas, estuaries, and flood plains.

Fertility and structure are of utmost importance in increasing the ability of soil to withstand erosion, and the application of organic matter seems to enhance the soil's capacity to maintain its integrity.

Farming Systems in Africa

The importance of the examination of farming systems in Africa lies predominantly in the need to sustain agricultural development. The viability of agricultural methods should be evaluated in the light of the changing demographics of the continent, the urbanization rate, the number of people involved in agriculture, the impact on the ecosystem, the economy of the countries of Africa, the changing social dynamics of the countries, the political realities of the countries, and the foreign aid for agriculture.

Table 4.5 shows the agricultural systems in Africa. The first three farming systems are types of shifting agriculture which have been in existence in Africa for centuries. Figures 4.7, 4.8, 4.9, and 4.10 depict various types of shifting cultivation. Shifting cultivation has always intrigued specialists of agricultural development from the different branches of science and policy because it has predominated agricultural practice in Africa for decades and has been modified in many ways to suit particular circumstances. In Itu, Nigeria, for example, shifting cultivation is practiced along the bank of Cross River (Figure 4.11). It is a modified form of floodland agriculture.

There is a plethora of literature on the problems of environmental degradation associated with this type of agriculture. By definition, shifting agriculture is "a system of and management in which relatively short periods of continuous cultivation are followed by relatively long periods of fallow" (Bunting 1984). Shifting cultivation could be categorized into two major types. The first type is rotational agriculture in which there is slash and burn of the forest. Upon the decaying of the burned material, tilling takes places in order to mix the decaying material with the soil. Two or more crops are grown and are rotated on the land during the growing seasons. The second type of shifting cultivation is one in which the land is abandoned for some time in order for the land to regain its fertility. Table 4.6 shows a number of African countries where shifting agriculture is practiced, the area under cultivation, the fallow period, and the decline in productivity of the land.

It should be pointed out that the population growth rates in these countries pose particular problems because they add significant new numbers of people to the group practicing shifting agriculture. Hence, a reduction in the fallow period occurs. Such efforts usually result in the heavy use of fertilizers. The last column in Table 4.6 shows the use of fertilizers even as far back as the early 1970s. Recent agricultural endeavors in many African countries emphasize intensification, and to keep the land productive, the use of fertilizers has increased tremendously.

Table 4.5: Prevailing Systems of Agriculture
on Small Farms, Main Regions of Use, Major Crops
and Animal Species, and Food Sources for Animals in Africa*

Major farming systems	Major crops	Major animals	Major regions	Food sources
1. Bush fallow (shifting cultivation), animals not important	*Rice/Yams/Plantains* maize, cassava, vegetables, tree crops, cocoyams, yams	Goats, sheep	Humid tropics	Fallow, crop residues
	Sorghum/Millet maize, sesame, soybeans, cassava, sugarcane, tree crops, cowpeas, vegetables, yams	Cattle, goats, sheep, poultry, horses	Transition forest/savanna Southern Guinas	Fallow, straws, stover, vines, cull roots, sesame cake
2. Rudimentary sedentary agriculture (shifting cultivation), animals important	*Rice/Yams/Plantains* maize, cassava, vegetables, tree crops, cocoyams	Goats, sheep, poultry, swine	Humid tropics	Rice bran, cull roots, straws, crop residues, vines, stover
	Sorghum/Millet maize, sesame, cotton, sugarcane, tree crops, cowpeas, yams, tobacco, groundnuts, vegetables	Cattle, goats, sheep, poultry	Transition forest/savanna	Stover, vines, sugarcane tops, cull roots, or tubers, tree forage, groundnut cake, brans
3. Compound farming and intensive subsistence agriculture (shifting cultivation), animals important	*Rice/Yams/Plantains* maize, cassava, vegetables, tree crops, cocoyams, yams	Goats, sheep, swine, poultry	Humid tropics	Rice straw, bran, vegetable waste, fallow, vines, cull tubers or roots, stover, tree-crop by-products, palm oil cake
	Vegetables sugarcane, tobacco, sesame, maize, tree crops, groundnuts	Goats, sheep, poultry, swine	Transition forest/savanna	Vines, stover, tree-crop by-products, groundnut cake
4. Highland agriculture, animals important	*Rice/Yams/Plantains* maize, cassava, vegetables, plantain, cocoyams	Goats, sheep, poultry, swine	Humid tropics	Fallow, leaves, stover, rice by-products, cull tubers, cassava leaves, vegetable residues

Table 4.5: (cont.)

Major farming systems	Major crops	Major animals	Major regions	Food sources
5. Flood land and valley bottom agriculture, animals of some importance	*Rice/Yams/Plantains* maize, vegetables, sugarcane, rice, yams, cocoyams, millet, groundnuts	Goats, poultry	Humid tropics	Crop residues, vines, grazing
	Rice vegetables, maize, millet, groundnuts, plantain, sugarcane, cocoyams	Cattle, goats, sheep, poultry, swine, horses, donkeys	Transition forest/savanna	Straw, stover, molasses, brans, groundnut cake
6. Mixed farming (farm size variable), animals important	*Rice/Yams/Plantains*	2 or more species (widely variable)	Humid tropics	Fallow, straw, brans, vines
	Rice/Vegetables yams, cocoyams	Some cattle	Transition forest/sa- ` vanna	Fallow, vines, straw
7. Plantation crops, East Africa (small holdings), animals of some importance	*Coconuts* vegetables, maize, plantains, cocoyams, cassava	Cattle, horses, donkeys	Humid tropics Transition forest/sa-vanna	Grazing or cut and carry
8. Plantation crops (compound farms, etc.), animals of some importance	*Cacao* vegetables, maize, plantains	Goats, sheep, poultry	Humid tropics	Grazing or cut and carry, stover
	Tree Crops sugarcane, plantains	Goats, sheep, poultry, swine	Transition forest/sa-vanna	Grazing or cut and carry, sugarcane tops
9. Market gardening, animals may or may not be present	*Vegetables*	Variable	Humid tropics Transition forest/sa-vanna	Natural range-lands, crop residues, browse plants, range forbs

*Adapted from McDovell, 1980.

Source: Lugo et al., 1987, p. 276.

Figure 4.7: Bush fallow (shifting cultivation) of plantain, banana, cocoyams, and oil palm, Ikot-Ekpene, Nigeria, 1991.

Figure 4.8: Rudimentary sedentary agriculture (shifting cultivation) in which tree crops and goats are raised, Ikeja, Nigeria, 1991.

Figure 4.9: Compound farming, intensive subsistence agriculture (shifting agriculture), Eket, Nigeria, 1991.

Figure 4.10: Compound farming, Ikeja, Nigeria, 1991.

Figure 4.11: Flood-land agriculture, maize, Itu, Nigeria, 1991.

Food Shortage

Food shortage problems in Africa have reached new dimensions. As recently as July of 1991, food aid worth $43.4 million was provided to Ethiopia by international organizations. The international organizations have been concerned about the food supply and demand problem. The World Food Council in May 1991 stressed the need for a more concerted endeavor to eradicate hunger in Africa and the rest of the developing world. The concern of WFC is deepened by the fact that the food crisis is compounded by the growing environmental deterioration of Africa's ecosystems and mounting socioeconomic problem. One of the most frustrating problems confronting relief agencies is how to get food to the truly needy in Africa. Most of the food aid to Africa is being sold by those entrusted with the authority to distribute it.

Conferences have been organized to address the problem of Africa's agricultural development. Some of these conferences assembled ministers and policy and decision makers from African countries along with donor countries' representatives who discussed and examined projects which would enable African countries to sustain their agriculture. Workshop 1991, which was organized by the Geneva-based Center for Applied Studies in International Negotiations (CASIN), is one example of such a conference. The central theme of Workshop 1991 was to assemble

Table 4.6: Shifting Cultivation in Some African Countries

Country	Area under shifting cultivation (ha)	Cropping/ fallow periods (years)	Decline of productivity during crop period (%)	Pop. per hectare of cropped land	Ann. pop. growth rate (%)	Annual fertilizer consumption (N=P205=K20) (kg/ha)
Congo People's Republic	90,000	2–5/2–10	20–50	1.4	1.2	1.1
Benin	900,000	2–3/3–10	25–60	1.8	2.9	3.0
Liberia	75,000	1.5–2.5	NR	0.3	1.7	0.6
Madagascar	200,000	3–5/NR	NR	2.3	2.4	5.0
Malawi	NR	1–2/3–20	Rapidly declining	1.6	3.0	4.5
Mali	NR	NR	NR	0.7	2.0	0.8
Niger	8,000,000	5–6/5	50–60	0.3	2.8	0.02
Uganda	3,200,000	1–2/0–10	30–50	1.9	2.6	1.4
Zaire	NR	1–3/5–20	Rapidly declining	2.5	2.4	0.9
Zambia	1,900,000	2–5/8–20	Declining	0.9	3.4	4.6

NR: Denotes no reply in questionnaire.

Data based on: questionnaire, FAO Production Yearbook and FAO Annual Fertilizer Review.

Data are for use as information and do not represent an official record.

Source: Braun, 1974, as cited in Bunting, A.H., and E. Bunting (eds.), 1984.

information that could lead to a more permanent agricultural solution.

Several countries have assisted in trying to solve the agricultural dilemma in Africa. In 1991, Great Britain pledged 60,000 tons of food for Africa, and food aid from all the European communities combined is estimated to have reached 600,000 tons. The European community (EC) member states gave as much as 400,000 tons of food and another 200,000 tons was said to have come from national contributions (West Africa 1991b).

Also in 1991 the governing council for the International Fund for Agricultural Development (IFAD) paved the way for the implementation of the second tier of efforts to assist the drought areas of sub–Saharan Africa with food aid. Countries such as Belgium, France, Kuwait, and the Netherlands contributed significant amounts of money toward this effort (West Africa 1991b).

Food aid is a temporary solution to a very difficult problem which is compounded by distribution problems and in some cases by civil wars. What is really needed in Africa is for the African countries to be able to grow enough food to feed their own citizens. Self-sufficiency in agricultural production is the key to sustaining Africa's deteriorating environment.

Commercial and Subsistence Cultivation

Commercial agriculture in Africa has a long history that precedes the arrival of the Europeans on the continent. African linguistic groups have always had intragroup trade and external trade. The intragroup trade depended on the "barter tradition" in which goods are exchanged. The arrival of Europeans brought into Africa the monetary system which expanded the commercialization of agricultural products.

The arrival of Europeans also meant the introduction of plantations for cash crops such as cocoa, coffee, tea, palm oil, sugarcane, and rubber. This has resulted in the extensification of agricultural practice in most African countries. Plantations and large agricultural schemes have been established for the production of crops that were meant to bring in foreign exchange. These plantations have succeeded in many respects.

The commercial agriculture in Africa could be small, modern, large-scale and be influenced by Western techniques. This type of agricultural practice produces for the market. Subsistence agriculture is mainly traditional and produces for local consumption. It is usually family oriented, although subsistence agriculture has given way to agriculture as an industry in many African countries.

The production of cocoa, for instance, has involved the participation and subsidies of governments such as Nigeria and Ghana in efforts to stabilize and sustain the crop. These two countries have profited from the large production of the cocoa product. Large cocoa plantations can be seen in the western parts of Nigeria in states such as Ondo, Ogun, and Osun. However, in recent years, the cocoa industry has suffered a down trend in price, and the farmers have had some economic difficulty in sustaining their production and lifestyle.

The commodity prices for cocoa, coffee, and tea have suffered a downward trend as shown in Figure 4.12. In 1992 the prices were at the lowest point since their highest level in 1984. The community market is expected to remain at a low point, and the prices of Africa's major export products are not expected to recover in the near future. The difficulty of sustaining an increase in the revenue of commodities is compounded by the fact that the market is saturated with the commodities and Western

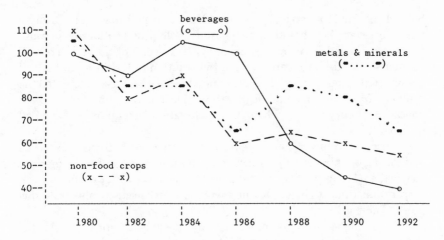

Figure 4.12: Real commodity prices.

Beverages: cocoa, coffee, tea

Non-food crops: cotton, jute, rubber, tobacco

Source: Adapted from *Africa Recovery*, 1991, p. 53.

countries who are the main buyers have alternative produce to market to their citizens.

One of the most damaging aspects of agriculture is the inability of any agricultural program or project to sustain itself. There is no doubt that the commercial agriculture in Africa emphasizes those commodities that can earn foreign exchange and be used for development projects and assist farmers. However, when there is a failure in the market, such a misfortune is usually translated into ecological degradation. The cocoa market is a good example where a failure in the market resulted in chaos in the farming communities of Nigeria and Ghana. Farmers engaged in cocoa farming are looking for alternative means of making an income and are not paying enough attention to their farmlands. Some are contemplating converting their farmlands to other uses, or just abandoning them. Their children and family members are not encouraged to choose farming as a profession.

Sierra Leone presents an interesting case study in cash-crop production. This country's farmers grow crops such as rice, bananas, and cassavas which are marketed locally for subsistence consumption. The cash crops the farmers grow are cocoa, oil palm, and coffee.

Cash crops are cultivated by a small number of rural farmers who see the cash crops as their livelihood. The tenacity of these farmers has led to the exponential increase in the production of cocoa from 17 tons in 1920 to more than 10,000 tons a decade ago (Lamin 1989). The government of

Sierra Leone and foreign assistance enabled the farmers to increase production. However, there has been tremendous ecological degradation because the farmers failed to recognize the carrying capacity of the soil. The soil nutrients have declined rapidly, and the addition of fertilizers to the soil has affected water quality. The unpredictable weather has exacerbated the problem of environmental degradation. During the 1980s there were unseasonably dry months which made cultivation difficult on the poor soil of Sierra Leone.

African farming systems seem to encourage the cultivation of crops and raising of animals for personal consumption as well as for the market. Hence there is a traditional relationship between livestock production and crop production in Africa. Karue's work in 1984 seems to illustrate this point (Table 4.7).

The hunter-gatherer communities have declined drastically in Africa. But there are some people in the Kalahari desert area and other parts of Central and West Africa whose hunter-gatherer behaviors or practices are still in effect. The hunter-gatherer groups in Africa have had negative impact on the numbers of wildlife in Africa as their populations have increased. They live off the land, and as long as their population was low and they were nomadic, their impact was negligible.

Nomadic and seminomadic pastoralists can be found in many parts of Africa. Reduction in the range of the herds has resulted in the overgrazing of many parts of the continent where pastoralism is practiced. Table 4.8 indicates pastoral and agropastoral communities in tropical Africa.

The ecosystems that are being threatened as a result of overgrazing are shown in column one. The second column shows the major linguistic groups involved in pastoralism. These groups have practiced this type of agriculture for centuries. The governments of their countries are attempting to establish more sedentary lifestyles for them in order to sustain the ecosystem and use part of the range of the animals for other development projects. Valuable indigenous livestock are kept by ranchers on plantations in Africa. Several ethnic groups of pastoralists keep livestock, but, unfortunately, indigenous breeds are being eliminated by the initiates of international organizations attempting to improve African livestock breeds. Travis (1992:678) notes:

> Indigenous breeds are being pushed toward extinction because native farmers, in the interests of greater productivity, have in many cases adopted specially bred Western animals like the American Holstein or European Friesian cow. And, as a result, some of the valuable genetic characteristics of the native breeds are vanishing as the newcomers replace them.
> The attraction for Third World farmers is that Western breeds have been improved through selection methods to be better producers of milk,

Table 4.7: Relationships Between Livestock Production and Crop Production in Africa

Community	Main source of food	Subsidiary sources of food
1. Hunters/ gatherers	Wild animals and wild plants	– Trade in meat, hides, and other parts of wild fauna – Government food assistance – Casual labor
2. Nomadic pastoralists	Livestock products: milk, blood, meat	– Trade in livestock products, e.g. hides – Gathering wild food
3. Semi-nomadic pastoralists	Livestock products: milk, blood, meat	– Cultivating cereals by shifting cultivation – Trade in animal products – Wild foods
4. Subsistence cultivators	Growing staple crops	– Keeping animals for milk/meat – Collecting wild foods – Trade in staple crops
5. Ranch, estate, plantations	Commercially bought supplies	– Keeping animals for trade – Growing crops for cash

Source: Bunting, A.H., and E. Bunting (eds.), 1984, p. 87.

eggs, and meat. But, because they are accustomed to constant grain, antibiotics, and temperate climate, modern breeds like the Holstein sometimes cannot handle the more rigorous life in poorer developing countries. "Many of these high-tech animals are not very successful, but it takes a few seasons to learn this," explains Don Bixby, executive director of the American Minor Breeds Conservancy. By then, however, the stock of native breeds can degrade considerably.

Replacing the African N'Dama cattle with a new breed could be ecologically unsound as the new breed may not be as hardy.

Subsistence cultivation is responsible for 60 to 70 percent of the food production in Africa, and it employs about 70 percent of the work force. In this system of farming, staple crops are grown (Figures 4.13 and 4.14), some animals are kept for milk and meat, and farmers collect wild foods such as fruits.

While subsistence agriculture employs a significant African population, the increase in traditional subsistence agriculture accounts for about 70 percent of the clearing of closed canopy forests as well as 60 percent of the cutting of the savanna woodlands in Africa.

Table 4.8: Pastoral and Agro-pastoral
Communities in Tropical Africa

Ecosystem (1)	Extensive nomadic pastoralists (2)	Agro-pastoralists (3)	Extensive ranching (4)
1. Desert and sub-desert zones	Arabo-Berbers, Moor, Tuareg, Moor-Tuareg, Tubu, Somali, Arab	Tubu, Arab	– –
2. Sahelian steppes	Somali, Arab, nomadic Fulani	Moor, Tuareg, Tubu, Arab	beginning
3. Eastern African steppes	Somali, Arab, Galla Nilo-Hamites	Galla, Nilo-Hamites Bantu (Gogo)	Kenya Tanzania
4. Southern African steppes	Hottentot	several Bantu societies	Zimbabwe, Southern Africa, Lesotho
5. Sudan and similar savannas	Nomadic Fulani Nilotics	Fulani, Nilotics	Angola, Zaire
6. Central African grassland and savanna	Nilotics	Nilotics, Bantu	Angola, Zaire

Source: Bunting, A.H., and E. Bunting (eds.), 1984, p. 87.

Conclusion

The key measure of all development policies and projects should be their sustainability. The problems of environmental degradation, biodiversity loss, and poverty must be integral parts of the structure for economic development. In the planning and management of sustainable agriculture in Africa, one is challenged to maximize the resources of the land while minimizing the waste or destruction which occurs as a result of the intensification and extensification of agricultural systems.

Sustainable agriculture in developing countries is of utmost importance because famine continues to threaten most of the world's population. In Africa alone, over 30 million people in the sub–Saharan region are threatened by starvation due to food shortages, agricultural failure, and environmental and economic problems. Many publications, including a briefing paper by the UN *Africa Recovery* (1992), lament the decline of agricultural production in Africa. Sustainable agriculture in the Third World could be achieved from three perspectives. First, as an *agronomic concept* sustainable agriculture refers to the long-term use and manage-

Figure 4.13: Subsistence farmers conducting daily business, Itu, Nigeria, 1991.

Figure 4.14: Community subsistence farmlands in the background, Itu, Nigeria, 1991.

ment of land for present and future crop production. This includes soil management, to maintain fertility, and usually requires proper and appropriate technology, indigenous knowledge, research and training, and strengthening of institutions (both domestic and foreign). The second avenue to sustainability of agriculture is from an *economic* perspective. This idea proclaims that the agricultural development should be economically feasible in the short range and in the long range and that it should be locally self-sufficient and based on local raw materials generating enough revenue to operate efficiently.

A developing country needs to be able to manage its resources for long-term sustained yield. It should be emphasized that the question of whether agricultural development can be sustained emerges from two quite different circumstances. The first is the introduction of new agricultural technology into upland forest regions of the Third World, and the other is the management of recent agricultural development where intensification of agriculture has been introduced. In the intensification aspect, the management decision to intensify implies the commitment of substantial inputs of materials and technological innovations to sustain production. The system must then be refined.

The third aspect of sustainable agricultural development is the *ecological system* as an entity that must be sustained.

International agencies, African governments, and individuals could enhance development in Africa by recognizing, working with, and assisting the following:

> 1. Major ethnic groups and subgroups, and social dynamics which exist within the groups. Cultural influence and traditions play a significant role in the success of agricultural programs. The role of rural women is paramount in this regard as they are the custodians of the natural resources.
> 2. The major social institutions in the countries. They should be fully understood because they play significant roles in determining how the land is developed agriculturally.
> 3. Land tenure systems, which are important because of the differences that exist between privately owned and public community property.
> 4. The inheritance systems, the rights of access, and property rights, which bear important policy implications.
> 5. The local government policies, which determine the allocation and use of land for agricultural purposes (Lugo et al. 1987).

Environmental design considerations in sustainable agricultural methods and development projects in Africa should be emphasized.

> 1. Sustainable agricultural development should be seen as a duality of (a) natural resource base, and (b) human ability and competence.

2. Institutional and organizational guidelines should be established to assess optimal and ultimate capacity of the land.

3. Planning and management of agricultural projects should be integrated with other development projects in order to understand and assess the full environmental impact.

4. African countries requesting aid and receiving aid must comply with environmental standards established by organizations like USAID in order to protect and sustain the environment. The organization must have the best interest of Africans in mind (Lugo et al. 1987).

Sustainable agriculture in Africa would provide relief from poverty, world hunger problems, malnutrition, and related health problems. The fragile social, economic, political, and ecological fabric of emerging nations would experience greater stability. The challenge for the development agencies is to provide their advanced technological expertise in agricultural research to enable African farmers to produce enough food for the growing population while sustaining the natural resource base. Future agricultural production and the fragile ecosystem should not be compromised or jeopardized. Traditional farmers must sustain agriculture by permitting farmlands to regain fertility by instituting at least a twenty-year fallow period. The utilization of controlled methods of fertilization would enhance future production. Sustainable development in Africa should address soil conservation, watershed development, land management, forestry, diversification of opportunities, management of salinity problems, and irrigation. Africa must look toward the future in order to preserve its past.

5. The African Forest

The African forest has provided sustenance for its people and serves as a home for millions of plant and animal life forms (only some of which have been identified and classified). These plants and animals play significant roles in the stability of the ecological system of Africa. They serve as protection for wildlife and are a source of food for both humans and wildlife. In many African countries (if not all) plants also serve a medicinal function. Ayensu (1978:17) in the introduction to his classic book notes:

> The history of herbal medicine is as old as human history. In the continent of Africa, the application of herbs for internal and external uses has always been a major factor in the practice of medicine. The treatment of wounds with concoctions prepared from leaves, bark, and roots is a daily occurrence in an African community. Because of the astringent or disinfectant properties of certain plant parts, such applications have been highly successful for generations. The alkaloids in plant families such as the nightshade, the poppy and the pea, have been well-known for healing qualities (if not in name, then in substance) to the herbalists over the centuries. Modern man recognizes the familiar plant derivatives from these families as alleviants in strychnine, quinine, nicotine, cocaine, and morphine.
>
> The West African flora is known to contain a multitude of drug plants and alkaloidal poisons, and the species presented in this book form a frequently encountered part of the total. There are other plants which contain important derivatives that are not native to West Africa, but are currently grown there for food. For example, bromelain, an enzyme isolated from the stumps of pineapples after harvest, is an anti-inflammatory pharmaceutical used in the treatment of sprains and contusions. There is currently a worldwide shortage of bromelain, and an increased exploitation of this otherwise waste product could become, to the improvement of the world's medical supply, a rewarding pharmaceutical and financial foreign exchange earner.

The major problem confronting humanity in Africa is the destruction of vegetation that is brought about as a result of agricultural practices, industrialization, clearing of land for shelter, transportation, and other

126

Figure 5.1: The forest in Akwa Ibom state, Nigeria, 1991.

Figure 5.2: The impact of bridge construction on the forest, Itu, Nigeria, 1991.

Figure 5.3: Unpaved roads in the forest cause environmental problems. Ikot-Obong, Nigeria, 1991.

Figure 5.4: The establishment of rural business necessitates forest clearance, Ikot-Ekpene, Nigeria, 1991.

Figure 5.5: Village center, Ikot-Ekpene, Nigeria, 1991.

Figure 5.6: Village elementary school, Ikot-Ekpene, Nigeria, 1991.

human activities. Figures 5.1 through 5.6 indicate some of the impacts of development activities on the forests of Nigeria.

Stages of Impact of Development on Nigerian Forests

As a result of the extraction of forest products and agricultural and other developments, the forests of Africa have declined drastically in size. This reduction has resulted in the loss of wildlife habitats essential for the stabilization of ecological systems. Table 5.1 documents the wildlife habitat lost by African countries. Africa has always been known for its richness in natural habitats, and parts of southeastern Nigeria, Cameroon, Congo, Central African Republic, Gabon, Congo, and Zaire still have forest areas that have not been exposed to modern man's activities. Yet many forested areas of Africa have degraded habitats which have occurred as a result of sporadic disturbances, often fires used for shifting cultivation and other projects. When the disturbance of the forest is sustained and the original vegetation is not replaced, the area becomes a ruderal habitat. Such places can be seen along the roadsides (Figure 5.7).

In many instances, farmers and governments establish a complete disturbance of the forest followed by the intentional introduction of new plants. This is a cultivated habitat, an example of which is shown in Figure 5.8.

Why Deforestation Occurs

There are many reasons for the destruction of the African forests, and an attempt will be made in this section to discuss and make available an accurate perspective of the problem.

Historically, indigenous Africans have used forest products (both plants and animals) for centuries without significant damage to the forest. However, the population of the African countries has increased tremendously, and the majority of the rural population depend on the forests for their livelihood. The high density of the population puts tremendous pressure on the forests. The rural population, by and large, are subsistence farmers, and their practice of shifting agriculture is part of the tradition. Hence, it should be understood that the rural poor do not intentionally destroy the forest, but in their desire to feed themselves, the forest ecosystem is destroyed. The indigenous people cannot be blamed for causing the problem. The problem of deforestation in developing countries is well documented in part two of a task-force report organized by the World Resources Institute, the World Bank, and the UN Development Programme (1985a:3–4):

Table 5.1: Wildlife Habitat Loss in Africa South of the Sahara

Country	Original Wildlife Habitat (1000 hectares)	Amount Remaining (1000 hectares)	Habitat Loss (percent)
1. Angola	124,670	76,085	39
2. Benin	11,580	4,632	60
3. Botswana	58,540	25,758	56
4. Burkina Faso	27,380	5,476	80
5. Burundi	2,570	359	86
6. Cameroon	46,940	19,245	59
7. Central African Republic	62,300	27,412	56
8. Chad	72,080	17,299	76
9. Congo	34,200	17,442	49
10. Côte d'Ivoire	31,800	6,678	79
11. Djibouti	2,180	1,112	49
12. Equatorial Guinea	2,500	920	63
13. Ethiopia	110,100	3,030	97
14. Gabon	26,700	17,355	35
15. Gambia	1,130	124	89
16. Ghana	23,000	4,600	80
17. Guinea	24,590	7,377	70
18. Guinea Bissau	3,610	794	78
19. Kenya	56,950	29,614	48
20. Lesotho	3,040	973	68
21. Liberia	11,140	1,448	87
22. Madagascar	59,521	14,880	75
23. Malawi	9,410	4,046	57
24. Mali	75,410	15,836	79
25. Mauritania	38,860	7,383	81
26. Mozambique	78,320	3,678	95
27. Namibia	82,320	44,453	46
28. Niger	56,600	12,788	77
29. Nigeria	91,980	22,995	75
30. Rwanda	2,510	326	87
31. Senegal	19,620	3,532	82
32. Sierra Leone	7,170	1,076	85
33. Somalia	63,770	37,624	41
34. South Africa	123,650	53,170	57
35. Sudan	170,300	51,090	70
36. Swaziland	1,740	766	56
37. Tanzania	88,620	50,513	43
38. Togo	5,600	1,904	66
39. Uganda	19,370	4,261	78
40. Zaire	233,590	105,116	55
41. Zambia	75,260	53,435	29
42. Zimbabwe	39,020	17,169	56
Total	2,079,641	773,774	63

Note: Data for Mauritania, Mali, Niger, Chad, and Sudan cover only the sub–Saharan portion of those countries. Islands other than Madagascar are not included.
Source: IUCN/UNEP, 1986b, as cited in McNeely et al., 1990, p. 46.

Figure 5.7: Forest burning and clearance for industries and roads, Ogbomosho, Nigeria, 1991.

Figure 5.8: Cultivated habitat, Lagos-Badagry Road, Nigeria, 1991.

Deforestation is a complex problem. The spread of agriculture, including crop and livestock production, is the single greatest factor in forest destruction. The rural poor are often unjustly held responsible. They are often the instruments of forest destruction, caught in a chain of events that force them into destructive patterns of land use to meet their basic needs for food and fuel. The real causes of deforestation are poverty, skewed land distribution (due to historical patterns of land settlement and commercial agriculture development), and low agricultural productivity.

These factors, combined with rapid population growth, have led to increasingly severe pressure on forest lands in developing countries. As productive land becomes scarce, small farmers have been pushed into fragile upland forest areas and marginal lowlands that cannot support large numbers of people practicing subsistence agriculture. The loss of forests and rising population pressure have forced farmers to shorten fallow periods, degrading the productive capacity of the land and setting in motion a downward spiral of forest destruction. This situation prevails now in many developing countries, and it can change only if rural populations are given alternatives to this ecologically destructive way of living.

There is no doubt that the destruction of the forests of Africa and the ultimate alteration of African landscape are due to the increasing population in the rural areas as well as the urban centers for that matter. It is estimated that 11 million hectares of tropical forest are destroyed every year in the developing world. A large portion of this number occurs in Africa. Of the 11 million hectares of the forest that are cleared for purposes of agriculture and other development projects, it is estimated that 7.5 million hectares consist of closed forests while 3.8 million hectares are open forest (World Resources Institute, et al. 1985a). Figure 5.9 shows the annual loss of forests in regions of Africa.

The tropical rain forest of Africa has been reduced to two regions of the continent. One region is along the west coast of Africa and covers about 200 to 400 km in width. The countries of Ghana, Côte d'Ivoire, Liberia, Guinea, and Sierra Leone share this small amount of rain forest, but Togo and Benin are virtually without any rain forest. The other region includes the southern part of Nigeria, southern Cameroon and Congo, a small part of Central African Republic, Equatorial Guinea, Gabon, northern Angola, and Zaire (Borota 1991).

Although human impact has denuded the two regions of African rain forest of many of its tree species, there are still some that have been spared. Borota (1991:17) claims that some of the characteristic tree species that can be found in the western region of Africa's moist tropical forest are "*Lophira alata* BANK ex GAERTN, f., *Turraeanthus africana* PELLEGR., *Tarrietia utilis* SPRAGUE and species of the *Uapaca* BAILL., *Entandrophragma* C. DC., *Khaya* A. Juss., and *Celtis* L. genera." He further contends that in

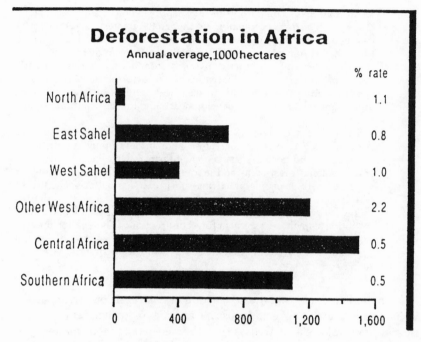

Source: Africa Recovery, 1991, p. 38.

Figure 5.9: Deforestation in Africa.

the central equatorial region of Africa the dominant species include: "*Brachystegia laurentii* LOUIS, *Gilbertiodendron dewevrei* J. LEONARD, species of the *Celtis* and *Entandrophragma* genera and *Terminalia superba* ENGL. et DIELS."

Forest as a Source of Energy

Fuelwood consumption in Africa is one of the reasons for the decline of the forest. The forest has been the source of fuelwood for centuries in Africa, but the exponential increase in the population over several decades has led to the rape of the forest in many rural areas. In the past when the rural population was low, the forest's carrying capacity was not exceeded and sustained yield was maintained. However, with the increase in population, sustained yield was impossible.

The forest is also the main supplier of the energy needed by the urban population for domestic use. Most of the urban population in Africa still cannot afford the price of alternative energy (kerosene, gas, etc.) and

Table 5.2: Household Energy Consumption

% of annual excess consumption over supply through growth of trees

Sahelian countries	30%
Niger	200%
Northern Nigeria	75%
Ethiopia	150%
Sudan	70%

Source: Adapted from Anderson, 1984, p. 1.

continues to rely heavily on fuelwood for cooking. Table 5.2 shows the energy consumption for five selected African countries by 1980. These figures have not changed drastically by 1992.

In the author's travels to West African countries, experiences in many cities and rural areas show that people still depend heavily on fuelwood for cooking (more than 90 percent). It is estimated that the rate of consumption of fuelwood is comparable to using 1.5 tons of oil per family per year. It is also argued that the consumption of energy by using fuelwood is about ten fold the total commercial energy consumed by electric power generation and transportation.

In northern Nigeria the annual rate of consumption has exceeded the annual rate of replenishment by 75 percent. Table 5.3 shows the statistics from other countries. The data indicate the trend of deforestation in the drier regions of Africa which has led to the destruction of much of the rain forest.

It is estimated that about 75 percent of the total energy supply in Africa in 1980 was by fuelwood (World Resources Institute et al. 1985a). The people of Africa also depend on the forest and trees for the construction of their traditional houses and a number of household furniture and implements. The building of modern Western-style houses also makes tremendous demand of the forest resources.

Illegal Activities

Many African countries have had their forests destroyed by individuals who engage in illegal logging or who collaborate with foreign multinations and domestic companies to defraud the government of its resources. This malpractice is not only economically devastating to African countries, but when logging is not properly managed, it is ecologically destructive. Ghana and Sierra Leone have both experienced

Table 5.3: Household Energy Consumption
for Selected Countries (1980)

Household Energy Consumption: Sudan Ethiopia Niger Senegal Nigeria

	Sudan	Ethiopia	Niger	Senegal	Nigeria
% Distribution by Source:					
Fuelwood, including charcoal	94	46	99	95	88
Animal dung and crop residues	5	54	n/a	n/a	n/a
	99	100	99	95	88
Electricity	0.2	0.05	0.6	3	7
LPG, Kerosene	0.5	0.15	0.6	2	5
	0.7	0.2	1.2	5	12

Source: Energy Assessment Studies for household energy consumption; Bank (1983) paper on "The Energy Transition in Developing Countries" for total commercial energy consumption. As indicated in Anderson, 1984, p. 27.

---

this problem. The Ghanaian situation drew the attention of non-governmental organizations such as the Friends of the Earth. Brian Mayo (1992:508) describes the Ghanaian situation accurately when he notes:

> Ghana has lost an estimated $50m through deceitful and fraudulent activities involving Ghanaian, European and other foreign companies at the center of the country's timber industry, according to a report by the Friends of the Earth.
> The 21 page report exposes for the first time the extent of malpractice that was carried out in Ghana's timber industry in the 1980s, with timber processing companies plundering the country's forests and siphoning illegally acquired profits into European bank accounts.
> The report says the scandalous trade in timber was uncovered by Ghanaian authorities in 1987 after a Timber Sub-Committee of the National Investigation Committee (NIC) investigated all aspects of the industry and trade. . . .
> The Friends of the Earth demand that all other bilateral and multilateral lending for commercial timber exploitation in rainforest areas be suspended "until such time that aid agencies clarify and define clear guidelines for 'sustainable forestry.'"

Illegal logging in Africa is certainly one of the major reasons for the disappearance of the rain forest. The difficulty in controlling this activity lies in the fact that there is an absence of police power in many countries, corruption seems to have become a way of life, and many people are unemployed and will do anything to have a decent life.

The Impact of Industries

The establishment of new industries requires land, and the forest is cleared for this purpose. A great deal of forest clearance is also undertaken in the construction of transportation routes. The impact of such endeavors is enormous when the necessary environmental impact analysis is not conducted.

The demand for forest products for industrial consumption has escalated in the past two decades. This demand has been both within Africa and from outside. The construction industry has relied heavily on forest products from Africa, and the foreign demand has exacerbated the destruction of most of Africa's forests. This consumption of forest products has superseded the production. This argument is supported by data from Nigeria (Figure 5.10). The rate of the disappearance of the forest in Nigeria has been aided by the use of forest products for furniture, construction of houses, and other house utilities.

Sound Forestry Policies

The absence of sound policy guidelines for the logging and harvesting of African forests has led to enormous environmental problems. It is argued in this section that the lack of sound and adequate policies in the management is one of the primary reasons for the destruction of African forests. The transportation of the felled trees also creates considerable environmental problems. As the forests are depleted in many African countries, the hydrological systems are put in an unbalanced situation, and flooding and erosion ensue. Delicate top soils are lost or damaged, and the flora and fauna species are lost. The destruction of the forest leads to the addition of an enormous amount of carbon dioxide to the atmosphere, and the temperatures increase.

The paper and pulp industries in African countries are operating without proper enforcement of environmental laws and regulations. Sawmills which produce lumber and panel products are not adequately policed and regulated to ensure that they are in compliance with the efforts of the governments to achieve sustained yield of forest products. The production of charcoal and fuelwood in many African countries is conducted in a haphazard fashion. These scenarios exacerbate the problem of deforestation.

The bar graph in Figure 5.10 shows that by 1975, Nigeria, which used to have positive trade in forest products, had become a country that had to import forest products in order to meet its domestic demands. Extractive industries have played significant roles in the construction of transpor-

Million cubic meters
(roundwood equivalent)

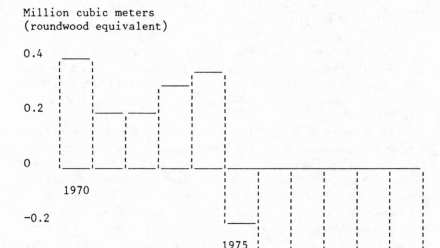

Source: World Resources Institute, 1985b, p. 11.

Figure 5.10: Nigeria's net trade in forest products (sawnwood + panel + pulp + paper).

tation systems in Africa. There is an historical link between role construction of roads (by colonial rulers) and the natural resources. The African roads open up virgin forest lands to large populations of subsistence farmers who in their practice of shifting cultivation exacerbate the forest depletion problem.

The establishment of industries has overwhelming environmental ramifications. Erosion that ensues as a result of clear cutting depletes the soil of its nutrients, water pollution is exacerbated, and the nutrient cycling ability of the soil is halted. Development projects have been appearing in parts of the rain forests of Africa at alarming rates. Some of the projects are planned and are phased into the forest ecosystem properly, but many are not and are conducted haphazardly. As a result of this observation, the author conducted a preliminary investigation to sample the public's attitudes toward the natural resources in Nigeria.

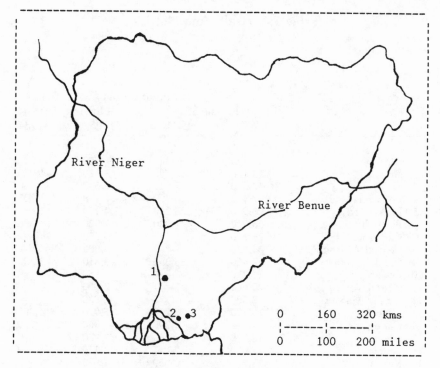

River Niger

River Benue

1. ●

2. ● ●3

| 0 | 160 | 320 | kms |
| 0 | 100 | 200 | miles |

Map of Nigeria Indicating Study Areas

1. Onitsha   2. Aba   3. Ikot-Ekpene

Figure 5.11: A study of the public's awareness of soil, water, and natural resource problems in Nigeria.

A Study of the Public's Awareness of Soil, Water, and Natural Resource Problems in Nigeria

Situation

In nineteenth-century Europe, despite endemic mass poverty and cyclical boom and slum, industrial output increased spectacularly overall and absorbed millions into production employment. Where it did fail to provide a viable livelihood, other mechanisms, from repression and incorporation in the political sphere to emigration and the Welfare State in the economy, were developed to avert mass misery turning into militant discontent. The industrial revolution in Europe also resulted in many environmental problems (Alexander 1991).

The situation in Africa today has been described by many scholars as

Table 5.4: Health and Nutrition

| | Population per | | | |
| | Physician | | Nursing Person | |
	1965	1984	1965	1984
1. Algeria	8,590	2,340	11,770	300
2. Angola	13,150	17,790	3,820	1,020
3. Benin	32,390	15,940	2,540	1,750
4. Botswana	27,450	6,900	17,710	700
5. Burkina Faso	73,960	265,250	4,150	1,680
6. Burundi	55,910	21,030	7,320	4,380
7. Cameroon	26,720	– –	5,830	– –
8. Central African R.	34,020	– –	3,000	– –
9. Chad	72,480	38,360	13,610	3,390
10. Congo	14,210	– –	950	– –
11. Côte d'Ivoire	20,640	– –	2,000	– –
12. Egypt, Arabs Rep.	2,300	770	2,030	– –
13. Ethiopia	70,190	78,770	5,970	5,390
14. Gabon	– –	2,790	760	270
15. Ghana	13,740	20,460	3,730	1,670
16. Guinea	47,050	– –	4,110	– –
17. Kenya	13,280	10,050	1,930	– –
18. Lesotho	20,060	18,610	4,700	– –
19. Liberia	12,560	9,350	2,330	1,380
20. Libya	3,860	690	850	– –
21. Madagascar	10,620	9,780	3,650	
22. Malawi	47,320	11,340	40,980	– –
23. Mali	51,510	25,390	3,360	1,350
24. Mauritania	36,530	11,900	– –	1,180
25. Mauritius	3,930	1,900	2,030	– –
26. Morocco	12,120	4,760	2,290	1,050
27. Mozambique	180,000	– –	5,370	– –
28. Namibia	– –	– –	– –	– –
29. Niger	65,540	39,670	6,210	460
30. Nigeria	29,530	6,440	6,160	900
31. Rwanda	72,480	35,090	7,450	3,690
32. Senegal	19,490	– –	2,440	2,030
33. Sierra Leone	16,840	13,620	4,470	1,090
34. Somalia	36,840	16,080	3,950	1,530
35. South Africa	2,050	– –	490	– –
36. Sudan	23,500	10,190	3,360	1,260
37. Tanzania	21,700	24,980	2,100	5,490
38. Togo	23,240	8,700	4,990	1,240
39. Uganda	11,110	– –	3,130	– –
40. Zaire	34,740	12,940	– –	1,800
41. Zambia	11,380	7,150	5,820	740
42. Zimbabwe	8,010	6,700	990	1,000

Source: Adapted from World Bank, 1991.

Table 5.4: (cont.)

Births attended by health staff (%) 1985	Babies with low birth weight	Infant mortality rate (per 1,000 live births) 1965	1989	Daily calorie supply (per capita) 1965	1988
—	9	154	69	1,683	2,726
15	17	192	132	1,843	1,725
34	10	166	112	1,976	2,145
52	8	112	39	1,982	2,269
—	18	190	135	1,841	2,061
12	14	142	70	2,383	2,253
—	13	143	90	1,990	2,161
—	15	157	100	2,016	1,980
—	11	183	127	2,274	1,852
—	12	129	115	2,236	2,512
20	14	149	92	2,334	2,365
24	7	145	68	2,336	3,213
58	—	165	133	1,803	1,658
92	16	153	98	1,805	2,396
73	17	120	86	1,912	2,209
—	18	191	140	2,006	2,042
—	13	112	68	2,169	1,973
28	10	142	96	2,024	2,307
89	—	176	137	2,110	2,270
76	5	138	77	1,803	3,384
62	10	201	117	2,375	2,101
59	10	200	147	2,196	2,009
27	17	207	167	1,843	2,181
23	10	178	123	1,796	2,528
90	9	65	21	2,212	2,679
—	9	145	69	2,066	2,820
28	15	179	137	1,704	1,632
—	—	145	101	1,882	1,889
47	20	180	130	1,930	2,340
—	25	166	100	2,166	2,039
—	17	141	118	1,660	1,786
—	10	160	82	2,452	1,989
25	14	208	149	1,976	1,806
2	—	165	128	1,410	1,736
—	12	124	68	2,615	3,035
20	15	160	104	1,853	1,996
74	14	138	112	1,800	2,151
—	20	156	90	2,345	2,133
—	10	121	99	2,343	2,013
—	—	141	94	2,135	2,034
—	14	121	76	2,042	2,026
69	15	103	46	2,044	2,232

different from that which occurred in Europe: it is one of urbanization without industrialization. The situation in many Third World countries has worsened because of the recession in many industrialized western countries. The slums have increased in many urban centers in African countries, and poverty has increased (Table 5.4). Infant mortality and diseases have multiplied, and above all environmental degradation such as soil erosion, water pollution, and the depletion of renewable natural resources is threatening the survival of the cultural diversity of developing nations of the world.

One of the most problematic issues confronting policy makers in Nigeria and other countries of Africa is the population explosion. Nigeria's population is estimated to be about 88.514 million people (Table 5.4); an average annual rate of increase of about 3 percent. Such an exponential increase in population puts tremendous stress on the natural resources.

The soil, water, and other renewable resources have all experienced a decline in quality and quantity. In order to produce food in quantities to support the growing population, farmers have intensified their use of small parcels of land, thus leading to the decline in the quality of the soil. There is a diminishing return in terms of the agricultural yield. Chemically based products such as fungicides, pesticides, herbicides, and fertilizers are being used increasingly, and as a result, rivers, streams, and underground water are being polluted. Slash-and-burn agricultural practices have reduced the amount of forest in Africa. The length of time for fallow periods has decreased because land-use purposes have increased. Land is being cleared for transportation, housing, and agricultural purposes.

The general public of Nigeria is experiencing a great deal of stress as a result of the deteriorating quality of the environment. There is a need to balance development with environmental management strategies. Certain paradigms have been advanced in order to theoretically explain resource use and deal with the applications of environmental management strategies. These paradigms are: frontier economics, ecodevelopment, deep ecology, environmental protection, and resource management.

Since this study has as its main thrust the investigation of the public's awareness of the natural resources, citizens in three states of Nigeria — Akwa Ibom, Imo, and Abia states — were surveyed. These states were chosen for their unique location.

Resultant Problem

Clearly the population explosion in Nigeria is a problem that has to be combated. The pressure on the environmental parameters is directly linked to population. In order to formulate good and effective policies, one

Table 5.5: Nigerian Population Census Figures

State Name	Males	Females	Total
1. Abia	1,108,357	1,189,621	2,297,978
2. Adamawa	1,084,824	1,039,225	2,124,049
3. Akwa Ibom	1,162,430	1,197,306	2,359,736
4. Anambra	1,374,801	1,393,102	2,767,903
5. Bauchi	2,202,962	2,091,451	4,294,413
6. Benue	1,385,402	1,393,102	2,778,504
7. Borno	1,327,311	1,269,278	2,596,589
8. Cross River	945,270	920,334	1,865,604
9. Delta	1,273,208	1,296,973	2,570,181
10. Edo	1,082,718	1,077,130	2,159,848
11. Enugu	1,482,245	1,679,050	3,161,295
12. Imo	1,178,031	1,307,468	2,485,499
13. Jigawa	1,419,726	1,410,203	2,829,929
14. Kaduna	2,059,382	1,909,870	3,969,252
15. Kano	2,858,724	2,773,316	5,632,040
16. Katsina	1,944,218	1,934,126	3,878,344
17. Kebbi	1,024,334	1,037,892	2,062,226
18. Kogi	1,055,964	1,043,082	2,099,046
19. Kwara	790,921	775,548	1,566,469
20. Lagos	2,999,528	2,686,253	5,685,781
21. Niger	1,290,720	1,191,647	2,482,367
22. Ogun	1,144,907	1,193,663	2,338,570
23. Ondo	1,958,928	1,925,557	3,884,485
24. Osun	1,079,424	1,123,592	2,203,016
25. Oyo	1,745,720	1,743,069	3,488,789
26. Plateau	1,645,730	1,637,974	3,283,704
27. Rivers	2,079,583	1,904,274	3,983,857
28. Sokoto	2,158,111	2,234,280	4,392,391
29. Taraba	754,754	725,836	1,480,590
30. Yobe	719,763	691,718	1,411,481
31. Abuja F.C.T.	206,535	172,136	378,671
Country Totals	44,544,531	43,968,076	88,512,607

Source: Nigerian Government Release, 1992.

needs to understand the public attitudes. An examination of many parts of Akwa Ibom, Imo, and Abia states indicates a great loss of the rain forest. The disappearing forest means a loss of biological diversity, but even more important, there is a loss of cultural diversity.

Two variables that this study evaluates are the severity of environmental degradation and the reversibility of environmental degradation. Severity cannot easily be compared, because effects are of different types, occur in different places, and affect different aspects of life systems.

Reversibility concerns the possibility of returning an ecological system to its former state. For example, can reforestation assist the reestablishment of the forests that have been denuded in the three states in question? The dimensions of time, certainty, severity, and reversibility combine to produce the extent of urgency in the degradation in these states. There are instances of erosion causing environmental problems in Akwa Ibom, Abia, and Imo states.

The environmental problems of Nigeria can be further divided between the effects of poverty and the effects of economic development. Under the poverty situation in many parts of the three states in question, the environment has exhibited the ravages of several years of mismanagement which include erosion, deforestation, surface water pollution, and air pollution. As a result of these problems the quality of life is endangered. Figures 5.12 and 5.13 depict the threat to environmental and cultural diversities of Nigeria.

As a result of the development process, Akwa Ibom, Abia, and Imo states have experienced environmental degradation due to agricultural growth, major residential construction, road construction, and industrial development. Along with the population increase, development is a source of environmental degradation. The major aspects of development that have led to environmental problems are urbanization and urban development, manufacturing industry development, and extractive industry exploitation (Figure 5.14).

Justification for the Study

In the study an attempt was made to do the following:

1. Investigate basic public values and the conservation ethic. The aim of this part of the study was to evaluate the public's attitudes toward resource conservation. The hypothesis advanced here is that the more informed the public is about the importance and limits of the soil and water resources as trust to the future generation, the more it will support programs and initiatives on conservation.

2. Evaluate whether public knowledge of conservation issues and practices is central to successful environmental programs.

3. Examine the public's priorities for the allocation of land and water resources. Are these priorities crucial to formulating policies that would be supported and further difficult political struggles?

4. Examine whether public attitudes toward federal and state action to promote soil, water, and forest conservation are germane to solving the environmental problems in the three states.

Figure 5.12: Fishing industry is threatened by offshore exploration, Eket, Nigeria, 1991.

Figure 5.13: Urbanization threatens quality of water and fish, Eket, Nigeria, 1991.

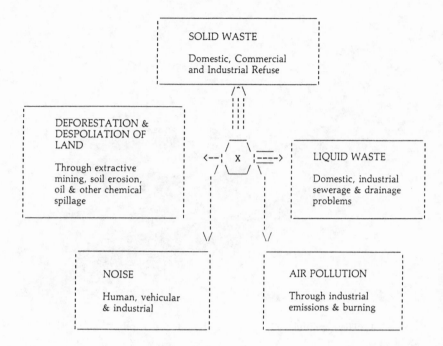

Note: The width of the arrow approximately indicates perceived magnitude of the problem.

Source: Adapted from Okpala, 1986.

Figure 5.14: The Nigeria environmental problem.

The Importance of the Study

The situation in Nigeria and the rest of Africa with regard to the water, soil, and other renewable resources is alarming. Newspaper reports and other major publications such as the *Daily Times* (1991) and *West Africa* magazine (1991d) claim that Nigeria is facing some very difficult environmental problems.

Since Nigeria is engaging in the process of a democratically elected government, it is imperative that the new administration know precisely what the public's attitude and perception is about the declining natural resource base of the country. This study provides invaluable information upon which new policies can be formulated. Policies already in place can be calibrated based on gathered data and information provided in this study.

This study can serve as a pilot study for other surveys that could be conducted in other parts of the country. It can also serve as a supplement to existing case studies on Africa's resource management issue.

The timing of this study is significant because Nigeria has lost well over 80 percent of its forests (World Resources Institute 1985). This study will contribute to the continuing efforts of many researchers to raise political awareness of the action needed to combat soil erosion, water pollution, and natural resource depletion in Nigeria.

This study is important because it will spark a response to the changing policy environment in Africa. It will provide the necessary framework to help Nigerian policy makers, first, to recognize the complexities of the environmental issues and then to design approaches to tackle those problems.

Methodology

In this study survey research was employed in gathering primary data. Secondary data were collected by conducting research in institutions in the United States and in Nigeria.

The survey method was particularly useful in this study. Anthropologists used the same method in the late 1940s and early 1950s and were very successful with it. Prior to 1950, survey research in Africa was associated for the most part with the needs of the colonial governments which required certain basic statistics for planning and administrative purposes.

However, there are pitfalls when surveys employ culture-bound techniques. Because Africa differs morphologically from Western culture there is a problem in using the survey method in its true sense in Africa (Lenski 1966, 1970; Goldschmidt 1959; and Stewart 1963). Sophisticated sampling procedures predicated upon the structural nature of Western society seem less applicable under typical African societies. These societies have designated roles for males, females, and children. Positions in Nigerian communities, villages, and towns are significant when consulting people for information concerning issues of national importance. Kinship order constitutes major status. Hence in order to gather information that includes a cross section of the towns in question, village heads (chiefs), heads of households, government officials, teachers, farmers, and spiritual leaders were interviewed.

One hundred individuals were surveyed in each of three Nigerian towns: Onitsha, Aba, and Ikot-Ekpene. These individuals were not randomly sampled. Rather they were selected based on the advice of local people who were familiar with the town. Since the researcher and his team of assistants were dealing with community grouping far less individualized and much more homogenous than Western societies, randomized survey research techniques seemed a cumbersome and expensive way to acquire data, the interpretation of which is uncertain and the utility of which, for either social policy or research knowledge, is at best questionable. Drake (1973:66–67) in his work "Research Method or Culture-bound Technique? Pitfalls of Survey Research in Africa" notes:

> I have, in fact, witnessed highly misguided and inappropriate surveys in Africa. Americans and Germans, with their concern for efficiency, were eager to get on with their job of surveying a community's health. They were far too busy to waste hours sitting and chatting with the headman or with crucially placed old men and women. As well-trained technicians, they went to the headman and bade him gather his people so they could detect the presence of particular germs or conditions of malnutrition. The results of some of these surveys are not difficult to predict. In reviewing some of these results, particularly of surveys conducted prior to my arrival in the area, I found that whole sections of a village were never discovered and that hosts of individuals had never appeared, although the researchers were confident they had assayed an entire village and all of its residents. The failure to spend time socializing had doomed the project to failure and had destroyed any chance of representative sampling. Most horrifying was that this ignorance of local society never troubled the researchers, and frequently, when it was gently demonstrated to them, they denied its relevance. They were "scientists," not socializers.

In each of the towns, one hundred people were interviewed (see Figure 5.11). The researcher was assisted by ten local residents of Nigeria who speak the local languages. The survey instrument consisted of twenty open- and closed-ended questions about the public awareness of soil, water, and other natural resources. Also included in the instrument were questions on policy and political issues concerning these resources (see Appendix).

Findings

One growing phenomenon in Africa is the steady loss of agricultural land. It was one of the intents of this study to see if the inhabitants of the towns of Onitsha, Aba, and Ikot-Ekpene understood the ramifications of the loss of agricultural lands. Of the people surveyed in Ikot-Ekpene, 95 percent felt it was a serious problem, and 98 percent in Aba and 100 percent in Onitsha felt the loss of agricultural land was a serious problem.

A high proportion of the respondents thought the soil and water resources of their area were misused: 75 percent in Ikot-Ekpene, 80 percent in Aba, and 83 percent in Onitsha. Tables 5.6 and 5.7 give summaries of some of the items in the questionnaire. The overall summary of the survey is that a great majority of the respondents felt that the environment was

Table 5.6: Awareness of the Seriousness of Ecological Problems of Soil, Water, and Natural Resources in Nigeria

	Very Serious Problem		
Ecological Awareness/Concerns	Ikot-Ekpene %	Aba %	Onitsha %
1. The loss of good farmland.	95	98	100
2. The misuse of soil and water.	75	80	83
3. The destruction of the forest.	84	89	92
4. The scarcity of firewood.	73	82	91
5. The loss of natural places.	87	84	89
6. The disappearance of wildlife.	89	90	92
7. Water pollution.	63	64	70
8. The shortage of fresh water.	90	94	97
9. The impact of road construction.	60	70	74
10. The impact of agricultural intensification.	70	74	75
11. The impact of agricultural extensification.	66	61	75
12. The impact of housing and infrastructure construction.	72	75	80

Note: Population Sample Total of N=300 (100 residents from each town).

suffering an enormous deterioration due to human development impact, and the government policies were not appropriately and adequately addressing the environmental decline problem.

Drastic and immediate steps must be taken to rectify the situation. This could be done by designing comprehensive plans for regions and towns in the regions. These comprehensive plans must address the physical components of the regions adequately and must take into consideration the environmental inventory which should document the flora and fauna of the region prior to development. Hence, development such as housing, agriculture, industries, and transportation impacts could be adequately assessed.

Recommendations

In order to reverse the trend of forest depletion in Africa and to ensure the integrity of the environmental quality several steps need to be taken. These steps must be part of an overall environmental plan which is

Table 5.7: Adequacy and Appropriateness of Ecological Services for Soil, Water, and Natural Resources in Nigeria

Adequate/Appropriate=A+ Inadequate/Inappropriate=I−	Ikot-Ekpene A+ : I−		Aba A+ : I−		Onitsha A+ : I−	
1. Adequacy of local government involvement in landuse issues.	30	43	21	73	40	50
2. Adequacy of federal government involvement in landuse issues.	36	39	19	75	50	39
3. Appropriate local government involvement in landuse issues.	14	65	26	60	30	55
4. Appropriate federal government involvement in landuse issues.	21	63	30	55	26	59

Note: Population Sample Total of N=300 (100 residents from each town).

---

beneficial to the development, conservation, and preservation of the natural resources of Africa.

1. Provide information about the present status and character of the community to identify needs and opportunities.

2. Set forth objectives for development of the country that will chart the character and quality of the community desired in the future.

3. Put property interest on notice as to the intent of the region to take action on various locations and in regard to specific projects.

4. Recommend programs designed specifically to alleviate existing environmental problems and to avoid the occurrence of potential problems in the future.

5. Provide coordinated activities in consonance with other public agencies in the region.

6. Stimulate understanding and support among the local citizens in order to bring forth the necessary fiscal and legal implementation devices that are essential for development and protection of the forest.

The above goals and objectives are for the overall environment, but specific forestry goals and objectives need to be articulated, beginning with the expansion of mass-media publicity and extension support for forestry conservation. Other strategies as suggested by the World Resources Institute (1985a:14) include the following:

1. Decentralize tree seedling production and other forestry operations and involve individuals more directly in these activities through local community groups, non-governmental organizations, and schools.

2. Give more attention to conservation programs that can help to increase protection of and research on tropical rain forests.

3. Use lower cost technologies such as direct seeding and more intensive mass-production techniques to accelerate tree planting programs.

4. Place greater emphasis on multipurpose trees to provide people with timber, poles, fuelwood, fruit, fodder, fiber, and other nonwood forest products.

5. Intensify research on agroforestry, management of secondary or degraded forests, and ways to involve local people in forestry.

6. Modify and expand forestry training and education programs to place greater emphasis on extension skills, agroforestry, and conservation of forest ecosystems.

7. Refrain from converting natural forests to plantations when other suitable land is available.

8. Revise government fiscal policies in forestry, such as lenient forest concession agreements, to encourage sustainable management of natural forests and plantations.

9. Quantify more precisely the negative effects of deforestation on agricultural productivity, employment, rural incomes, and the balance of trade.

10. Work more closely with planners in agriculture, energy, industry, and other sectors to design broadly based agriculture and energy programs in which forestry will play a vital, though not always the lead, role.

Some countries like Nigeria, Ghana, Congo, and Cameroon have begun these strategies and are receiving encouragement from international organizations and governments of industrialized countries. Private voluntary organization involvement is also very crucial. The African forest is very crucial to the survival of the human race and as such should be protected through the coordinated efforts of African governments and assistance from international agencies.

6. The Savannas of Africa

Introduction

The savanna of Africa stretches from the southern edge of the Sahara Desert to the northern edge of the deciduous forest of West and Central Africa. The savanna covers an extended portion of Ethiopia, Somalia, Kenya, Tanzania, Burundi, and Sudan, and most of Zambia, Zimbabwe, Angola, Malawi, Madagascar, and Uganda consist of savanna. Forest and savanna differ in the numbers of trees, density of trees, and foliage. There are also differences in the flora and fauna that exist in these two biomes. The general definition of savanna is an area with scattered trees with a limited amount of rainfall. A more complete definition is given by Hills (1965:2181–89):

> A plant formation of tropical regions, comprising a virtually continuous ecologically dominant stratum of more or less xeromorphic plants, of which herbaceous plants, especially grasses and sedges, are frequently the principal, and occasionally the only, components, although woody plants often of the dimension of trees or palms generally occur and are present in varying densities.

Origins of Savannas

There appears to be marked delineation of the forest-savanna boundary. The factors that lead to the formation of savannas are different from those of the forest. The factors that are involved in the formation of the savannas are many and very different. Figure 6.1 is a schematic diagram which attempts to show the interacting factors which enhance the formation and maintenance of the savanna. There are two basic paradigms on the subject of savanna formation. One of these paradigms is that the savanna is a naturally occurring vegetation. The argument is supported by the fact that the flora and fauna of the savannas are very different from those of the forests. The savanna vegetation and animals are able to

152

Interactive Factors Enhance the Formation and Maintenance of the Savanna

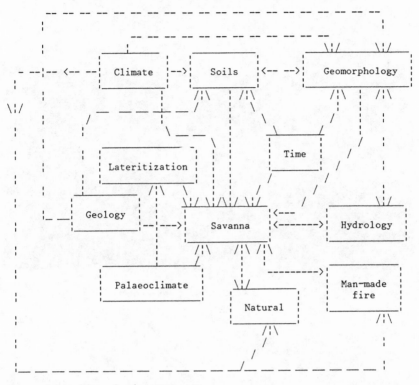

Source: Adapted from Goudie, 1982, p. 43.

Figure 6.1: Schematic diagram of savanna formation.

withstand the limited amount of rainfall and water available in the region. The soil types are also very different from those of the forests. The climatic factors seem to be instrumental in supporting this argument.

The second paradigm is that savannas are caused by man and that human activities—especially burning—have created the savanna conditions. Human action such as pastoralism certainly helps in the maintenance of the savanna conditions. Confusion sets in when one examines the experiments that have been conducted in some African countries such as Nigeria as to the effect of burning on the savanna ecosystem. It is argued that the negative impact of savanna burning is exaggerated (Moss and Morgan 1965). Figure 6.2 shows an example of a savanna vegetation. Figure 6.3 shows the impact of burning on the maintenance of a savanna-like vegetation.

The factors that have a direct impact on the formation process of the

Figure 6.2: Savanna vegetation, western Nigeria, 1991.

Figure 6.3: Burning in a savanna region of western Nigeria, 1991.

savanna are: geomorphology, geology, palaeoclimate, climate, lateritization, soils, hydrology, natural fire, and man-made fires. On a worldwide basis, the formation of savannas can be attributed to the activities that occur through human development of the environment, although there are savannas that are due to natural causes.

Eden's 1974 study of "Palaeoclimatic influences and the development of savanna in Southern Venezuela" gives one an insight into the possible origins of the savanna. Two interesting conclusions are provided by this study. First, savannas can exist in relatively wet environments which are in close proximity to forest lands. Second, although savanna soils are low in fertility, such a condition is not peculiar to the savanna soils. Adjacent forest soils are sometimes just as infertile. However, this study concludes that periodic burning does maintain the status or conditions of the savanna.

The boundary of the savanna and forest has been a subject of great ecological debate for a long time, but there is a general consensus that burning and cultivation are the predominant biotic influence for the maintenance of the savanna. The environment of the savanna provides a very different set of circumstances for land-use practices when compared to the forest environment. The type of agriculture and settlement patterns of the savanna are also different from those of the forests (Morgan and Moss 1965). And as far as agricultural practices are concerned, the fallow periods differ substantially for the savanna and forest areas.

The types of vegetation of Africa can be divided into three major groups: forests, grasslands, and desert. The African savannas lie between the forest and desert biological and climatic regions of Africa. Phillips (1960:175) in his classic book *Agriculture and Ecology in Africa* divided the savanna ecosystem into four basic groups. These groups were the wooded savanna region; the desert to near-desert climax or transitions; open savanna or grassland climax; and the Macchia, Maquis, or "Fynbos" climax. The wooded savanna region is divided into five subregions:

1. Subhumid wooded savanna and related vegetation (SHWS).
2. The mild subarid wooded savanna and related vegetation.
3. The subarid wooded savanna and related vegetation.
4. Arid wooded savanna and related vegetation.
5. Subdesert wooded savanna and related vegetation.

The five categories of the wooded savanna are in turn divided into three types based upon their location relative to the equator: (1) north of the equator; (2) south of the equator; and (3) sub-tropical (Phillips 1960).

Figure 6.4 indicates the biogeography of Africa. The savannas are important ecosystems within the African continent. The plants and animals that exist in the savanna play an important role in the natural scheme of the

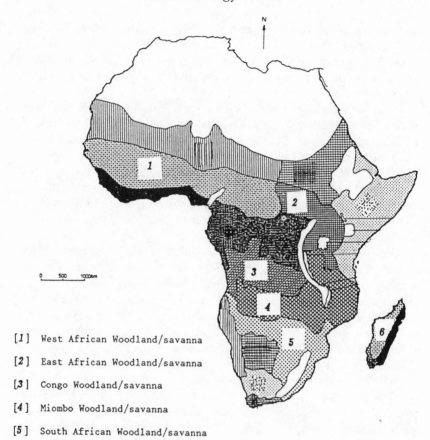

[1] West African Woodland/savanna

[2] East African Woodland/savanna

[3] Congo Woodland/savanna

[4] Miombo Woodland/savanna

[5] South African Woodland/savanna

[6] Malagasy Woodland/savanna

Source: International Union for Conservation of Nature and Natural Resources (IUCN), United Nations Environment Programme, *IUCN Directory of Afrotropical Protected Areas,* 1987, p. 19.

Figure 6.4: The biogeographical map of Africa.

continent. The intricate relationship between the plants and animals must be fully understood for development purposes.

Flora and Fauna of the Savanna

Botanically, Andropogon and Pennisetum plants predominate the savanna region. The trees found in the savannas are not as tall as those of the forest region. Shantz (1971:51) contends that the most abundant tree

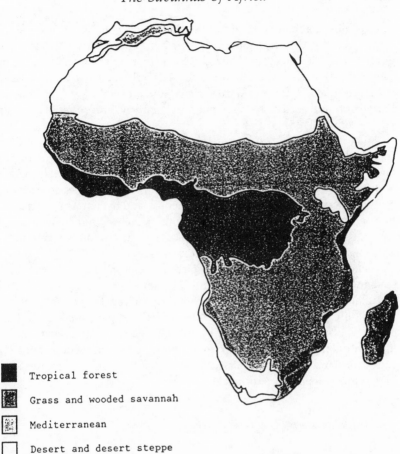

Tropical forest

Grass and wooded savannah

Mediterranean

Desert and desert steppe

Source: Africa Recovery based on FAO data.

Figure 6.5: Africa's natural vegetation.

types are: *Bauhinia reticulata* DC, *Acacia suma* Kurz, *Parkia africana* R.
Br., *Butyrospermum parkii* Kotschy, *Lophira alata* Banks, *Cussonia
djalonensis* Cheval., *Entada sudanica* Schwein f., and species of *Annona,
Kigelia, Erythrina, Strychnos, Borassus, Hyphaene, Gardenia,* and many
other genera. In northwestern Africa high grass–low tree savanna appears
to form a ring which encompasses the rain forest, although the latter has
shrunk tremendously starting in Senegambia and moving eastward
through Nigeria and Cameroon where it is broken by the Cameroon
mountains (Figure 6.5).

A typical East African short-grass plain habitat consists of thick bush,
Acacia belt, light Acacia bush, coarse grass, and open short-grass plains.

The wildlife that can be found in the thick bush consists of lesser, kudu, eland, buffalo, duiker, leopard, and rhino. The Acacia generally have giraffe, zebra, and impala. The light acacia belt is dominated by gerenuk. The coarse grass region is rich in steinbok and warthog. Gazelle, wildebeest, jackal, bat-eared fox, hyena, lion, cheetah, topi, hunting dog, hartebeest, and aardvark are plentiful in the open short-grass plain of East Africa (Smith 1985).

The habitats of southern African savanna can be categorized into rocky hills type, coarse grass slope type, acacia park-like type and short-grass plains type. The wildlife present in the rocky hills habitat is made up of klipspringer, baboon, and jackal. The coarse grass slopes contain large numbers of mountain reedbuck, vaal rhebok, and hyena. The acacia park-like habitat contains impala, giraffe, steinbok, zebra, and hartebeest. The short-grass plains and soda flats ecological system contain wildlife such as wildebeest, springbok, blesbok, and aardvark.

The ecological systems of a typical central and southern woodland savanna of Africa consist of the woodland, open grassland, light woodland, and rocky hills and outcrop. Respectively they have the following wildlife. For the woodland: giraffe, buffalo, sable antelope, lion, and eland. The open grassland has oribi, tsessebe, warthog, and reedbuck. The light woodland has grysbok, roan antelope, zebra, and scrub hare. The rocky hills and outcrop of Africa savanna habitat contains greater kudu, klipspringer, leopard, and jackal.

Development Opportunities

There are many advantages that accrue as a result of well-planned and executed development. Sustainable development in the savannas falls into three broad categories: (1) ecological, (2) economic, and (3) agronomic.

Ecological sustainability of development projects is very crucial because of the fragile nature of the soils and vegetation of the savanna region closest to the deserts of the Sahara, the Karoo-Namib, and the Kalahari. Experience in the Sahelian countries shows that overgrazing and shifting cultivation have exacerbated the southward and northward spread of the desert-like conditions (desertification). Intensification of agriculture and slash-and-burn practices have also increased the spread of the desert. The overgrazing problem is exemplified by Figure 6.6. Agricultural development must incorporate the concept of carrying capacity which enhances planning for the suitable and wise use of the land and as such reduces the deterioration of the land. Improper development in the savanna could result in wind and water erosion, so a thorough

Figure 6.6: Cattle grazing in western Nigeria, guinea savanna-woodland.

understanding of the climatic and terrestrial conditions is necessary in order to have sustained development.

Agriculturally, mixed cultivation is of great importance because it helps to maintain soil fertility and reduces the chances of erosion should one type of crop suffer from an epidemic or should a crop be infected by some plant disease. In Uganda, for instance, garden beds are a foot or two higher than the ground and several crops such as maize, peanuts, and sweet potatoes are grown. Such a strategy helps in the nutrient cycle.

Argument on African Wildlife Utilization

There are opposing schools of thought on how to practice conservation of wildlife in Africa. Elephants, one of the largest of Africa's wildlife, seem to have been in the center of a controversy of whether or not their population has to be controlled by curling. Curling is the organized practice of controlled hunting. Animal groups that are overpopulated are reduced in numbers, and their hides, horns, tusks, and meat are sold. Such efforts, proponents claim, would help keep the elephant population from exceeding the carrying capacity of their habitats. Many incidences in Africa have shown that when elephant populations exceed the carrying capacities of the sanctuaries where they are restricted, they often go outside of their protected habitats into human agricultural land and destroy crops. Reports from Ghana, Kenya, and Uganda have shown how elephants sometimes venture outside of their protected areas into villages and in some cases, have even killed human beings. Hence, it is argued that when elephants are curled, the meat is used as food and the ivory tusks are sold for substantial amounts of money which could then be used for development.

Early in 1992, the elephant populations in South Africa and Zimbabwe were substantially high, and these two countries were interested in having the ban on ivory lifted so that they could resume international trade. They argued that the ivory trade would enable them to reduce the number of elephants. The large number of elephants was becoming a menace, damaging their habitat. Many proponents of curling argue that Africa should not be different from other parts of the world where such measures of conservation have been adopted. Miller (1977:19) notes:

> Perhaps the "elephant problem" should be viewed in broader perspectives as symptomatic of the future of most of Africa's wildlife. Will African nations, in the face of rapidly expanding human populations and their needs, continue to ensure the integrity of large, free-ranging populations of wildlife? Or will the African elephant and many of its associated species be eventually confined, like the American bison, to relatively small, isolated areas where intensive management is required to keep the populations at relatively low levels to protect their habitats? It seems almost certain that the latter course will soon apply throughout the range of the African bush elephant, and the several other species might share the same fate.

The opposing viewpoint seems to rest on moral and ethical values. It submits that the magnificent and elegant wildlife of Africa should not be subjected to curling. It appears that those who oppose harvesting of wildlife do not understand that curling is one of the best methods of keeping the wildlife from destroying the ecosystems on which they exist. It is also important to note that human activities must also be curtailed so that encroachment is substantially reduced. If strict management is not an adopted policy, future generations may not have a proud wildlife heritage. This argument is supported by the fact that in the late 1960s, the 1970s, and the early 1980s, it was fashionable to possess novelty items of handbags, coats, wall hangings, and rugs made of animal hides from Africa. The zebra, lion, and tiger hides were very popular. The Grevy's zebra, the common zebra found in Kenya, and the mountain zebra of South Africa were being killed in large numbers for their hides by poachers. Poaching can be controlled only when funding and sound management practices are established. This should be the emphasis of African resource managers. A combination of approaches seems to be the right management practice for

Africa's wildlife. In parts of Africa where the wildlife have not exceeded the carrying capacity of the habitats on which they depend, they should be allowed to roam freely and no curling should be done. However, in other areas where the carrying capacity has been exceeded, "cropping" should take place. Governments of Africa have shown some bold and courageous efforts in the past. During the reign of the former Kenyan head of state, the late Jomo Kenyatta, the hunting of wildlife was banned, and later the sale of wildlife trophies and curios was banned. This was a sincere beginning of the efforts to save Kenya's wildlife from poaching.

The growing number of poachers and people encroaching upon wildlife habitats is problematic for the tallest creature on earth, the giraffe. Their shrinking habitats have led to a decline in their numbers. About 130 years ago, giraffes existed in the savanna regions of West Africa, from Senegal to the Sudan, Kenya, and Tanzania. In the 1990s, giraffes can only be found in small areas of Kenya, Tanzania, and southern African countries. They are almost extinct in West Africa.

Probably one of the most significant modes of increasing the conservation movement in Africa is through education. It is an accurate assessment to contend that most people who live in African countries well endowed with wildlife are not quite aware of the importance or significance of the wildlife to their countries or to the world at large. This fact was discovered by Sandra Price in 1979 in her research in Kenya. Many young students in Kenyan urban centers had never seen elephants or other wildlife. She started a program in which 560 wildlife conservation clubs were formed in Kenya, and by 1980 they had over 30,000 members. Malawi, Uganda, Cameroon, and Zambia have now adopted this model, and the young people have become the custodians of African wildlife. Momentum is growing as educational programs in elementary, secondary, and university institutions buttress environmental awareness and education efforts. Lamenting about the Kenyan conditions prior to her efforts, Price (1979:4–11) notes: "The majority of younger Kenyans have almost no environmental awareness. Despite their country's heritage, most have never even seen a lion — or an elephant." Price admits that the idea of having wildlife clubs started in 1968 at the initiation of Kenyan youths and that she only provided the mechanism for the expansion of the idea.

The plight of elephants in countries such as Kenya and Tanzania must be stressed again and again because of the conflict between the wildlife and humans. Kenya, like most African countries, is becoming increasingly urban and industrial. Modern human activities geared toward development are growing very rapidly which is a direct threat to the elephants. Approximately 1.5 million elephants remain in the whole of Africa. This number has declined slightly because of a number of factors that have already been enumerated. The ivory trade to Asian countries exacerbated the destruction of the elephant population. As a matter of fact, in 1976, two hundred tons of ivory were shipped to major Asian centers. Land clearing and poaching are also among the factors that have been problematic in the management of elephant herds in Kenya. In five years in the 1970s, one-half of Kenya's elephants were killed. In search of a new habitat in the 1980s, groups of elephants from the Samburu game reserve moved toward the southern part of the country, and the cultivated lands of the country were destroyed. Approximately two thousand elephants were involved in the southern movement into farmlands. They destroyed entire fields of corn, and the lives of villagers were threatened. In Aberdere, two people were killed by elephants. This trend presents a problem for park managers and government authorities. Should elephants and other wildlife be treated as cattle? In order to grow staple food and preserve the food necessary to cope with recurrent drought problems, the elephants must be contained in the parks.

The conservation of Africa's wildlife must be conducted in such a way that the existence of the wildlife must bring in some revenue. The central issue is whether Africa's wildlife must be exploited in order to save it. The argument on how to practice conservation in Africa is really an old debate which has not found a "real solution." In many African parks it is not un-common to find that subsistence hunting, sustainable cropping, sport hunting, livestock grazing, and to a lesser degree mineral extraction do oc-cur even though these activities may be illegal. Large mammals are facing a tremendous threat, a combination of solutions is necessary. It is possible to have a strict management practice which will allow people to profit by "farming" wildlife and being a part of a mechanism which is economically beneficial in cropping wildlife, conserving it, and also participating in the tourism industry. The mechanism of operating parks and other wildlife habitats should make it difficult for those who engage in poaching to carry out their activities.

Norman Myers (1982:43) maintains that sustainable cropping is the best way to protect Africa's wildlife because it incorporates strategies that have already been tested and have proven to be successful in some African parks. He notes:

... Over 10,000 elephants and hippos have been cropped in six parks in five coun-tries, and the wildlife watcher senses not the slightest disturbance. At Ngorongoro, tourists are offered beef or zebra steak for dinner. No objection during 12 years of this practice. Translocation of excess animals has been officially eliminated as an option on grounds of misguided ecology, let alone gross expense, except in the case of severely endangered species such as the rhino.

Research centers in African parks and reserves offer tremendous hope for the future of conservation in the continent. Although the Fossey's

Karisoke Research Center is located at ten thousand feet in Parc National Volcans in Rwanda, it is shared among Rwanda, Zaire, and Uganda. It gives the world a view of what goes on when conservation is attempted in Africa. The research center offers a unique opportunity to study mountain gorillas and their struggle against encroachment problems. In 1980, poaching threatened the gorillas; several of them were killed (Harcourt and Harcourt 1980). The conservation region of the park overlaps part of Zaire and Uganda and can be categorized as having characteristics of both the savanna and forest regions of the continent of Africa. The research center has been able to maintain important records which are crucial in the sustainable conservation of the gorillas in the park. Besides this important function, the 150-square-mile area is unique for its beauty because of the flora diversity it contains. All across Africa, one notices the threat that confronts the diverse communities of wildlife and plants. It stands to reason that conservation and preservation efforts must be increased and improved in order to save the rich and diverse environment of this great continent.

There is no doubt that the cure to many of the world's diseases will continue to come from the plant world. By destroying the floral ecosystems, mankind is risking his existence and survival. Many people in Africa, as well as other Third World regions, depend on the herbs obtained from the forest regions. The position of the herbalist, who understands the efficacy of the herbs, has been elevated to the equivalency of that of a Western trained physician. International health organizations have begun to investigate how they can work with herbalists to improve the health of the millions of people in the world. More than three-fourths of the world's population cannot afford modern hospitalization, and the medicinal and pharmaceutical world can benefit immensely from the conservation and preservation of the flora of the savannas.

Norman Myers (1981:26) in commenting on the significance of the flora and herbalists of Africa makes the following observation.

Today, though, attitudes are changing — so much so, in fact, that witch doctors are good guys again. They are being courted by the World Health Organization and drug companies. Their methods are being studied by scientists and are even taught in universities. In late 1979, a World Congress on Folk Medicine was held in Peru. As a result a number of organizations concerned with traditional remedies have sprung up. In Zaire, healers advertise their skills on billboards, in newspapers and over local radio stations. In South Africa, some medicine men are said to earn up to $23,000 a year. Why the sudden change of heart? For one thing, it's often a case of local cures or none at all; folk healers provide the only medicine available. For another thing, some of their herbal concoctions almost certainly contain hither to unknown "miracle drugs" along with other substances that could lead to new pesticides and industrial chemicals.

The periwinkles of Madagascar have been useful in the treatment of childhood leukemia. In the Ghanaian villages of the Brong Ahafo region, Nana Kofi Drobo, of Drobo Herbal Treatment Center at Nwoase, thinks he has discovered an herbal treatment for Acquired Immune Deficiency Syndrome (AIDS). He is believed to have successfully treated about one hundred patients since 1986. International medical centers are attempting to work with him to learn what the herbs he uses for treating his patients are made up of chemically. This is another important reason why the savannas and forests must be protected.

The world will continue to benefit from the flora and fauna of the savannas and forests of Africa. Unfortunately, on a worldwide scale, only 1.5 billion of the original 6.2 billion forests remain undisturbed. The Congo and Brazil (South America) contain most of the undisturbed forests. Côte d'Ivoire has been losing approximately 16 percent of its forest every year and it is estimated that only one-fortieth of its original forest remains in the 1990s. The vegetation of the savannas has suffered a similar fate, although statistics on it are not available. The protection of the animals and plants of Africa must be considered a paramount priority because of their riches. For instance, the Samburu Game Reserve is famous for its crocodiles and has been attracting tourists in millions annually. Other places known for their crocodile populations are Lake Turkana in the northern part of Kenya, the Nile River in Uganda, South Africa, Zimbabwe, and Mali's Lake Menaka, which is known for drying out during the dry season.

Saving Africa's wildlife can sometimes be very controversial. One particular example is the case of Kenya's war against poachers. In Meru (Kenya) one can find thousands of wild animals that move freely close to Mount Kenya, such as the black rhinoceros which occupies the savanna. They have been threatened by poachers for a long time, and their population has declined drastically. Since Meru Park is close to the Somalian border, non–Kenyans have been part of the poaching problem. It is estimated that the black rhinoceros population declined from over eighteen thousand in 1969 to less than one thousand in 1981 in Kenya (Wallace 1981). The demand is great for rhinoceros horns which are used for medicinal purposes in many far eastern countries of Asia. Horns are used as cures for fever, headaches, and heart problems. Poaching occurs because those engaged in this immoral and greedy act make substantially higher incomes than they would if they were working for the government or private industry in Kenya.

Enforcing the law has meant confrontation between poachers and antipoaching rangers. In 1980 in the Masai Mara Game Reserve antipoaching teams killed twenty-two poachers. The war against poachers is continuing in the 1990s, and it will take the international communities' efforts to completely stop poaching activities.

A spectacle of the savanna region of Africa is the wildebeest (both blue and black gnu). Although the population of both blue and black gnu has increased tremendously over the last four decades, blue gnu's populations have increased exponentially. The blue gnu population was 350,000 in 1950 and 650,000 in 1960 (Myers 1981). The number was probably higher than 1.5 million in 1991. The problem is that this large population of wildebeest only occupies ten thousand square miles of the savanna region, and the failure of rains could bring devastating problems to the region. However, the Serengetti Planes have managed to support the wildebeest fairly well. It has even been postulated that because the vegetation of the savanna in the Serengetti has been able to sustain such a large number of wildebeest, it might be able to sustain a couple of million more for a short period of time. In other words, the carrying capacity has not yet been exceeded. Nonetheless, it should be pointed out that the wildebeest are found in South Africa, Namibia, Zimbabwe, Botswana, Mozambique, Angola, Tanzania, and Kenya. They migrate in large numbers.

African savannas represent about 2 million square miles of grassland and woodland which is home to many animals, but the savanna is also the area where farmers grow their crops and raise their livestock. The agricultural practice often leads to the loss of habitats. The savanna habitat is home to many African wild cats such as lions, leopards, and cheetahs. The numbers of lions have been greatly reduced in the last five decades. Only a few thousand lions remain in Africa in the 1990s, and most of these are in national parks. Ranchers in Africa have played a significant role in the reduction of predators, as have poachers. In the last fifteen years an estimated twenty-five thousand leopards have been poached out of East Africa. However, the cheetah population has been fairly stable in many parts of Africa.

Small cats such as the civet, serval, caracal, sand cats, black footed cats, golden cats, and genets have been able to survive better than the large cats because they are more elusive and more adaptable to their environment. They require smaller range, and their nutritional needs are not as specialized as those of the big cats. The "micro-habitats" of the small cats are more variable than those of the big cats. In the dry parts of southern Africa such as Namibia, Botswana, and Zimbabwe the black footed cats can be found, while in the northern and southern parts of the Sahara, notably Libya, Algeria, Niger, and the Sudan, the sand cats can be found. Other small cats such as the golden cat occupy the savanna forests of many West and East African countries; in the lower Nile region and the river deltas swamp cats can be found (Myers 1976).

Small cats as well as big cats are confronting human populations as the need to extensify agricultural practice in Africa grows. A combination of solutions is suggested to enhance conservation strategies in Africa. The suggestions offered here would assist in the reduction of the confrontation between humans and wildlife but will only be successful if used in combination with other existing programs that are integral parts of the African societies: (1) zoo breeding, (2) translocation to protected areas, (3) preservation of large areas for national parks (full-scale reserves), and (4) mini reserves. Some of these are already in existence in countries such as Kenya, Tanzania, South Africa, and Zimbabwe. In these countries, better enforcement strategies and local participation must be encouraged and solicited. Funding and marketing strategies of the conservation and tourism industries will encourage and enhance country efforts.

Conclusion

The savannas of Africa have great potential agriculturally if and when managed properly. The goal of the development of the savanna is to maximize the potential and to reduce or minimize problems that could emanate as a result of such development.

A resource management plan for savanna lands must be drafted and implemented in all countries of Africa where the savanna exists. Such plans will guide all natural resource management activities and establish management standards and guidelines for the savanna regions of Africa. Such plans must describe resource management practices, levels of resource production and management, and availability and suitability of lands for resource management. For any development to occur in the savanna region a plan which incorporates the following ideas should be followed.

> 1. There should be an analysis of the management situation. The appropriateness of the development and the demand and supply conditions for various commodities and services related to the development must be thoroughly investigated. The productivity potentials and use and development opportunities must be thoroughly investigated and analyzed.
> 2. There must be established goals, standards, and guidelines to maximize opportunities and minimize problems.
> 3. There must be an established plan for monitoring and evaluating the projects in the savanna environment. This is to establish the necessity for projects to take into consideration the significance of the "first and second law of thermodynamics." Basically to ensure the ecological equilibrium of nature.

With regard to the savanna soil, management concerns should center around maintaining soil productivity. The activities in the savanna region which can affect soil productivity include slash and burn, logging for

Table 6.1: Development of International Tourist Arrivals and Receipts in Africa (1980-89)

Year	International Tourism Arrivals (thousands)	Percentage rate of Change %	Index (1950 =100)	International Tourism Receipts (millions US $)	Percentage rate of Change %	Index (1950 =100)
1950	524	– –	100	88	– –	100
1960	1035	97.52	197.52	213	176.14	276.14
1961	1172	13.24	223.66	235	−3.29	267.05
1962	1270	8.36	242.37	233	−.85	264.77
1963	1474	16.06	281.30	253	8.58	287.50
1964	1892	28.36	361.07	256	1.19	290.91
1965	1965	3.86	375.00	280	9.38	318.18
1966	1980	.76	377.86	330	17.86	375.00
1967	1790	−9.60	341.60	360	9.09	409.09
1968	2250	25.70	429.39	373	3.61	423.86
1969	2556	13.60	187.79	479	28.42	544.32
1970	2842	11.19	542.37	482	.63	547.73
1971	3434	20.83	655.34	594	23.24	675.00
1972	4107	19.60	783.78	712	19.87	809.09
1973	1293	4.53	819.27	909	27.67	1032.95
1974	4876	13.58	930.53	1072	17.93	1218.18
1975	5685	16.59	1084.92	1269	18.38	1442.05
1976	5554	−2.30	1059.92	1438	13.32	1634.09
1977	5691	2.47	1086.07	1948	35.47	2213.64
1978	6128	7.68	1169.47	2130	9.34	2420.45
1979	7243	18.20	1382.25	2170	1.88	2465.91
1980	8449	16.65	1612.40	3528	62.58	4009.09
1981	9548	13.01	1822.14	3870	9.69	4397.73
1982	9375	−1.81	1789.12	3601	−6.95	4092.05
1983	9788	4.41	1867.94	3518	−2.30	3997.73
1984	10576(r)	8.05	2018.32	3393(r)	−3.55	3855.68
1985	11429(r)	8.07	2181.11	3480(r)	2.56	3954.55
1986	10862(r)	−4.96	2072.90	3776(r)	8.51	4290.91
1987	11806(r)	8.69	2253.05	5216(r)	38.14	5927.27
1988	14629(re)	23.91	2791.79	6390(re)	22.51	7261.36
1989	15323(pe)	4.74	2924.24	6652(pe)	4.10	7559.09

(r) revised figures
(re) revised estimates
(pe) preliminary estimates

Source: Adapted from World Tourism Organization, 1990, p. 59.

Table 6.2: International Tourism Receipts and Exports (1984 and 1988) in Africa

Region	Receipts millions US $		Exports millions US $		Ratio Receipts/Exports	
	1984	1988	1984	1988	1984	1988
World	109,812	194,166	1,877,053	2,795,339	5.85	6.95
Africa	3,393	6,490	68,668	66,573	4.94	9.60
Eastern Africa	380	764	5,379	6,706	7.06	11.39
Burundi	1	2	98	129	1.02	1.55
Comoros	1	3	—	—	—	—
Djibouti	4	5	13	14	30.77	35.71
Ethiopia	6	4	417	500	1.44	.80
Kenya	210	410	1,083	1,071	19.39	38.28
Madagascar	5	11	333	332	1.50	3.31
Malawi	8	6	309	295	2.59	2.03
Mauritius	46	172	373	901	12.33	19.09
Reunion	—	—	77	104	0	0
Rwanda	6	6	83	101	7.23	5.94
Seychelles	40	81	26	31	153.85	261.29
Tanzania	13	31	378	282	3.44	10.99
Uganda	1	4	386	386	.26	1.04
Zambia	13	5	655	1,141	1.98	.44
Zimbabwe	26	24	1,148	1,419	2.26	1.69
Middle Africa	94	104	5,421	3,994	1.73	2.60
Central Afr. Rep.	2	8	86	131	2.33	6.11
Cameroon	65	50	882	924	7.37	5.41
Chad	12	6	166	61	7.23	9.84
Congo	5	7	1,265	517	.40	1.35
Gabon	2	5	2,018	1,271	.10	.39
Sao Tome Principe	1	1	—	—	—	—
Zaire	7	27	1,004	1,090	.70	2.48
Northern Africa	1,992	4,347	30,760	29,313	6.48	14.83
Algeria	135	132	11,886	8,186	1.14	1.61
Egypt	860	1,784	3,140	3,828	27.39	46.60
Lybian Arab Jam.	4	3	11,136	10,841	.04	.03
Morocco	479	1,102	2,172	3,603	22.05	30.59
Sudan	51	55	629	460	8.11	11.96
Tunisia	463	1,271	1,797	2,395	25.77	53.07
Southern Africa	672	726	9,883	13,882	6.80	5.23
Botswana	35	23	549	822	6.38	2.80
Lesotho	9	12	—	—	—	—
South Africa	610	673	9,334	13,060	6.54	5.15
Swaziland	18	18	—	—	—	—

Source: Adapted from World Tourism Organization, 1990, p. 60.

firewood, site preparation for reforestation, road construction, grazing for domestic livestock and wildlife, recreational use, and fire. These activities must be controlled and carefully undertaken in order to maintain the fertility of soils. The management of the soil resource as part of the strategy for preserving the integrity of the savanna is of utmost importance.

Traditionally in Africa, soil management efforts concentrated on the reduction of soil losses due to erosion, and even this was not adequately carried out. Efforts should be made to control losses following major project establishment and to reduce erosion from rangelands. The plan for the conservation of the savanna ecosystem must call for the identification and protection of threatened, endangered, and sensitive species. The establishment of objectives and policies by African governments for inventorying the species, determining habitat and environmental needs, and protecting critical habitats is crucial to the African economy and environment.

Several African countries such as Kenya and Tanzania have already taken giant strides to accomplish this goal. Countries such as Gambia, Kenya, Tanzania, Congo, Rwanda, Madagascar, Ghana, and Malawi have benefitted from the tourism increase resulting from the interest in wildlife. Table 6.1 shows the growth of tourism for the whole of Africa from 1950 to 1989 while Table 6.2 shows that of individual countries. Overall, there has been an increase in the international tourism arrival to Africa, which has certainly brought some economic and infrastructure development with it.

Land reform in Africa is very crucial in order to preserve the savanna ecosystem. Most African countries have already embarked on reforming their land tenure system. It is generally agreed that when people have a stake in the land that they are cultivating or developing, then they are most likely to pursue conservation practices. Success brought about as a result of land reform has been achieved in countries such as Nigeria, Ghana, and Tanzania.

Research and development are key to the wise use and management of the natural resources of the savanna. The improvement of crop species, soil fertility, cultivation methods, combating pests and the control of other problems emanating as a result of development depends on the compilation of statistical data and information, and the resultant interpretation will enhance the proper management of the savanna ecosystem. Education plays an important role in the conservation and wise use of resources. Traditional education will continue to preserve traditional African methods of conservation while appropriate foreign assistance will fortify the traditional ways by stressing the understanding of new scientific knowledge. With these suggested ideas, it is possible to slow down the destruction of the savannas of Africa and to encourage the rational development of this region which can serve as the bread basket for the whole of Africa.

7. The Desert of Africa

Introduction

The discussion in this chapter applies to the Sahara, the Kalahari, and the Karoo-Namib regions of Africa. The desert environment constitutes the third major vegetation in Africa; the others being forests and savanna. The deserts of Africa are increasing in size due to various reasons (discussed in the previous chapter), but it is important to emphasize the fact that the increase in desertification is in the form of a "rash." The degree of increase varies from country to country depending on the intensity of human activities or natural occurrences which exacerbate the process. For example, the rate of desertification in Mauritania is much higher than the rates in northern Nigeria and Burkina Faso. Figure 7.1 shows the location of the desert vegetation in Africa. The locations of the Kalahari, Karoo, Sahara, and Namib areas were shown on Figure 6.2 in Chapter 6.

The arid zones of Africa are germane in the discussion of African resources because severe deprivation occurs in the Sahel and Karoo-Namib regions of Africa. The type of discussions and analyses presented in this section will expose the limitations of the dry land. It is hoped that the people and the governments in these two areas of Africa will attempt to understand the limitations of the desert and target development efforts that maximize the use of the resources while arresting the spread of the desert.

The negative impact caused by the increase in the desert-like conditions in Africa has caused several thousands of people from countries such as Mali and Burkina Faso to seek residence in Ghana and Côte d'Ivoire. The streets of Lagos, Nigeria, are inundated with many citizens of Niger who have come south in search of better lives for themselves and their families. Hence the moral imperative for citizens and governments of the Sahelian countries that border the Sahara and include the Sahara, and those of the Kalahari, is to make the desert environment habitable. It stands to reason also that some parts of the deserts must be made cultivable.

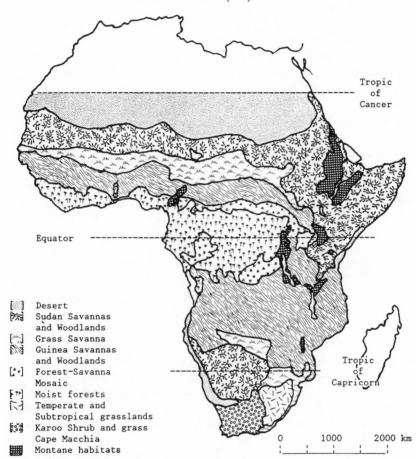

Tropic
of
Cancer

Equator

Tropic
of
Capricorn

[▨] Desert
[▨] Sudan Savannas
     and Woodlands
[▨] Grass Savanna
[▨] Guinea Savannas
     and Woodlands
[▨] Forest–Savanna
     Mosaic
[▨] Moist forests
[▨] Temperate and
     Subtropical grasslands
[▨] Karoo Shrub and grass
     Cape Macchia
[▨] Montane habitats

0   1000   2000 km
|_____|_____|_____|_____|

Source: Adapted from UNESCO/AETFAT/UNSO, *Vegetation Map of Africa,* 1983.

Figure 7.1: Africa's vegetation zones.

The Ecology of the Desert

The deserts of Africa like those which exist in other parts of the world are found in arid regions where plants and animals have very limited amounts of water to thrive on. The desert ecosystem is known for its low rainfall and high evaporation for most of the year. The composition of the vegetation and the structure and function of both the flora and fauna are in a state of agreement with the abiotic component of the environment. The "natural laws" which are the first and second laws of thermodynamics are evident in the way the ecological systems maintain their natural balance and react to perturbations introduced as a result of human activities. Nowhere is the significance of these laws more evident than at the edges of the savanna and the desert.

Human activities have worsened the conditions which lead to the spread of the desert. Entropy (the second law of thermodynamics) is the measure of disorder. The true meaning of this disorder is evident where the desert and the savanna meet because agricultural practices, drought, and settlement have helped to increase the frontiers of the desert.

One of the most striking features of the desert ecosystem is the absence of life to one who is unfamiliar with the desert ecology. It is a common agreement among those who are familiar with the desert environment that the appropriate phrase to use in describing the desert ecosystem is "scarcity of life." Although it may appear that the environment does not support any life, there are certainly some plant and animal species that have adapted to the harsh desert environment. The number of species that have evolved adaptive mechanisms are few, however, and man is certainly not one of the members of the animal kingdom that has done so.

The ability to adapt means that plant and animal species can utilize the limited quantity and range of energy flow to their advantage. The activator to the utilization of energy is water. Rain ignites the biological process in the desert by beginning the production of material essential for life. Energy and information are transmitted in the water medium, and for a short period of time primary production ensues. This production rate is very rapid, and the water quickly used up. Thus, the desert-like condition returns, but prior to that reproduction accelerates at a very rapid pace. Water then becomes a limiting factor. It is of significance to note that as one travels from a desert environment towards the savanna environment a difference in climatic conditions is encountered.

The desert and semi-desert environments have little vegetation, and the soil becomes a distinguishing characteristic instead of the vegetation. The soils of the desert environment are predominantly aridisol (James 1991a). In some parts of the desert the entisol soil type exists. The aridisols are the dry desert soils which have a high salt content. The entisols have the characteristics of recent alluvium and are thought to have little or no development profile (James 1991a).

The formation of semi-desert conditions in Africa emanates with conditions where the mean annual rainfall is below 250 mm. In certain circumstances, because of the synergistic effects of other environmental parameters, semi-deserts may result when the mean annual rainfall is higher than 250 mm a year. Temperature, wind direction, the distribution of rain, and soil characteristics are significant factors which influence desert-like conditions.

It is very difficult to precisely and accurately define a desert. "Absolute deserts" are few in the world. By "absolute deserts" the author is referring to conditions where the land is completely devoid of any kind of vegetation, and it is only at the oasis that vegetation is found.

The equator divides Africa into two almost equal halves. To the south of the equator are the small deserts called the Kalahari and Namib. These deserts are very diversified with regard to their flora and fauna. On the eastern coast of Africa, in the country of Somalia, is a coastal desert, and to the north of the equator is the Sahara Desert. The Sahara is the largest desert in the world and is sometimes considered the most extensive wasteland because of its extreme conditions. As shown in Figure 7.1, the Sahara spans from the west coast of Africa (Atlantic Ocean) toward the eastern part of the continent where it is interrupted by the Nile (in Egypt and the Sudan) and then moves toward the Red Sea.

The desertification problem in both the northern and the southern edges of the Sahara has made it very difficult to determine the precise boundaries of the Sahara. To illustrate this difficulty in determining the Saharan boundaries, White (1983:216) notes:

> The limits of the desert are somewhat arbitrary, the "best fit" with biological reality is obtained if northern limit is drawn to coincide with the 100 mm isohyet and the southern limit to coincide with 150 mm isohyet (Quézel, 1965a). The 100 mm isohyet more or less corresponds to the northern limit of cultivation of the date palm (Phoenix dactylifera) and southern limit of "Alfa," *Stipa tenacissima*, one of the most characteristic species of the Mediterranean-Sahara transition zone. The 150 mm isohyet more or less responds to the southern limits of *Cornulaca mocantha, Stipagrostis pungens* and *Panicum turgidum*, at the northern limits of several Sahel species, notably grass, "Cram-Cram," *Cenchrus biflorus*, and, among woody plants, *Commiphora africans* and *Bos senegalensis*. The southern boundary of the Sahara much less abrupt than the northern because of the absence of pronounced features of relief. Over a whole the transition zone Saharan and Sahelian elements occur in mosaic. The precise distribution of each is determined principally by local features of physiography.

Rainfall distribution determines climatic zones in the Sahara. White (1983) recognizes three climatic zones: northern, central, and southern. The northern zone enjoys some of the Mediterranean influence and usually has rain during the winter season. The duration and amount of rainfall vary from year to year. There is also variation in the regions of the Sahara. For example, it is a well known fact that in the western part of the Sahara, there may be no rain for years, while in some eastern parts such as in the desert of Libya, there has been no rain during the lifetimes of the residents in the closest village.

Saharan Vegetation

The vegetation of the Sahara is best described as exiguous. It is scanty and as was pointed out earlier, the physiognomy of the vegetation is mixed. Since the western Sahara receives some amount of rainfall, its vegetation is much more diverse than that of the eastern Sahara.

The Saharan study by Quézel (1978) indicates that the Sahara can be classified into nine phyto-geographical regions: northwestern, northern, Atlantic, western, central, southern, Saharomontane, northeastern, and eastern. In the same study, Quézel observes that there are about 1,620 species of plants in the Sahara. An interesting aspect of the species breakdown as articulated by Quézel indicates that 11.6 percent of the 1,620 species are native to the Sahara; another 22.7 percent of the 1,620 species could be found as far away as the Arabian desert; and the Mediterranean region shares 22.2 percent of the plant species of the Sahara. In the southern edges of the Sahara the majority of tropical species are found and comprise about 32.3 percent (White 1982).

Eleven of the sixteen well-known endemic genera of plants as noted by White (1982) are *Foleyola, Monodiella, Nucularia, Tibestina Warionia, Agathophora, Anabasis, Anastatica Neurada, Ochradenus, Rhanterium, Schouwia,* and *Zilla.*

Several endemic plant species such as *Myrtus nivellei, Medemia argun,* and *Cupressus dupreziana* can be found in the Sahara. Some of these plants are found in many different parts of the Sahara while others are confined to specific regions because of the limiting and synergistic environmental and climatic factors which affect growth.

Plant and Animal Adaptation to the Desert

Desert animals show a great deal of diversity. The fauna of African deserts ranges from scorpions of primitive type and dung-hoarding scarab beetles, to large animals such as the camel. These animals have evolved over hundreds of years and possess various adaptive skills which enable them to survive in the harsh desert environment. They can exist for long periods of time without water and have adaptive characteristics which make them elusive to predators. Some have camouflage behaviors, and others are poisonous or possess great speed. There are numerous desert animals that only exist on the moisture they obtain through their herbivorous eating habits. Some desert animals obtain moisture directly from the earth by burying themselves underground in moist soiland absorbing water through their skins.

Desert plants can exist on very limited amounts of water, and such plants are predominantly xerophytic in character. They vary in structure and shape (stem, leaves, and roots) depending on the degree of dryness in the environment and the sporadic nature of the rainfall pattern. The plants found at the oases and near pools of standing water are quite different from those found in the drier and sandy desert areas.

The increase in the size of the deserts of Africa has been attributed to both natural and man-made events. Whether the changes in the deserts are natural or man-made in origin, they have resulted in the massive migration of thousands of people from the countries experiencing drought into wetter regions of other countries. Whole cities and communities are known to have migrated south of the Sahel because of sand storms, drought, and other effects of desertification. Some countries that have been affected in the past fifteen years by the spread of the Sahara are Burkina Faso, Nigeria, and Chad. The number of livestock has declined, and approximately 25 million people in the African savanna regions bordering the desert have been negatively affected by the recurring drought.

The Sahara and Its Habitat

The Sahara, the world's largest desert which occupies about 3.5 million square miles, used to be forested and contained riverbeds between 60,000 and 10,000 B.C. However, the earth's rotation, glacial movement, and human impact have led to the current large expanse of the desert.

There are approximately 2.5 to 3 million people who make the Sahara Desert their home. These people who occupy the northern third of the continent rely on the oases for their survival. The oases represent part of the desert with some vegetation, predominantly spiny date palm.

Nomadic lifestyles prevail in many parts of the Sahara. The nomadic Tuareg, after centuries of living in the Greater Sahara have been able to adapt to the sand storms and the extreme heat during the hot June and July months. Their tents, which are made of goat skins, provide shelter from the heat during the day. In the oasis women play significant roles in raising the children, assisting with the livestock, drawing water from the wells for domestic use. They also cultivate dates which need frequent watering to thrive but yield on an average of one hundred pounds of fruit per date palm tree. No part of the date palm tree is wasted. The trunks serve as building materials. Nomachi (1980:57) claims that the palm trunks are used as supports imbedded in walls constructed of sun-dried bricks surrounded with a plaster of mud. The Tuaregs are known to construct household implements such as pestles, mortars, and well-pump levers from the fibrous trunks of the date palm.

Literature is scarce on the classification of desert habitats, but White (1982:218) attempts to discuss and map what he considers the major units of ecological habitats of the Sahara Desert: (1) Oases, (2) Absolute deserts, (3) Atlantic coastal deserts, (4) Red Sea coastal deserts, (5) Halogyp-sophilous vegetation, (6) Saharomontane vegetation, (7) Regs, hamadas, wadis, (8) Desert dunes without perennial vegetation, (9) Desert dunes with perennial vegetation. A brief description of the habitats of the Sahara is given here.

The oases are places within the Sahara where there is water which is relatively low in salt content. Villages may develop as a result of the presence of water. The vegetation is dominated by date palm (Phoenix dactylifera). The availability of water has also resulted in some cultivation.

As mentioned in an earlier section, some absolute deserts exist in the Sahara. The rainfall in these parts of the Sahara is under 20 mm. per annum, and rainfall may not occur for several years. Absolute deserts are mostly in the eastern Sahara. Perennial seeds which are present in the surface sand usually grow when it rains.

The Atlantic coastal desert is basically a thin stretch of land which approximates about 41 kilometers. In the south it meets the Sahel, and in the north it meets the succulent shrub land of the Mediterranean Sahara. Although the rainfall is relatively low, a number of species exist there, including Ramalina sp, Euphorbia regisjubae, Senecio anteuphorbium, and Euphorbia echinus (White 1982).

In the eastern end of the Sahara Desert is the Red Sea coastal desert which consists of a plain at the coast and becomes rugged inland with small mountains. It is estimated to be between 15 to 20 kilometers wide (White 1982), and since the climatic conditions favor very little rainfall, vegetation of any kind is absent for most of the year. The wadis of the coast plain are exceptions to the claim because the saline areas of the wadis benefit from the influence of the sea. According to White (1982) the wadis are known to contain dense growth of Juncus arabicus, Tamarix "mannifera," Capparis decidua, Calligonum comosum, Lasiurus hirsutus, Panicum turgidum, and Retama retam. Ferns, bryophytes, and other plants that are dependent on water can be found on the mountains during the spring season.

Salt accumulation is a common phenomenon in a desert environment where there is tremendous water evaporation from depressions that do not drain. This condition usually results in the formation of salt pans. The crust of the salt pans, which are usually white, is called "sebkhas" or "chotts." The upward movement of water through capillary action of the soil could result in the "sebkhas" becoming wet. This usually happens in areas with ground water. Northern and western Sahara are known for their sebkhas especially close to the oases.

White (1982) contends that three major types of halogypsophilous vegetation are clearly defined in the northern region of the Sahara:

1. The hyperhalogypsophilous vegetation which is dominated by the plant *Halocnemum strobilaceum*. It is important to mention that *Halocnemum* are halophytic plants that owe their existence to the occurrence of sebkhas in the desert.

2. The second type of halogypsophilous vegetation is the halogypsophilous vegetation on drier soils. This vegetation is dominated by plants such as *Salsola sieberi* and *Zygophylum cornutum* which are essentially low shrubs found in the northern fringe of the Sahara. Other types of plants found in this type of habitat include *Zygophyllum album*, *Traganum nudatum*, *Limoniastrum guyonnianum*, *Suneda mollis*, *Limonium pruinosum*, *Nitraria retusa*, and *Salsola tetragona*.

3. The third type of halogypsophilous vegetation found in the Sahara is the vegetation of gypsaceous loamy sands. It is found in ancient alluvial terraces and wadis beds. *Suaeda vermiculata* and *Salsola baryosma* (foetida) are the characteristic plants. Two types of this third category have been distinguished based on their location. The type found in the beds of the wadis seems to be characterized by plants which are different from those plants found in the halophytic vegetation of the sebkhas.

The Saharomontane vegetation is present in western Sahara on the Tassili n' Ajjer, Tibesti, Ahaggar, Tafedest, and Mouydir. Saharomontane vegetation may vary from the dominant type which occurs on the Ahaggar and Tibesti. For instance, Jebel Uweinat in the Libyan desert has a somewhat different vegetation because of its location. It is lacking in vegetation at its highest point because of its low altitude. Typical Saharomontane vegetation is sometimes rich in plant life. It is diverse because it receives some rainfall. Several types of flora are native to the Saharomontane area, and endemism of the plant species is probably reenforced by the fact that the Saharomontane vegetation embraces elements of the Mediterranean Saharan, Sahelian, and Afromontane microclimates.

Saharomontane vegetation is classified into four main types (White 1982:222).

1. Saharomontane wadi vegetation is one of the four types. It is dominated by *Olea Laperrinei*. Perennial grasses such as *Stipa parviflora*, *Stipa capensis*, *Oryzopsis (Piptatherum) coerulescens*, *Pistacia atlantica* and *Rhus tripartita* coexist with the Saharomontane wadi vegetation. The companion relationship developed by the plants and vegetation strengthens their survival.

2. The second type of Saharomontane vegetation is called Saharo-

montane grassland. Perennial species such as *Stipagrostis Obtusa* and *Aristida coerulescens* are common here.

3. The third Saharomontane vegetation is the Saharomontane dwarf shrub land and it should be noted that it inundates the mountain tops of Ahaggar and Tibesti. Common plant species are *Pentzia monodiana*, *Artemisia herba-alba*, *Artemisia tilhoana*, and *Euphedra tilhoana*.

4. The fourth Saharomontane vegetation consists of the *Erica arborea* community.

Regs constitute another desert habitat. They are basically gravel deserts which are lacking in vegetation. Regs originate from deposits of heterogeneous rocks through the erosive perturbation brought about by wind. The accumulation of calcium carbonate ($CaCO_3$) results in the formation of hardpan of great depth. This condition prevents the growth of plants because their roots cannot penetrate the hardpan. *Haloxylon scoparium*, *Stipagrostis plumosa*, *Stipagrostis obtusa*, and *Stipagrostis ciliata* are species found in regs of the northern Sahara. In the central Sahara, there is hardly any vegetation, but it is worth noting that rain may lead to the growth of the species *Stipagrostis obtusa* (White 1982).

Hamadas habitats are also produced as a result of wind erosion. The process is similar to that of soil formation which begins with weathering and the subsequent removal of the fine particles of soil by wind. In hamadas, the parent rock is marine in origin. A chemical process leads to the solidification of surface stones mixed with gypsum and salt sheets. This results in a blackish layer consisting of iron and manganese compounds. Over time this layer is covered by sand. This habitat is often without vegetation, but the varying differences in temperature between the night and day lead to cracks and crevices which can then hold enough moisture for some plant growth. Examples of plant life forms are *Erodium glaucophyllum*, *Reaumuria hirtella*, *Helianthemum kahiricum*, and *Fagonia mollis*.

Wadis are desert habitats rich in trees and bushes and are known for their desert diversity. The diversity of the flora enhances the desert's ability to have more diverse animal life. However, it is noteworthy to recognize that the wadis habitat has three basic communities: (1) Tamarix communities, (2) Acacia communities, and (3) Hyphaene communities (White 1982). Tamarix communities, when water is plentiful, could become closed riparian forests, but under unfavorable conditions, vegetation and other plants are sparse. Acacia communities prevail in the rocky beds of wadis. Most of the woody plants of the Sahara belong to the Acacia communities.

The dominant trees of fully grown forest which are found on the slopes of the Tibesti constitute the *Hyphaene thebaica*, *Salvadora persica*, and some *Hyphaene* palms. The fruits of the palm are eaten by inhabitants of villages close to the area.

Sandy habitats are also common occurrences in the Sahara. There are two kinds of sandy habitats, one which is devoid of vegetation, and another with vegetation. The sand dunes without vegetation are moved by wind, making a very hostile environment. Dune vegetation is very sparse and supports very little life.

The Namib Desert

As shown earlier on Figure 7.1 the desert extends from the southwestern coast of Angola, through the whole of Namibia, into the northwestern part of South Africa. The predominant feature of this desert is its moving sand. Other features include granite and gneiss. Rainfall in the Namib Desert varies from below 100 mm to 250 mm per year depending on a number of climatic and environmental factors. During the winter months the western Namib Desert receives a lot of rainfall.

The Namib Desert can be divided into three categories: northern, central, and southern. These categories vary not only in the amount of rainfall they receive but also the period when the rainfall occurs. Like the Sahara, the cooler season enhances the growth of plants in the Namib. Fog condensation plays a significant role in the germination of certain plants. White's (1982) work referencing Giess' 1968 and 1971 classic works contends that the "Outer Namib fog desert" can be divided into three categories: sand dunes, gravel desert, and rocky outcrops. The characteristics of these three desert environments are similar to those of the Sahara Desert. Plants of the sand dunes include *Barleria solitaria, Ectadium virgatum, Indigofer cunenesis, Merremia multisecta,* and *Petalidum angustitubum.* Examples of plants found in the gravel desert of the Namib are *Anthraerua leubnitziae* and *Zygophyllum stapfii.* The rocky outcrops of the Namib are famous for their stem succulents and leaf succulents.

Data on the flora of the "Inner Namib desert" is scanty. Unlike the "Outer Namib desert" which is rich in halophytes, the Inner Namib Desert is famous for *Stipagrostis* of which the most prominent is *Stipagrostis obtusa.* Another area of the Namib of significance is the desert of Mossamedes. Halophytic plants such as *Salsola zeyheri* and *Suaeda fruticosa* are found in the coastal region of the Mossamedes. Halophytes store large amounts of salt (sodium chloride, NaCl). They grow in ordinary places and are occasionally found in the shores around the world.

Through the action of wind, animals, and water currents, seeds of halophytes are sometimes transported to soils that are not rich in salt. Absence of competition from other plants in their new environment usually leads to the establishment of the halophytes. It is thus prudent to claim that in environments where plant competition is high, halophytes would only succeed if the soil is rich in salt content.

Overall, it should be stressed that the characteristic feature of the Namib vegetation starting from the coast to the borders of the semi-desert steppe and the Kalaharian woodland depends on a number of factors which are climatic and soil dependent. It should also be emphasized that the differences in the physical nature and humidity of the soil are paramount determinants of the type of vegetation in the Namib. Stunted halophitic plants are common, and colonies of *Giesekia, Zygophyllum,* or *Aristida subacaulis* make the Namib Desert their habitat. Intensive winds bring sand which buries the colonies of these plants. However, *Ectadium virgatum* is known to be able to withstand sand storms. Shrubs are plentiful in the eastern part of the Namib Desert. *Byttneriaceae, Acanthaceae,* and *Scrophulariaceae* are found in the eastern part of the desert of Namib.

The Karoo semi-desert which is an extension of the Namib is richer in plant life than the Namib. Hence, animal life is also increased. *Harpagophytum, Liliaceae, Iridaceae,* and *Amaryllidaceae* are found there, along with perennials such as *Mesembryanthemum, Crassula,* and *Sarcocaulon,* which are succulents.

Kalahari Desert

The Kalahari regions which are sometimes referred to as the "thirstlands" of western Botswana and northeastern Namibia present an important desert ecosystem in which the so-called Bushmen have successfully learned to live. It is estimated that there are between thirty thousand and sixty thousand people who are still being referred to as the Bushmen of the Kalahari. Of this number, only a few hundred or so still practice the "hunter-gatherer" lifestyle. Many of the total population are presently sedentary and have been cultivating parts of the Kalahari (Wannenburg 1982).

The Kalahari Game Reserve has been established in order to help conserve some of the wildlife of the area and also because many of the people of the Kalahari now have guns which can be easily used to destroy the wildlife. The old traditional ways are conservative in character because the Bushmen only take what they need for subsistence. However, there are poachers, and their type of hunting is not for subsistence, but for the greedy exploitation of the hides, skins, and horns of the wildlife. Zebra hides have been very lucrative to poachers in the past, and if the poachers are not controlled, the limited amount of wildlife will decline drastically. The drought of 1992 further exacerbates the dilemma of the wildlife and has affected the agricultural output of many African countries in the southern part of the continent.

The Kalahari region resembles parts of the Sahara because it does not have surface water. The sands of the Kalahari are mostly red, and it is believed by some that it is not a true desert. The vegetation is composed of woodland, scrub, and grass which are well adapted to the infrequent and limited rainfall. The traditional way of life of the Bushmen has suited the environment and maintained the ecosystem at equilibrium for centuries. Modernity, agriculture, and population increase seem to be threatening the woodlands of the Kalahari.

Conclusion and Inference

The deserts of Africa present humans unique habitats that have to be completely understood in order to enjoy the benefits that they present. Humans, like any other mammals, confront the same problems of water scarcity, excessive heat, large quantities of salt in the soil, and generally poor soil conditions in the desert. Unlike plants, man has not been able to adapt to the lack of water, excessive heat, and salt conditions of the deserts. Except for recent satellite imagery which suggests that the Sahara might be shrinking, reports from countries of the Sahel indicate that the Sahara is increasing in Burkina Faso, Mauritania, Niger, and Chad.

It thus behooves humans to attempt to make some parts of the desert habitable. It is unthinkable to continue to lose large areas of Africa which used to be cultivated land to desertification. The unproductive natures of these lands must be reversed. In order to make the desert productive, the first step is to stop all human actions that increase the desert. The following plan of action could be useful:

1. All human activities that bring about erosion and the destabilization of the ecological integrity must be discouraged.

2. Cultivation and livestock activities must be carried out with great care. In some dry lands they should be totally discouraged.

3. The demand for fuelwood has increased the problem of desertification, so the removal of woody plants for firewood must be prohibited at all costs. Teaching community in desert ecosystems the importance of leaving the trees to thrive is very important. Alternative sources of energy must be sought.

4. Research into how past cultures survived in the desert must be integrated with modern technological knowledge in afforestation and reforestation projects.

5. Countries such as Algeria, Libya, Nigeria, and Egypt which are fairly rich with foreign exchange balances should engage in research such

as desert engineering in order to convert desert areas into lands which can support modern agriculture on a small scale without causing other ecological problems. It must be stressed that such research would enhance the adequate and proper exploitation and management of water resources available in the oases and other resources in the desert. Water harvesting from runoff during the short rainfall periods in the Sahara and Namib represents the key to the development of these arid places. Research would also enhance the exploitation of ground water, desalinization of brackish and sea water could enhance desert development. Libya has already started in this direction. It created the first man-made river to deliver water to towns in North Africa where water shortage has been a problem.

  6. Other technological innovations which could help the desert development projects are:

  a. Cloud seeding to increase rainfall.
  b. Careful introduction of new plants and animals.
  c. Expanding the carrying capacity of the desert through the use of foreign crops.
  d. Production of algal biomass so as to increase vegetation cover and plant species.

8. Impact on Water and Soil Resources

One of the major aspects of development in Third World countries is the provision of safe drinking water to the millions of people that live there. The United Nations through the establishment of the International Drinking Water Supply and Sanitation Decade has been attempting to assist developing nations throughout the world in their attempt to address this most basic of human needs.

Despite the tremendous efforts and money that the countries of Africa and other developing areas have put into assuring that the citizens of their countries have safe drinking water, water quality and quantity have still not improved adequately. The people of these countries still drink water containing high concentrations of bacteria and harmful chemical substances.

In examining the progress that has been made in developing countries in the provision of safe drinking water, a general statement could be made that in the rural areas, progress has been achieved in the water sector, but in the outskirts of growing metropolitan areas and big cities, there is a definitive problem with the water supply.

Whether one is examining the problem of water supply in the urban area or the rural area, the constraints for drinking water supply in the African countries can be categorized into the following subheadings:

1. Human resources
2. Operation and maintenance inadequacies and the need for rehabilitation
3. Institutional constraints
4. Failure to attract more external finance
5. Water resources management
6. Imbalance in coverage in urban and rural areas
7. Lack of community participation and choice of technology
8. Low government support for water resource development (Lowes 1987)

It is particularly difficult to make generalized statements about the water supply problems in Africa because of the limited data available for making such an assessment. Nonetheless, the limited information seems to indicate that although the African countries vary in terms of geography, climate, and economic situations, the overall population of Africa has increased by 36 percent during the last decade. The rural areas of Africa increased by 26 percent, while the urban areas increased by 73 percent (World Bank 1991). Hence there is a tremendous need to make available adequate and safe drinking water.

Table 8.1 indicates the current population growth and projections of the countries of Africa. If the population continues to increase at the rates indicated, it is estimated that the demand on the domestic industrial and agricultural water resources will increase by about three fold. Table 8.2 shows the 1970–87 annual withdrawal of the internal renewable water resources.

Self-sustaining growth and development will be almost impossible in Africa if the poor become poorer as the world moves towards the twenty-first century. It is estimated that the number of poor people in the rural parts of the developing world will increase by one-third of the current population, and that means that the number will be close to 1.3 billion people within the next ten years (Editorial, *West Africa*, 1992). This prediction was previously given by Idriss Jazairy, the president of the International Fund for Agricultural Development (IFAD).

The ramifications of the poverty problems in Africa are that the environmental quality of the continent will deteriorate as more demands are made on limited resources. The prediction for the heavily populated urban centers seems to be even worse. Quality of life will decrease sharply from the already bad conditions, which will exacerbate the problem of water supply and sanitation. One editorial that was featured in *West Africa* magazine in February (1992:210), in describing the environmental problems in the developing countries, notes: "Nigeria is one of four African countries adjudged by international environmental organizations as having unacceptably high levels of water pollution. According to a report by News Agency of Nigeria (NAN) the others are Ghana, Tanzania, and South Africa."

Technology

One thing is clear to scholars of Third World development: more coordinated effort has to be put into providing adequate and safe drinking water to people of Third World countries. In meeting the demand for water supply, one area that needs both indigenous and foreign assistance

Table 8.1: Population Growth and Projections of African Countries

	Average annual growth of population (%)			Population size (millions) (*=projection)				Age structure of population (%)			
	1965–80	1980–89	1989–2000*	1989	2000*	2025*	?	0–14 yrs 1989	2025*	15–64 yrs 1989	2025*
1. Algeria	3.1	3.0	2.8	24	33	52	78	44.0	25.7	52.1	68.5
2. Angola	2.8	2.6	3.0	10	14	27	65	44.8	40.1	52.3	56.8
3. Benin	2.7	3.2	3.0	5	6	11	21	47.4	33.4	49.8	63.2
4. Botswana	3.5	3.4	2.6	1	2	2	4	47.3	25.3	48.9	68.9
5. Burkina Faso	2.1	2.6	2.9	9	12	23	51	45.3	38.5	51.7	58.7
6. Burundi	1.9	2.9	3.5	5	8	16	39	46.3	41.4	50.8	56.2
7. Cameroon	2.7	3.2	3.2	12	16	33	69	46.9	37.0	49.3	59.5
8. Cape Verde	–	–	–	–	–	–	–	–	–	–	–
9. Central Afr. Rep.	1.9	2.7	2.7	3	4	7	13	42.3	33.7	54.8	62.6
10. Chad	2.0	2.4	2.7	6	7	14	29	41.8	37.2	54.7	58.9
11. Comoros	–	–	–	–	–	–	–	–	–	–	–
12. Congo, People's R.	2.8	3.4	3.4	2	3	7	16	45.0	39.2	51.0	57.8
13. Côte d'Ivoire (Ivory C)	4.1	4.1	3.8	12	18	37	85	48.9	39.5	48.8	57.6
14. Djibouti	–	–	–	–	–	–	–	–	–	–	–
15. Egypt, Arab Rep.	2.1	2.5	1.8	51	62	86	120	39.2	24.4	56.5	67.6
16. Equatorial Guinea	–	–	–	–	–	–	–	–	–	–	–
17. Ethiopia	2.7	3.0	3.4	49	72	159	435	46.6	43.2	50.6	54.3
18. Gabon	3.6	3.7	2.8	1	1	3	6	38.7	38.2	56.5	57.5
19. The Gambia	–	–	–	–	–	–	–	–	–	–	–
20. Ghana	2.2	3.4	3.1	14	20	35	63	46.7	32.8	50.2	63.5
21. Guinea	1.5	2.5	2.8	6	8	15	34	46.2	40.4	51.3	56.8
22. Guinea-Bissau	–	–	–	–	–	–	–	–	–	–	–
23. Kenya	3.6	3.9	3.4	24	34	62	114	50.3	31.9	46.7	64.6
24. Lesotho	2.3	2.7	2.7	2	2	4	6	43.2	29.2	53.2	66.0
25. Liberia	3.0	3.2	3.0	2	3	6	11	44.8	32.6	51.9	63.2
26. Libya	4.3	4.2	3.6	4	6	14	36	46.0	39.5	51.4	56.7
27. Madagascar	2.5	2.9	3.1	11	16	29	54	46.2	35.1	50.3	61.7
28. Malawi	2.9	3.4	3.6	8	12	27	72	46.5	43.0	50.8	54.4
29. Mali	2.1	2.5	3.0	8	11	24	60	46.6	41.3	50.4	56.1
30. Mauritania	2.4	2.4	2.8	2	3	5	14	44.4	42.4	62.4	55.0
31. Mauritius	1.6	1.0	0.9	1	1	1	2	29.8	18.9	65.1	66.8
32. Morocco	2.5	2.6	2.3	25	32	48	72	41.0	25.9	55.2	67.9
33. Mozambique	2.5	2.7	3.1	15	21	41	87	44.0	37.7	52.9	59.0
34. Namibia	2.4	3.1	3.0	2	2	4	7	45.6	31.2	51.2	64.4
35. Niger	2.6	3.4	3.3	7	11	24	76	47.1	44.7	50.4	52.9
36. Nigeria	2.5	3.4	3.2	114	160	298	580	47.6	35.2	50.2	61.3
37. Rwanda	3.3	3.2	4.1	7	11	24	74	48.3	44.3	49.4	53.4
38. Senegal	2.9	3.0	3.2	7	10	20	46	46.9	39.6	50.6	57.9
39. Sierra Leone	2.0	2.4	2.6	4	5	10	24	43.2	40.5	53.7	56.3
40. Somalia	2.6	3.0	3.1	6	9	17	39	45.9	39.7	51.2	57.2
41. South Africa	–	–	–	–	–	–	–	–	–	–	–
42. Sudan	3.0	2.8	2.8	24	33	57	106	44.8	33.7	52.1	62.5
43. Swaziland	–	–	–	–	–	–	–	–	–	–	–
44. Tanzania	2.9	3.1	3.3	24	34	66	140	46.7	37.7	50.3	59.2
45. Togo	3.0	3.5	3.3	4	5	9	18	47.9	35.4	49.1	61.4
46. Tunisia	2.1	2.5	2.1	8	10	14	19	38.4	23.7	57.5	68.3
47. Uganda	2.9	3.2	3.5	17	25	51	119	48.6	40.6	49.1	57.0
48. Western Sahara	–	–	–	–	–	–	–	–	–	–	–
49. Zaire	2.8	3.1	3.0	34	48	86	164	46.1	34.4	51.3	62.0
50. Zambia	3.0	3.7	3.6	8	12	24	52	49.2	38.5	48.6	58.8
51. Zimbabwe	3.1	3.5	2.7	10	13	20	29	45.8	25.4	51.5	68.7

*=projections; ?=estimate of stationary population; *Source:* Adapted from World Bank, 1991, p. 254.

Table 8.2: Water Resources of African Countries

Internal renewable water resources annual withdrawal (1970–87)

	Total (cubic kms)	As a % of total water resources	Total	Domestic	Indust. & agricul.
1. Algeria	3.00	16	161	35	125
2. Angola	0.48	0	43	6	37
3. Benin	0.11	0	26	7	19
4. Botswana	0.09	1	98	5	93
5. Burkina Faso	0.15	1	20	6	14
6. Burundi	0.10	3	20	7	13
7. Cameroon	0.40	0	30	14	16
8. Cape Verde	–	–	–	–	–
9. Central African Rep.	0.07	0	27	6	21
10. Chad	0.18	0	35	6	29
11. Comoros	–	–	–	–	–
12. Congo, People's Rep.	0.04	0	20	12	8
13. Côte d'Ivoire (Ivory Coast)	0.71	1	68	15	53
14. Djibouti	–	–	–	–	–
15. Egypt, Arab Rep.	56.40	97	1,202	84	1,118
16. Equatorial Guinea	–	–	–	–	–
17. Ethiopia	2.21	2	48	5	43
18. Gabon	0.06	0	51	37	14
19. The Gambia	–	–	–	–	–
20. Ghana	0.30	1	35	12	23
21. Guinea	0.74	0	115	12	104
22. Guinea-Bissau	–	–	–	–	–
23. Kenya	1.09	7	48	13	35
24. Lesotho	0.05	1	34	7	27
25. Liberia	0.13	0	54	15	39
26. Libya	2.62	374	262	39	222
27. Madagascar	16.30	41	1,675	17	1,658
28. Malawi	0.16	2	22	7	15
29. Mali	1.36	2	159	3	156
30. Mauritania	0.73	10	473	57	417
31. Mauritius	0.36	16	415	66	348
32. Morocco	11.00	37	501	30	471
33. Mozambique	0.76	1	53	13	40
34. Namibia	0.14	2	77	5	72
35. Niger	0.29	1	44	9	35
36. Nigeria	3.63	1	44	14	30
37. Rwanda	0.15	2	23	6	17
38. Senegal	1.36	4	201	10	191
39. Sierra Leone	0.37	0	99	7	92
40. Somalia	0.81	7	167	5	162
41. South Africa	–	–	–	–	–
42. Sudan	18.60	14	1,089	11	1,079
43. Swaziland	–	–	–	–	–
44. Tanzania	0.48	1	36	7	28
45. Togo	0.09	1	40	25	15
46. Tunisia	2.30	53	325	42	283
47. Uganda	0.20	0	20	7	14
48. Western Sahara	–	–	–	–	–
49. Zaire	0.70	0	22	13	9
50. Zambia	0.36	0	86	54	32
51. Zimbabwe	1.22	5	129	18	111

Source: Adapted from World Bank, 1991, p. 268.

is the technological aspect. Africa is blessed with many natural resources, but the distribution of the resources varies from one part of the continent to another. The distribution of water is a major problem. Although there are many rivers in Africa, the major problem seems to be how to get the water to places that are deficient in water. Another problem is how to tap underground water.

In many countries in Africa capital-intensive and complicated water-supply technologies are embarked upon. Water-supply technologies in Africa must be appropriate with regard to addressing the labor-intensive aspect of the economy, issues of cost, maintenance source of water supply, and operation of the constructed facility. In many rural communities, the maintenance and operation of water plants are beyond the capability of the local residents.

The health situation in Africa is closely connected with a safe drinking-water supply. In technologically advanced countries, many diseases associated with poor drinking water have been greatly reduced. These diseases are cholera, hepatitis, dysentery, and diarrhea. About 5 million children die annually from water-borne diseases. Infant mortality rates are still very high in Africa. Poor sanitary conditions result in the contamination of water supplies. Life expectancy is relatively low in many developing nations due in part to poor sanitary conditions. The inadequate sewage disposal system creates a great deal of problems in many African countries. This indicates that a great deal of work needs to be done in supplying water to the inhabitants. Since there is a direct correlation between sanitary conditions and health, more efforts need to be put into providing decent sanitary conditions. Hence, the efforts of the United Nations in providing leadership with its International Drinking Water Supply and Sanitation Decade are very important in improving the water supply problems of Africa.

An assessment of the achievement of the Water Decade seems to indicate that all the goals of the countries were not achieved by 1990, but significant strides have been made. Policies are being put into place to enhance the provision of safe drinking water to the people of Africa.

Table 8.3 shows the level of service that was available in some African countries in 1980. Many countries attempted to provide the level of service indicated. Based upon the level of service that was provided in 1980, the Decade target for 1990 was set as shown in Tables 8.4 and 8.5. These were targets established for urban and rural water supply and sanitation. The importance of these statistics is that they give the countries a means to assess their performance, and countries that have monitored their progress have been able to increase the number of services to their citizens. Although the 1990 targets were not met due to economic and political instabilities in some of the African countries, genuine and sincere progress has been made.

Table 8.3: 1980 Expected Levels of Service
(Populations in Thousands and %)

Population

Country/Territory	Total	Urban	Rural
Angola	7,900	1,200	6,700
		15%	85%
Benin	3,540	1,580	1,960
		45%	55%
Burundi	4,214	219	3,995
		5%	95%
Cape Verde	296	108	188
		36%	64%
Gambia	601	110	491
		18%	82%
Ghana	11,573	4,164	7,409
		36%	64%
Guinea	5,017	1,117	3,900
		22%	78%
Guinea-Bissau	794	159	635
		20%	80%
Kenya	15,900	2,414	13,486
		15%	85%
Lesotho	1,300	150	1,150
		12%	88%
Madagascar	8,740	1,720	7,020
		20%	80%
Malawi	6,007	576	5,431
		10%	90%
Mali	7,204	1,210	5,994
		17%	83%
Mauritania	1,443	354	1,089
		25%	75%
Mauritius	957	410	547
		43%	57%
Niger	5,534	701	4,833
		13%	87%
Rwanda	5,185	233	4,952
		4%	96%
Senegal	5,728	1,810	3,918
		32%	68%
Sierra Leone	3,161	923	2,238
		29%	71%
Togo	2,500	700	1,800
		28%	72%
Upper Volta	6,129	930	5,199
		15%	85%
Total	103,723	20,788	82,935
		20%	80%

Source: Calculations/Projections *World Health Statistics Report 1976* (adapted).

Table 8.3: (cont.)

| | Drinking water | | | | Sanitation | | |
| | Urban | | Rural | | Urban | | Rural |
Total	aHC	bPS		Total	cSC	Other	
1,020	360	660	670	480	240	240	1,000
85%	30%	55%	10%	40%	20%	20%	15%
413	165	248	300	760	0	760	80
26%	10%	16%	15%	48%	0%	48%	4%
197	49	148	799	88	18	70	1,393
90%	22%	68%	20%	40%	8%	32%	35%
108	25	83	40	37	12	25	19
100%	23%	77%	21%	34%	11%	23%	10%
94	–	–	–	–	–	–	–
85%	–	–	–	–	–	–	–
3,015	1,100	1,915	2,439	1,940	160	1,780	1,226
72%	26%	46%	33%	47%	4%	43%	17%
769	180	589	90	600	145	455	40
69%	16%	53%	2%	54%	13%	41%	1%
29	17	12	49	34	2	32	81
18%	11%	7%	8%	21%	1%	20%	13%
2,051	1,436	615	2,055	2,140	1,180	960	3,590
85%	59%	26%	15%	89%	49%	40%	19%
55	36	19	126	20	15	5	162
37%	24%	13%	11%	13%	10%	3%	14%
1,380	330	1,050	500	150	60	90	–
80%	19%	61%	7%	9%	4%	5%	–
443	307	136	1,995	576	90	486	4,400
77%	53%	24%	37%	100%	16%	84%	81%
451	248	203	8	955	10	945	6
37%	20%	17%	0%	79%	1%	78%	0%
283	71	212	925	18	18	–	–
80%	20%	60%	85%	5%	5%	–	–
410	287	123	536	410	225	185	492
100%	70%	30%	98%	100%	55%	45%	90%
286	203	83	1,547	252	–	252	145
41%	29%	12%	32%	36%	–	36%	3%
112	70	42	2,700	140	0	140	2,500
48%	30%	18%	55%	60%	0%	60%	50%
1,400	600	800	980	1,811	91	1,720	79
77%	33%	44%	25%	100%	5%	95%	2%
462	185	277	45	284	7	277	134
50%	20%	30%	2%	31%	1%	30%	6%
490	100	390	565	170	0	170	180
70%	14%	56%	31%	24%	0%	24%	10%
255	155	100	1,612	349	0	349	260
27%	16%	11%	31%	38%	0%	38%	5%
13,723	5,924	7,705	17,981	11,214	2,273	8,941	14,787
66%	29%	37%	22%	54%	11%	43%	20%

aHC=house connection   bPS=public standpost   cSC=sewer connection

Table 8.4: Decade Targets for Urban Water Supply and Sanitation

Country/ Territory	Urban Pop. (000) 1980	Urban Pop. (000) 1990	Water Supply Population covered (000) 1980	%	Water Supply Population covered (000) 1990	%	Sanitation Population covered (000) 1980	%	Sanitation Population covered (000) 1990	%
Kenya	2,414	6,119	2,051	85	6,119	100	2,140	89	4,325	71
Ghana	4,164	6,922	3,015	72	6,922	100	1,940	47	5,540	80
Mali	1,210	1,957	451	37	1,957	100	955	79	1,957	100
Upper Volta	930	1,305	255	27	930	71	349	38	1,014	78
Malawi	576	1,080	443	77	1,080	100	576	100	1,080	100
Niger	701	1,550	286	41	1,550	100	252	36	1,550	100
Rwanda	233	322	112	48	322	100	140	60	322	100
Burundi	219	351	197	90	343	98	88	40	350	100
Benin	1,580	2,952	413	26	2,362	80	760	48	2,361	80
Sierra Leone	923	1,485	462	50	1,486	100	284	31	1,485	100
Togo	700	1,020	490	70	1,020	100	170	24	1,020	100
Cape Verde	108	180	108	100	161	89	37	34	150	83
Total	12,758	25,243	8,243	60	24,253	96	7,691	56	21,154	84

	Water Supply	Sanitation
Additional people to be covered by 1990	15,970	13,463
Ratio of additional people to be served by 1990 to number served in 1980	1.93:1	1.75:1

Source: Calculations/Projections *World Health Statistics Report 1976*, p. 590.

There are many social and economic problems that make the provision of safe drinking water difficult in Africa. The removal of these constraints would make planning much easier. This idea is probably the most crucial in all the planning phases of the development of water resources. But it should be recognized that it is of utmost importance to rank or prioritize the constraints so that the most difficult ones are removed in order to achieve set goals. Table 8.6 shows the ranking of constraints to water supply and sanitation problems in Africa.

A survey of experts on water supply and sanitation in Africa provides valuable information on the water supply problems in Africa. Table 8.6 shows that a group of experts rank funding limitations as the largest constraint on the development of water resources in Africa. This is followed by the lack of trained personnel to install and maintain the facilities. In order to achieve sustained development and growth economically and raise the standard of living of millions of Africans, these obstacles must be overcome. Some countries such as Nigeria, Kenya, Ghana, and Côte

Table 8.5: Decade Targets for Rural Water Supply and Sanitation

Country/ Territory	Urban Pop. (000) 1980	1990	Water Supply Population covered (000) 1980	%	1990	%	Sanitation Population covered (000) 1980	%	1990	%
Kenya	13,486	19,193	2,055	15	11,516	60	2,590	19	8,300	43
Ghana	7,409	8,937	2,439	33	7,000	78	1,226	17	7,000	78
Mali	5,994	7,043	8	0	4,226	60	6	0	3,522	50
Upper Volta	5,199	6,292	1,612	31	6,292	100	260	5	2,391	38
Malawi	5,431	6,500	1,995	37	6,500	100	4,400	81	5,200	80
Niger	4,833	5,739	1,547	32	5,739	100	145	3	5,739	100
Rwanda	4,952	6,828	2,700	55	6,828	100	2,500	50	5,463	80
Burundi	3,995	4,918	799	20	4,425	90	1,393	35	3,442	70
Benin	1,960	1,703	300	15	1,700	100	80	4	736	43
Sierra Leone	2,238	2,595	45	2	1,817	70	134	6	1,298	50
Togo	1,800	2,300	565	31	2,100	91	180	10	1,840	80
Cape Verde	188	153	40	21	92	60	19	10	92	60
Total	57,485	72,201	14,105	25	58,235	81	12,933	22	45,023	62

	Water Supply	Sanitation
Additional people to be covered by 1990	44,130	32,090
Ratio of additional people to be served by 1990 to number served in 1980	3.13:1	2.48:1

Source: Calculations/Projections *World Health Statistics Report 1976.*

d'Ivoire have been contemplating developing water-resource master plans which would enable them to provide water to the rural and urban inhabitants and also ensure the availability of water for agricultural purposes. By all indications, based upon the global economic situation, even by the year 2000 funding will continue to be the major obstacle for the sustainable development of water resources in Africa. Many African countries are burdened with competing priorities such as food, shelter, development of infrastructure, and health. It could also be said that the World Bank which has tried to help in the provision of safe drinking water to African countries also suffers from the issue of competing priorities.

Thus the level of investment required to make available safe drinking water to the urban and rural populations of Africa has not kept pace with the exponential increase in population. The progress that has been made in supplying the rural inhabitants of the developing world is commendable because the percentage of those without water has been reduced from about 80 percent in the 1960s to slightly less than 60 percent in 1990. The

Table 8.6: African Scholars' Ranking of Water Supply Constraints

	Ranking Index
Constraints:	1=Highest 17=Lowest

1. Funding limitations
2. Insufficiency of trained personnel (professional)
3. Logistics
4. Operation and maintenance
5. Insufficiency of trained personnel (sub-professional)
6. Inadequate or outmoded legal framework
7. Intermittent water service
8. Inappropriate institutional framework
9. Insufficient knowledge of water resources
10. Inadequate cost-recovery framework
11. Lack of planning and design criteria
12. Import restrictions
13. Inappropriate technology
14. Insufficient health education efforts
15. Lack of definite government policy for sector
16. Non-involvement of communities
17. Inadequate water resources

Source: Summarized from *World Health Statistics Report 1976.*

United Nations' International Drinking Water Supply and Sanitation Decade has made that progress possible. However, there are still about 1.5 billion people in the world without safe drinking water (Briscoe and de Ferranti 1988). The exponential population dilemma will continue to render all domestic and international water-supply efforts minimal in making a substantial dent in serving a significant number of people with safe drinking water. Table 8.7 indicates the World Bank's lending in rural water supply and sanitation. The World Bank has played a significant and important role in the provision of safe drinking water around the world.

Besides the funding constraint that makes the provision of water in Africa difficult, other constraints include insufficiency of trained personnel to maintain the equipment that is brought into Africa from the industrialized countries. Probably what this means is that appropriate technology should be examined and attempted before embarking on imported technology. The problem of the lack of modern technological skills is especially common in the rural regions of Africa, and efforts should be made not to install sophisticated water supply systems. Inappropriate institutional framework, insufficient knowledge of water resources, and intermittent water service are also problems.

The constraints discussed in this section are responsible for 65 percent

Table 8.7: World Bank Lending in Rural Water Supply and Sanitation: Total Lending and Percentage of Project Lending, 1974–85 (in millions of dollars)

Year	Rural Water Supply Project Component — Free-standing projects	Water and sanit.	Agri-culture	Total lending to rural water supply	Total lending to urban water and sewerage	Total lending to water and sewerage sector	Total lending of IBRD and IDA
1974	0.0	0.56	7.2	7.7	173.2	180.9	4,423.6
1975	0.0	1.5	22.7	24.3	143.6	167.8	5,945.9
1976	0.0	12.1	11.1	23.2	322.5	345.7	6,702.4
1977	0.0	3.6	28.9	32.5	297.1	329.6	7,086.8
1978	9.0	0.0	29.8	38.8	366.2	405.0	8,410.7
1979	20.0	19.6	11.9	51.5	979.2	1,030.7	10,010.5
1980	0.0	23.6	12.0	35.6	607.5	643.1	11,481.7
1981	11.8	27.3	34.7	73.8	495.4	569.2	12,291.0
1982	30.5	2.5	33.5	66.5	408.2	474.7	13,015.9
1983	46.1	8.6	28.4	83.1	747.5	830.6	14,447.0
1984	60.9	11.9	17.6	90.4	620.1	609.7	15,524.0
1985*	80.0	2.4	25.5	107.9	772.3	880.2	14,386.3
Total	258.3	113.6	263.3	635.2	5,832.4	6,467.2	123,725.8
Cumulative percentage of total Bank lending				0.5%	4.7%	5.2%	100.0%
Cumulative percentage of rural water supply investments as part of water sector and agriculture components				9.8%	90.2%	100.0%	

*Figures for 1985 were calculated on a basis different from that used for previous years.

Source: Churchill, 1987, p. 62.

---

of the rural population in the Third World—to which most of Africa belongs—not being able to have safe and convenient sources of drinking water (Churchill et al. 1987). By the year 1985, Churchill and his colleagues contended that 75 percent of the people of the developing world did not have reasonable sewage disposal systems, making the likelihood of water contamination very high. The situation has gotten worse in the 1990s because of the population explosion, and very little improvement has occurred in many of the countries of the Third World.

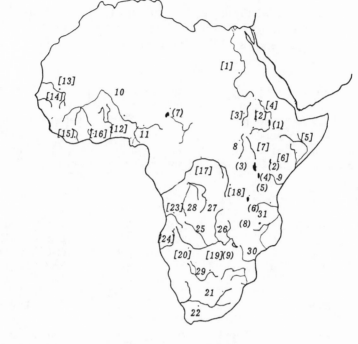

Figure 8.1: Rivers and lakes of Africa.

R I V E R S	11 Benue	22 Orange	L A K E S *
[1] Nile	[12] Volta	[23] Cuanza	(1)*T'ana Hayk
[2] Blue Nile	[13] Senegal	[24] Cunene	(2)*Lake Rudolf
[3] White Nile	[14] Gambia	25 Cuito	(3) Lake Albert
[4] Nahr 'Atbarah	[15] Sassandra	26 Cuando	(4) Lake Kyoga
[5] WabeShebeleWenz	[16] Bandama	27 Kasai	(5) Lake Victoria
[6] Giuba	[17] Congo	28 Kwango	(6) Lake Tanganyika
[7] Omo	[18] Lualaba	29 Limpopo	(7) Lake Chad
8 Bahr Al Jabal	[19] Zambezi	30 Shire	(8) Lake Nyasa
9 Tana	[20] Okavango	31 Rufiji	(9) Lake Karioa
10 Niger	21 Vaal		

Water Sources and Population Distribution

The availability of water resources in Africa determines the population distribution in many rural areas. As a result, many countries are now embarking on national water resources master plans. The main objective of such ambitious plans is to maximize the available water resources of the countries and make water available for domestic consumption, agricultural development, and hydroelectric power.

The water resources of Africa are many, but they are not evenly distributed in the continent. As can be seen from Figure 8.1, Africa has many rivers that can be harnessed for their resources. For centuries Africans have utilized the resources of the rivers for many purposes. The

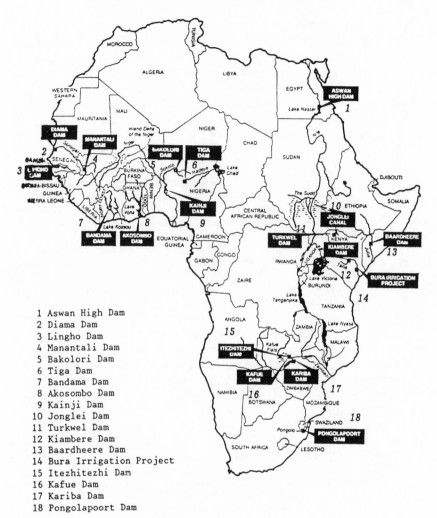

1 Aswan High Dam
2 Diama Dam
3 Lingho Dam
4 Manantali Dam
5 Bakolori Dam
6 Tiga Dam
7 Bandama Dam
8 Akosombo Dam
9 Kainji Dam
10 Jonglei Dam
11 Turkwel Dam
12 Kiambere Dam
13 Baardheere Dam
14 Bura Irrigation Project
15 Itezhitezhi Dam
16 Kafue Dam
17 Kariba Dam
18 Pongolapoort Dam

Figure 8.2: Major dams of Africa.

Nile is famous for its irrigation schemes for watering the farmlands of Egypt. Many of the other rivers in Africa are used for the same purpose, including domestic water supply, hydroelectric power, fishing, and recreational purposes. Figure 8.2 shows a number of dams that were constructed in Africa by 1985. The number of dams has increased since then. The benefits from the dams are many, but there are also problems.

Planning for water projects in Africa and the rest of the developing world needs to embrace the concept of environmental impact assessment. Water projects, although well intentioned, if not properly planned, could have a devastating negative impact on both the biological diversity and cultural diversity of the environment. There should be a careful exploration of the cultural conditions. With deliberate and long-range planning, it is possible to deliver safe drinking water to every family living in Africa.

In his address to the audience at the conference on the "Ecology and Utilization of African Inland Waters" in 1981 Professor R.J. Olembo stated that some of the overriding issues that Africa must seek answers to include the following:

> 1. Behavior and effects of domestic sewage and industrial wastes on aquatic ecosystems and on the health of the inhabitants thereof;
> 2. Effects of agricultural and forestry practice on aquatic ecosystems;
> 3. Ecological aspects of major developmental activities on freshwater ecosystems (e.g. engineering works such as dredging, damming, canalization, mining);
> 4. Recreational, tourism, and other leisure-type interactions and pressures on the freshwater ecosystems; and
> 5. All the issues related to the productivity of these ecosystems in the light of increasing demands for food and fuel by ever-increasing dependent human populations [p. 7].

The concern in this section is the impact of dams on the environment. Dam projects can lead to increases and decreases in the volume of available water. The increase in the amount of water would occur in the lakes that are created as a result of dam building, and the decrease in the amount of water is due to the construction of irrigation canals. Obeng and Gaudet (1981:162) claim:

> hydro-projects, small and large, often cause changes in water quality (a physical example is silt effects in impoundments; a chemical example is industrial pollution of streams; biological examples are numerous waterborne diseases); interbasin water diversion and transfers also cause changes in both the water and related sources inasmuch as the diverted water may exhibit characteristics unlike those of the parent water body (for example the Jonglei diversion canal).

Jonglei canal and the other dams are shown in Figure 8.2.

Impact Assessment

Since the development of the water resources would have both beneficial and adverse effects, it is worthwhile to conduct a complete environmental impact analysis for any water development project in Africa. This is basically an environmental design consideration which employs the understanding of ecology. A simple environmental impact checklist could

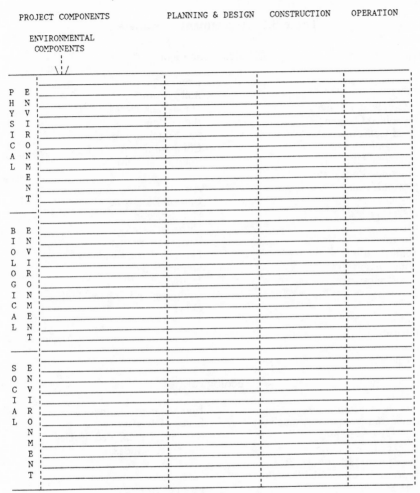

Figure 8.3: Project impact matrix.

be used to assess the positive and negative effects of water projects on the ecosystem. A project impact matrix as shown in Figure 8.3 could be used to show possible impacts that could occur when a dam is constructed on a river.

Use of the impact matrix offers the opportunity to examine the possible impact of the three phases of the project: planning and design, construction, and the operations on the environmental components (physical, biological, and social). The impact matrix shown here is similar to the Leopold Matrix and the checklist methodologies used in many impact assessments in developed countries. The assessment parameters are chosen from the list presented in Table 8.8.

Table 8.8: Assessment Parameters

Physical/Chemical

Water
BOD
Groundwater Flow
Dissolved Oxygen
Fecal Coliforms
Inorganic Carbon
Inorganic Nitrogen
Inorganic Phosphate
Heavy Metals
Pesticides
Petrochemicals
pH
Stream Flow
Temperature
Total Dissolved Solids
Toxic Substances
Turbidity

Noise
Intensity
Duration
Frequency

Land
Soil Erosion
Flood-Plain Usage
Buffer Zones
Soil Suitability for Use
Compatibility of Land Uses
Solid Waste Disposal

Air
Carbon Monoxide
Hydrocarbons
Nitrogen Oxides
Particulate Matter
Photochemical Oxidants
Sulfur Oxides
Methane
Hydrogen and Organic Sulfides
Other

Ecological

Species and Populations
Game and Nongame Animals
Natural Vegetation
Managed Vegetation
Resident and Migratory Birds
Sport and Commercial Fisheries
Pest Species

Habitats and Communities
Species Diversity
Rare and Endangered Species
Food Chain Index

Ecosystems
Productivity
Biogeochemical Cycling
Energy Flow

Aesthetic

Land
Geologic Surface Material
Relief and Topography

Air
Odor
Visual
Sounds

Water
Flow

Biota
Animals — Wild and Domestic
Vegetation Type
Vegetation Diversity

Man-Made Objects
Man-Made Objects
Consonance with Environment

Composition
Composite Effect

Table 8.8: (cont.)

Clarity	Unique Composition
Interface Land and Water	Mood Atmosphere
Floating Materials	

Social

Individual Environmental Interests	*Individual Well-Being*
Educational/Scientific	Physiological Health
Cultural	Psychological Health
Historical	Safety
Leisure/Recreation	Hygiene
Social Interactions	*Community Well-Being*
Political	Community Well-Being
Socialization	
Religious	
Family	
Economic	

The necessity of conducting the environmental assessment is to ensure that impacts are fully documented and evaluated in order to make a rational choice as to what decision a government and its citizens have to make. Hydroelectric power plants like all major projects have primary, secondary, and tertiary impacts which are both positive and negative. These impacts must be fully analyzed. Past experience in Africa shows that impact statements were not fully utilized in major projects. They ought to be, given the fact that governments are aggressively trying to develop industrially and are importing foreign technologies.

A good example is given by the Nigerian government's interest in providing water for agriculture and other purposes to its citizens. To this effect, Alhaji Abubakar Hahidu (Nigeria's minister of agriculture, water resources, and rural development) thinks the construction of dams will assist the country in making water available to millions of people for many purposes. He notes:

> The Federal Government has tried to ameliorate the problems of the sector by providing bulk water supply through the construction of multi-purpose dams and bore holes for water supply, irrigation and hydro-electricity; securing a loan of $256m for the strengthening of the state water agencies for the rehabilitation of some existing water systems throughout the nation [interview, Idowu, 1992:100].

Although these steps are ambitious and would improve water supply situations in Nigeria, it is certain that there are environmental problems that would emanate as a result of these projects. The problems that occur as a result of the massive irrigation schemes include the buildup of salt in the soil. Experience shows that the continuous irrigation of the land around the Nile in Egypt resulted in the initial agricultural boom along the banks, but these places have since declined in fertility due to the increase in salt concentration. Africa should take as an example the southwestern United States where water was brought in from the Colorado River to irrigate the arid lands of the San Joaquin Valley so that cotton and fruits could be cultivated. Over a ten-year period between 1975 and 1985, the salt content of the soil has increased tremendously, and there has also been a buildup of selenium. Selenium is an element that occurs naturally in the water environment. Plants need selenium in trace quantity for their development, but in large quantities, it becomes hazardous to both plant and animal life.

It is imperative that African countries take note of these kinds of problems before embarking on massive irrigation schemes through the construction of dams. Water resource developments are bound to change the ecological systems of the areas where the development occurs. The buildup of selenium in large concentrations can render environments completely useless and could effect ecological succession processes, food chains, and food webs.

The challenge facing planners in Africa are many, but probably one of the biggest challenges is that which is created by the pollution of the sources of water supply to the people of Africa. Industrialization without a sound environmental plan is self-defeating in many respects. Urbanization without a sound environmental plan which is comprehensive in perspective is disastrous. The disasters are common when one examines the state of water supply to the growing urban and rural populations. Water-borne diseases, heavy organic loading, and sediments are found in increasing amounts year after year in many water-supply sources in Africa. This is the direct result of lack of proper sanitary conditions, poor environmental control and monitoring, and population explosion. Heavy metal and sediment increases in water are due to soil erosion. Many African countries do not have soil conservation strategies and programs, and water quality problems are enormous.

In mining and industrial areas of Africa, improper disposal of waste materials pollutes the water and results in high concentrations of barium, cadmium, chloride, chromium, copper ions, lead, manganese, mercury, nitrate, nitrite pesticides, phenols, sulfates, and zinc in water supply sources. These substances cause health problems in humans. The environmental assessment process can assist in the investigation of how a project would affect the physical, physiological, biological, and chemical characteristics of African water resources. The physical characteristics comprise temperature, turbidity, solids, and color; the physiological characteristics are taste and odor; the biological characteristics consist of protista, viruses, plants, and animals; and the chemical characteristics are made up of organic, inorganic, and gaseous chemicals. African water quality is affected by development projects which have besieged the continent without careful ecological consideration. Obeng and Gaudet (1980:163–64) argue:

> There are many examples in Africa where the quality of the water is threatened by development projects. The cause can be traced to the discharge of sewage and industrial wastes into surface waters; agricultural chemicals may be washed into surface and ground waters; excessive withdrawal of water may result in the intrusion of salt water into ground and surface water with resultant alteration in water quality which, in turn, affects ecological balances. Impoundments can also affect water quality, depending on how the water is released. Surface spillways release epilimnetic water, whereas release from the bottom allows the discharge of hypolimnetic water; the latter is a water of completely different quality than the surface water.
>
> Several instances of gross pollution in Africa such as the Jukskei River, Athi-Nairobi River, etc., are known and in most instances the ecological effects are similar to what is expected, i.e. lower species diversity, high biotic density, etc. In instances of cultural eutrophication, the result is often increased macrophyte or algal growth and the establishment of an undesirable invertebrate fauna.

Oil spills in the Niger delta of Nigeria have decimated whole rural societies.

Sustained Development and Water Supply

African countries are very interested in sustained development in both rural and urban settings, and efforts are being made by national governments and foreign investors in Africa to develop the water resources by financing projects that are aimed at increasing water use. For instance, in Nigeria, the construction of bridges and roads has made water resources available to rural communities (Figure 8.4).

The United Nations Development Program (UNDP) and African nations recognize the significance of massive investments in human development in order for Africa to attain and sustain the full potential of its development. The investment in water and sanitation projects must be high on the agenda of African nations because one-half of the estimated total population of Africa of about 450 million people do not have opportunities for health services, and two-thirds do not have safe drinking water (World Bank 1991).

Figure 8.4: Bridge linking villages to water source, Calabar River, Nigeria, 1991.

In the urban and semi-urban areas of Africa, where there are modern water supply operations, many factors contribute to the problems of water supply. Among these problems are: the lack of powerful generators that could pump large volumes of water, small water reservoirs, and the fact that the water projects have not kept pace with the expanding populations.

The disappointing conditions of water supplies in some African urban centers is given by one prime example in Anambra state of Nigeria. Nwade (1991:5) argues:

> The apparent indifference of the ministry over this problem (water supply) has made it impossible for enough water to circulate through the underground network of pipes in the town. That a big town like Awka with 33 villages and the presence of two higher institutions of learning — a campus of the Anambra State University of Science and Technology (ASUTECH) and the Awka College of Education cannot have reliable water supply is a point which has often been played upon by some restless students. In fact the spring water project at Offiaimoka Awka which was planned and executed through communal effort in the 1970s would not have broken down had it been expanded and maintained properly.

Communities in both urban and rural centers that have modern water supply facilities are faced with new problems which are managerial and technical.

Figure 8.5 shows a water supply project in Ikot-Ekpene (Akwa-Ibom state) of Nigeria. This technology operates on diesel oil, and during the periods when diesel is scarce or unavailable, the town residents whose houses are connected to the pipeline do not have water. Occasional breakdown or cleaning of the equipment is sometimes problematic due to the insufficient knowledge of operation and maintenance of equipment. To avoid being without water, residents always make sure they store water in large containers (Figure 8.6).

However, in rapidly expanding areas of Africa the municipalities are incapable of supplying water to a majority of their citizens. Such is the case in Orile, Iganmu, Nigeria, where individuals store water in water tanks so that others can purchase it by the gallon (Figure 8.7). Alternatively, wells are still being used in the outskirts of major urban centers (Figure 8.8). The well water in this particular case is used for all other domestic purposes but drinking. While in some rural and semi-rural towns where public water is not provided, people can travel a few miles or go to their neighbors' homes for safe drinking water (Figure 8.9).

Unfortunately for some uninformed individuals, pesticide cans are used for fetching water in both urban and rural parts of Africa. In 1991, it was reported that in Nigeria, some people who used empty pesticide cans to collect and store drinking water died from the poisonous effects of the contaminants (Radio Nigeria 1991). This type of incidence could be avoided if local governments conducted campaigns of educating the rural and urban dwellers on how to store drinking water properly.

Between 1960 and 1991, the United Nations spent more than 1.2 million naria on development projects in Nigeria alone. This is about $600,000 at 1992 exchange rates. It is reported that out of $8 billion spent on development projects by the UN in 1990, 43 percent of that money was spent by forty countries in Africa (World Bank 1991). The development of water resources is receiving enormous attention despite economic difficulties. There is a genuine attempt to develop water resources in African countries, and this effort encompasses all aspects of water supply. The plan for African countries is to develop the water resources for irrigation purposes, the domestic and industrial uses, hydro-electric power generation, transportation, fishing, recreation, and the disposal of waste products as a result of development.

Comprehensive water-supply plans would mean extensive irrigation of African agricultural land. Such efforts could have ecological implications. It appears that in some cases the governments have not clearly defined the problems associated with irrigation projects.

Water is a basic necessity of life. For any tangible social and economic progress to be made in Africa, the inhabitants of this majestic continent must have safe drinking water and sustainable agriculture.

Figure 8.5: Modern water supply facility, Ikot-Ekpene, Nigeria, 1991.

Figure 8.6: Drums of water for domestic use, Ikot-Ekpene, Nigeria, 1991.

Figure 8.7: Tank containing water for sale, Orile, Iganmu, Nigeria, 1991.

Conclusion

The successes in providing safe drinking water are growing with education. Many indigenous people of Africa are resorting to self-help. Examples can be seen in Nigeria, Ghana, Benin, Kenya, and Tanzania where local governments use both modern water-supply hand pumps and wells. Many development projects in Africa depend on foreign technology in order for them to be initiated. Water projects in Africa will still require initial assistance from abroad, but the projects must be based on the willingness of Africans to pay and support them. Standards must be such that Africans can operate and manage them. The lessons from Kenya, Tanzania, and Malawi are important. In some projects which succeeded, the communities were participants in all phases of development. The projects involved low-cost technologies, community resources were mobilized, and foreign agencies were facilitators.

It is certain that the use of environmental-impact assessment methodology will assist in safeguarding the rivers, lakes, and streams of Africa. The quality of drinking water will be maintained so as to protect human health, amenity, and environment. The logical sequence of environmental impact assessment as shown in Figure 8.10 should be allowed. The physical conditions of African rivers – Nile, Niger, Congo, etc., must be well understood. The destruction of savannas and forests of Africa has led to

Figure 8.8: Well water in an urban area, Orile, Iganmu, Nigeria, 1991.

the situations whereby soil erosion has affected the rivers. The estuaries of some African rivers have been heavily silted. Many scientists and researchers suggest that in order to protect Africa's rivers the following steps should be taken:

1. Prepare a synthesis of African river limnology.
2. Study the sensitive systems associated with rivers of Africa. For example floodplains and deltas and how human activity can change it.
3. Land use patterns should be monitored as to how they change the plant and animal life of rivers.

Figure 8.9: Young boys and girls fetching water from neighbors, Ikot-Ekpene, Nigeria, 1991.

4. A long-term research to understand the transfer of energy in African river systems is necessary. The flow of energy in different tropic levels — primary and secondary producers would be understood if such research is conducted.

5. Since rivers such as the Niger, Congo, and Zambazi travel through two or more countries, it is important for intergovernmental organizations to be established in order to manage the river systems effectively [Breen et al. 1981].

The water quality problems associated with African dams are toxic substances such as fertilizers from agricultural lands, nutrients, sedimentation, and deoxygenation. Plans must be made to rid the dams of these problems during the construction and operation phases.

It must be emphasized in the concluding section of this chapter that the best solutions for Africa's water supply problems were suggested in a 1987 World Health Organization publication which enumerates seven ideas about what the appropriate technology for water supply should incorporate:

1. Be as inexpensive as possible without jeopardizing the effectiveness of the improvements sought.

2. Be easy to operate and maintain at the village, community, or

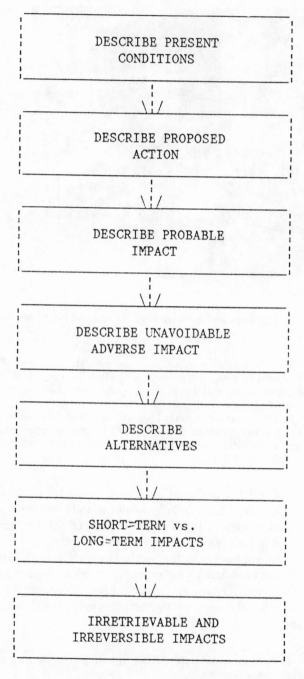

Figure 8.10: Schematic flow diagram of environmental impact assessment.

municipal level, and not demand a high level of technical skills or require a massive deployment of professional engineers.

3. Rely on locally produced materials rather than on externally provided equipment and spare parts, where this is applicable.

4. Make effective use of local labor especially in areas where there is a surplus of labor.

5. Facilitate and encourage the local manufactures of equipment and parts under the leadership of entrepreneurs.

6. Facilitate the participation of village communities in its operation and maintenance. And

7. Be compatible with local values and preferences [p. 13].

These recommendations must be taken seriously because water projects in Africa have to be funded and given deserved attention. There are approximately 20 million more Africans who were without safe drinking water and 30 million more Africans who were without adequate sanitation at the end of the International Drinking Water Supply and Sanitation Decade (1980s) than at the beginning. These numbers are alarming and deserve all efforts (African and international) in order to meet the water needs in Africa.

Part II

International and Domestic Policies for Developing Africa's Resources

9. Past, Present, and Future Activities: Efforts and Consequences

Introduction

Africa's present condition, economically, environmentally, socially, technologically, and internationally has been greatly affected by past activities that occurred in the continent. These activities had two groups of actors: Africans and foreigners (Europeans and Arabs).

In this book, the emphasis is on the environment, and an attempt must be made in this chapter to investigate Africa's past environmental condition and how past activities recognized the ecological balance which is very crucial for stability. The starting point must be to examine the type of economic activities that existed in Africa, followed by the type of agriculture, and finally the industrialization and technological activities.

Africa has never been in a state of torpor. From the Sahara in the north to the coasts of South Africa, human activities have helped in shaping the outlook of Africa. One area of interest to many scholars has always been the economic history of Africa. Wickin's (1986) work summarizes the economic history of Africa from 1890 to 1980. This work along with others has been the backbone of the discussion in this section.

Transformation of Africa

The process of economic development in Africa was not set into motion by Europeans, but it was accelerated by them. Africans historically were involved in "intra-tribal" and inter-tribal trade, although this type of trade was very limited due to the self-sufficiency of the linguistic groups in Africa. Nature was very generous to many village communities in the forest and savanna regions of Africa. It provided food for sustenance in

213

the form of many diverse fruits and animals, and many African societies did not develop into the type of communities and societies as those of Europe in the pre-1880s. The African villages in the pre-1800s because of their small sizes were self-contained and depended upon family members to contribute to the needs of the villages. In many parts of Africa today nature still provides for sustenance (Figures 9.1 and 9.2).

The transformation of Africa was triggered by several factors. One of these factors is the population growth. As each village began to grow in population, more land was needed for settlement and agriculture. It was necessary for the land to be cleared for these purposes. This was the beginning of the the transformation of the forests and savannas of Africa. As more and more people got into the land clearance process the ecological systems began to suffer. However, it must be noted that this process of change was slow when compared to what happened upon the arrival of Europeans.

Population growth also meant that greater demands were made on the natural resources than previously when the population was small. As more villages were formed, informal large communities emerged. In some places such as the savannas of West Africa, the Songhai, Fulani, and Ghana empires emerged out of trade and the conquering of one African linguistic group by another. Timbuktu in Mali was not only a town for higher education but it was an important trading post. Trading between Africans for food stuffs was by barter, and overall trade was small. Slave trading was part of the trade that was conducted at the post.

However, upon the entry into Africa by Europeans, the process of change was accelerated precisely because the European impact changed and influenced not only the social structure but also the African landscape. The literature of the historical development in Africa is inundated with a plethora of arguments for and against the European impact on Africa.

European Influence

A great deal has been written about European involvement in the slave trade. The trans-Atlantic slave trade devastated Africa in all developmental arenas. In many respects, it stopped some of the progress that was being made by African societies. In other cases it slowed down progress. The impact of the trans-Atlantic slave trade still lingered even in the 1900s. What was the negative impact of slavery, and how big was the impact on the development of the continent? These questions are major subjects of research for African historiographers. African slaves who were brought to North and South America were the most numerous immigrants from the so-called Old World. The Atlantic slave trade disrupted cultures

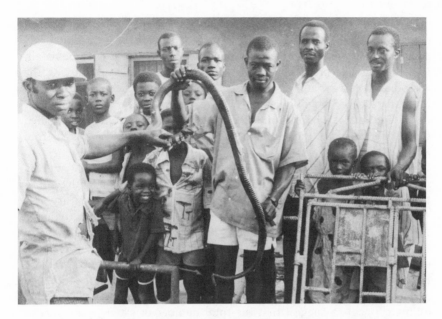

Figure 9.1: Residents of Orile, Iganmu, Nigeria, display a snake killed.

Figure 9.2: The rivers provide fish for inhabitants of Ibuno, Nigeria, 1991.

and educational institutions (by African standards), damaged social development and evolution, and destroyed technological developments and innovations which were taking their natural paths. Above all, it caused or exacerbated environmental degradation by removing the custodians of the natural resources. Women who tilled the land with the assistance of able-bodied men were captured and taken as slaves to foreign lands. The magnitude of the trade can be fully appreciated when one examines the estimates of the number of slaves taken from Africa.

It is estimated by Kucznski (1936:12) that by the year 1600 approximately 900,000 slaves were taken from Africa; by the seventeenth century the estimate was about 2.75 million slaves; the eighteenth century witnessed the number of African slaves rising to 7 million; and in the nineteenth century it is estimated that the number of slaves that were taken to the Americas was 4 million. The total number of slaves, by Kucznski's estimate, that landed in North and South America is 14.65 million. However, a later calculation by Deerr (1949–50) suggests that the total was about 11.97 million. Curtin's (1969) new calculations and revisions of old estimates seem to suggest that the total number of slaves was approximately 9.56 million. The human misery of the trade was translated into environmental, social, and developmental problems of immeasurable proportion. It is not surprising that in recent times African countries are demanding reparation compensation from European countries. There is a strong argument by African scholars that slavery and colonialism set Africa back, and that while other parts of the world were taking a traditional path of uninterrupted development, Africa's progress was greatly hindered by outsiders who were interested in its natural and human resources. Europeans depended almost entirely on Africa for the labor force necessary for plantation agriculture. In Latin America, there was a diversification of slave labor into areas of mining, ranching, and small-scale industry. The viewpoints of scholars about the reparation to Africa are under consideration by the Organization of African Unity (OAU).

Vestiges of slavery still affect some countries of Africa in this decade. In Mauritania, a country which has suffered the ravages of the Arab slave trade, drought, and extreme poverty, blacks are being marginalized, discriminated against, tortured, and alienated by the government officials who are mainly "Beydanes." The Beydanes are of Arabic descent and as such emphasize Arabic culture and have managed to organize the "Haratines" who are former black slaves (and their descendants) against black Mauritanians who have a strong French connection and education. This problem has its roots in slavery and colonialism. Omaar and Fleischman (1991:36) note:

The determination to link Mauritania's fortunes to the Arab world has had a distinctively negative impact on the black community and this is manifested in the educational system. Since the mid–1960s, policies designed to favor Arabic-speaking students have discriminated against the black population, depriving them of academic and economic opportunities, thereby furthering their marginalization.

At independence from France in 1960, the French left political power firmly entrenched in the hands of *beydanes*. However, most educated Mauritanians were black and spoke French, largely because their settled life-styles facilitated adaptation to modern schooling. In contrast, most *beydanes* led a nomadic existence, making it difficult to attend schools. In addition, they saw the teaching of French as a threat to Islam and their cultural heritage.

Since Mauritania was an Islamic state, *beydanes* argued, Arabic should replace French as the official language. Blacks, also Muslim, rejected the government's attempts to equate Islam with Arab identity. Since they regarded Arabic as the language of political domination and cultural assimilation, and arabianization of the educational system as a threat to the economic future of their community, black intellectuals began to promote the use of their African languages, Pulaar, Wolof, and Soninke. In the meantime, they expressed their preference for French.

Smith (1991:36–37) echoes the lamentable historical problems of Africa as she examines the Europeans' impact on Africa. She contends that as Europeans mastered the world's oceans, they saw an opportunity to control the world's natural resources, and Africa which was considered the Dark Continent was envisaged as a source for raw materials. She contends: "Between 1500 and 1870 Europeans reaped the heart out of the continent, taking some 229 million able-bodied farmers out as slaves. By the late 1800s, Africa was divided into spheres of influence based not on the equitable development of the African economy, but on European interests."

European colonial expansion in Africa caused major changes in the continent. The partition of the continent — brought about by the Conference of 1885 in Berlin — accelerated the pace of changes which occurred in Africa in several ways. Britain, France, Portugal, Spain, Germany, and Italy acquired several parts of Africa. France and Great Britain got most of the territory in Africa, but Portugal and Spain are known for having the longest history of colonialism in the continent (Wickens 1986). The spread of the British and French empires preceded colonialism. Britain and France attempted to acquire territories all over the world, and such greed ignited the interests of other nations to scramble for Africa. Germany acquired part of Kamerun, Togoland, southwest Africa, and the territory of German East Africa. Britain became the owner of British East African Protectorate which was part of Somalia. The Italians acquired Eritrea and part of Somalia, and Spain was left with some poor places such as the western

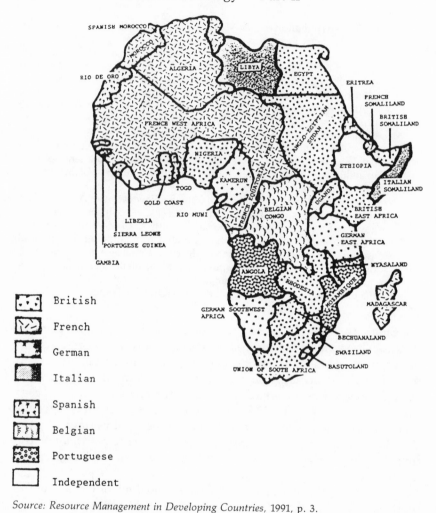

British

French

German

Italian

Spanish

Belgian

Portuguese

Independent

Source: Resource Management in Developing Countries, 1991, p. 3.

Figure 9.3: The division of Africa, 1885.

Sahara, Centa, Melilla, Fernando Po, and Spanish Guinea. Figure 9.3 shows how Africa was divided among European powers. This was the continuation of the dominance of Africa by outsiders and the control of Africa's resources. The colonial period witnessed a time when Africans had no role in the future direction of the continent. A brief discussion of the agriculture and industrial sectors will help to shed some light on this matter.

Colonialism brought large-scale plantation agricultural practice into Africa. Traditional African agriculture was basically subsistence in purpose whereby only the leftover produce was traded, but the introduction of agriculture for cash linked the African economy with the European economy. Cash crops such as cocoa, coffee, cotton, oil palm, tea, and sugar cane were grown for European markets. Plantations required many acres of land, a lot of labor, some mechanization, and use of fertilizers.

Africans responded with great enthusiasm to the production of these crops, and Africans proved that they could grow crops successfully and sustain their production. But there was a price paid by Africans to produce the cash crops in high quantities. They turned their attention away from producing subsistence crops and by so doing created a scarcity of staple foodstuffs. Plantation work broke down family structures which had been established through the communal work stratification on family farms. The African family continued to disintegrate under the plantation agriculture systems. Strains in family foundations left scars on the family because everything was done to suit the agendas of the colonial rulers who owned the plantations.

Subsistence agriculture did not keep pace with the population boom that ensued, and so one can rightly argue that the political instabilities or fragile political systems of Africa owe their roots to past colonial activities. African efforts were misdirected right from the very beginning of colonialism. An examination of the peasant communities in Africa, including the Fulani nomads on the fringes of the Sahara, the cereal growers of the savannas, and itinerant farmers of the forest seems to indicate that colonialism changed their priorities and their sense of agricultural practice was shifted to catering to the needs of the Western market. Unfortunately, Africa is still being exploited after independence. The world market prices for agricultural goods and forest products are still not enough to enable African countries to partake fully in global affairs. Dumont and Mottin (1983:5–6) note:

> The "old international economic order" (though "disorder" would be a better word) is taking a long time a-dying, in spite of countless declarations in favor of a "new order" that would bring about a fairer distribution of the world's wealth. In fact the looting of the Third World has never stopped since the period of slavery and colonization. It is continuing in our own day in the form of an unfair system of trading in which raw materials — initially agricultural and subsequently mineral — are bought far below their value, while manufactured products and hard goods produced by factories in the developed countries are sold at too high a rate. With freightage, brokerage, insurance, banking, factorage, patents and transfer of technology and other invisibles, this type of exploitation is continually being added to.

In the late 1950s and in the 1960s, many African countries obtained political independence, but it could be argued that they are still economically dependent on the Europeans. This economic dependency pervades the continent today, and it is part of the reason Africa cannot sustain any kind of development strategy. Structurally, the agricultural organizations were set up for European interests, and as such Africa in the twentieth century cannot feed itself if present conditions prevail. Africa will not be able to feed itself in the twenty-first century.

Smith (1991:36–37) discusses a classic example of how European interests undermined Africa's development:

> Sudan Africa's largest country is a good example of the kind of development that has made Africa the "Third World's Third World," a sight of recurring famines and unpayable debt. Although never wealthy, the Sudanese had maintained the ability to feed themselves for centuries. When Britain governed the country, it decided that Sudanese farmers should grow cotton, to supply burgeoning British mills. Using the latest in agricultural technology, the British developed huge cotton-growing schemes on Sudan's most fertile land.
>
> When Sudan became independent in 1956, the new government encouraged by "development" banks and foreign donors continued to emphasize cotton production. Two things happened: over time, the world market price of cotton fell, and Sudan's supply of foreign currency plummeted. Since agricultural resources were tied up in cotton, food production kept steadily declining. With no foreign currency, the country had to take out loans to import food. The mills of northern England, however, still had a constant supply of cotton.

When Africans and African governments were encouraged to produce more export and cash crops, little did they know that the prices of the commodities would fluctuate depending on the "market forces" and policies set in industrialized countries. In modern-day Africa, it seems that most of what is being discussed in economic circles includes the unfair trade practices, how Africa is not receiving equitable prices for its agricultural produce and other natural resources—both renewable and nonrenewable. For example, in July of 1992, world cocoa prices fell by 7.3 percent, the prices for sugar plummeted by 10.9 percent from the previous month's level, and the price for sorghum dropped by 64 percent (*West Africa* 1991).

Africa's Development

Intrinsically tied to Africa's development is the sustainability of its trade with other countries. It must be able to make a profit on its agricultural produce and its minerals, but so far it appears that it has not really been able to. There is a school of thought which contends that there is "north" dominance of the "south" over the price of commodities. This argument is supported when one examines the prices of raw materials which are produced in the Third World. The prices are said to be determined by policies set in the "north" — Western industrialized countries. As recently as July 1991, the prices for African metals and minerals, with the exception of steel, plummeted to their lowest levels in three years by 4.4 percent. The rise or fall of prices of Africa's raw materials is determined by factors outside of the continent of Africa.

In many countries of Africa, there are civil strife, unrest, disorder, civil wars, and border conflicts. These problems exacerbate the hunger problem and social, political, economic, and environmental destruction. In order for Africa to develop, there must be a more orderly strategy for development at three fronts: the local, the national, and the international. The strategy must embrace environmental development goals and must not develop at the expense of the environment.

African countries such as Nigeria, Zaire, Ghana, Kenya, Ethiopia, Chad, and Côte d'Ivoire are experiencing tremendous environmental degradation, and as was pointed out in an earlier chapter, this is compounded by the exponential increase in population. Another factor that is often not included in the equation of the devastation of Africa is the high rate of war on the continent.

In the last decade, Africa has been faced with many wars. Between 1975 and 1989 Angola had a bitter civil war. Wars were also fought in Burundi (1988), Chad (1980–87), Ethiopia/Eritrea (1974–91), Ghana (1981), Liberia (1990–91), Morocco/Western Sahara (1975–87), Mozambique (1981–89), Namibia (1966–89), Nigeria (1980–81 and 1984), Somalia (1988), Sudan (1984–89), Uganda (1981–87), and Zimbabwe (1987). Wars have devastating effects on human beings, the environment, and the development process. For instance, the wars in Ethiopia completely destroyed the agrarian communities of the country, since 90 percent of that country's military (400,000 soldiers) are farmers. It is therefore understandable that Ethiopia cannot feed itself and has to depend on foreign food aid. Mozambique's situation is just as bad, because 4.35 million people — half of the total population of the country — depend on food aid from overseas. In Liberia it is estimated that the war for the control of the government between Charles Taylor's group and Mr. Sawyer's faction has resulted in the displacement of more than half the population of the country (approximately 1.2 million people).

The urban and rural environment has been greatly damaged. Agricultural practices have been practically halted, and neighboring countries of Sierra Leone, Côte d'Ivoire, and the Guineas are now having to deal with the problem of refugees. Monies that could have been used for development purposes are being diverted for military purposes. It is estimated that the annual military expenditure of African governments is approximately $14 billion (Smith 1991). Obviously, African leaders must take some of the blame for the ravaging of the African environment and people. But it must be stated that the involvement of industrialized countries in the conflicts often exacerbates the problems of war as El-Affendi (1991:37) rightfully argues:

> Consider Africa's longest running civil war, which came to a conclusion satisfactory to all parties within months of stoppage of foreign inter-ference — Eritrea. Was it Africans who set up air bases in Ethiopia and funded Emperor Haile Selassie's war against his people and the Eritreans? Or was it Africans who pumped billions of dollars' worth of arms to prop up Mangistu and sustain his wars against his people and his neighbours? Now that Moscow and Washington have packed up and left, the war is over.

Africa's Present Position in Global Affairs

One of the most paradoxical situations that Africa finds itself confronted with is its natural resources. The continent is endowed with enormous natural resources, yet 30 million of its people are at the brink of starvation and many countries are dependent upon assistance from abroad to meet the most basic necessity of life — food.

Perhaps Africa's position in regard to the rest of the world can best be described as being at the periphery of world affairs with respect to economics, technology, and key decision-making positions. El-Affendi (1991:37) argues that Africa has been put in such a position because the continent has been robbed and is still being robbed of its resources. There is also a one-directional flow of wealth. Foreign investment is minimal in Africa, and there is a definite monopoly of technology and skills by Western nations and an unfair practicing policy on African goods. El-Affendi thinks Western countries should share energy technology with the African countries and not price farming technology out of Africa's reach.

However, there are other viewpoints about Africa's position in global affairs. One such viewpoint is articulated by Shaw who thinks that Africa's dilemma is one that could be explained from how Africa participates in world affairs. The participation can be grouped into three categories: incorporation, intervention, and isolation. Shaw (1987:4) notes:

> The ambiguities of Africa's position are revealed with particular clarity in the case of food, a sector in which the continent used to be self sufficient but now is increasingly dependent upon external supplies. But dependence on foreign food is not simply a function of population growth or environmental deterioration. Rather, it is one of aspect of the continent's

incorporations into the world system. Africa's involvement in the international division of labor means that it produces primary products for export — coffee, tea, cotton, groundnuts, etc. — and imports basic commodities — wheat, rice, meat, fish — that it can no longer provide for itself.

The paradox that emerges from this discussion is that Africa is endowed with the rich natural resources that can enable it to feed itself if proper and adequate attention is paid to producing basic food stuffs. There is no doubt that the savannas of Africa can serve as the bread basket of Africa. The soil can support extensive agriculture that would make Africa self-sufficient but not isolated from the rest of the world. Africa's role in global affairs must move from one of dependency to one of equality with the rest of the world.

The current description of the African environment can only be discussed in terms of deterioration, disruption, imbalance, destruction, decaying, deplorable and all other negative descriptions associated with a process by which the African environment is experiencing tremendous entropy or disorder. The poor economic situation in all African countries plays a significant role in the resultant environment of Africa.

The current economic situation of Africa has its own set of descriptions which conjure images of poverty, slow industrial growth rate, low rate gross domestic product, and high unemployment rates. Tables 9.1, 9.2, and 9.3 give vivid evidence of how dismal the economic situation is in some African countries where development is stagnant and planners say that the standard of living has deteriorated.

In some countries there has been a rise in the cost of basic food stuffs, housing, and transportation, and these conditions have resulted in civil unrest. In April and May of 1992, several Nigerian universities (Lagos, Ibadan, Benin, and Port-Harcourt) were closed because students were rioting over the continued decline in the standard of education, living, the environment, and the social fabric of the country. Several students were killed, and some faculty and students were detained by the government. The current situation in many African countries needs to be corrected. Although the rate of development varies from country to country since some countries have more natural resources than others, the general atmosphere of the African economy is poor. Hence, there is an urgent need for proper and adequate planning strategies and policies for managing Africa's natural and human resources. Certainly there are some basic constraints hindering Africa's development as has already been pointed out all through the discussions in this book. For purposes of convenience and reiteration, these obstacles include the underdevelopment of human resources, the instability of the governments, the lack of continuity of institutions that are concerned with development, the fact that the Western

Table 9.1: Structure of Manufacturing

	Value added in manufacturing (millions of current dollars)	
	1970	1988
1. Algeria	682	5446
2. Angola	–	–
3. Benin	19	80
4. Botswana	5	99
5. Burkina Faso	65	376
6. Burundi	16	92
7. Cameroon	119	1,708
8. Cape Verde	–	–
9. Central African Republic	12	87
10. Chad	51	163
11. Comoros	–	–
12. Congo, People's Republic	–	198
13. Côte d'Ivoire	149	–
14. Djibouti	–	–
15. Egypt, Arab Republic	–	–
16. Eq. Guinea	–	–
17. Ethiopia	149	579
18. Gabon	22	331
19. The Gambia	–	–
20. Ghana	252	528
21. Guinea	–	85
22. Guinea-Bissau	–	–
23. Kenya	174	849
24. Lesotho	2	49
25. Liberia	15	–
26. Libya	81	1,500
27. Madagascar	–	275
28. Malawi	–	154
29. Mali	25	135
30. Mauritania	10	–
31. Mauritius	26	419
32. Morocco	641	3,894
33. Mozambique	–	–
34. Namibia	–	–
35. Niger	30	167
36. Nigeria	543	2,989
37. Rwanda	8	328
38. Senegal	141	939
39. Sierra Leone	22	53
40. Somalia	26	53
41. South Africa	3,914	19,046
42. Sudan	140	–
43. Swaziland	–	–
44. Tanzania	116	111
45. Togo	25	106
46. Tunisia	121	1,411
47. Uganda	158	213
48. Zaire	–	982
49. Zambia	181	1,149
50. Zimbabwe	293	1,327

Source: Adapted from World Bank, 1991, pp. 214–15.

Table 9.1: (cont.)

Distribution of manufacturing value added

Food, beverages & tobacco		Textiles & clothing		Machinery & transport equipment		Chemicals		Other	
1970	1988	1970	1988	1970	1988	1970	1988	1970	1988
32	20	20	17	9	13	4	3	35	47
–	–	–	–	–	–	–	–	–	–
–	54	–	10	–	0	–	6	–	30
69	–	9	–	2	–	1	–	19	–
53	–	25	–	0	–	6	–	16	–
50	–	15	–	4	–	3	–	27	–
–	–	–	–	–	–	–	–	–	–
–	–	–	–	–	–	–	–	–	–
–	–	–	–	–	–	–	–	–	–
65	–	4	–	1	–	8	–	22	–
27	–	16	–	10	–	5	–	42	–
–	–	–	–	–	–	–	–	–	–
17	29	35	20	9	9	12	17	27	25
–	–	–	–	–	–	–	–	–	–
46	48	31	19	0	2	2	4	21	27
37	–	7	–	6	–	6	–	44	–
–	–	–	–	–	–	–	–	–	–
34	40	16	6	4	1	4	7	41	47
–	–	–	–	–	–	–	–	–	–
33	40	9	10	16	12	9	9	33	28
–	–	–	–	–	–	–	–	–	–
–	–	–	–	–	–	–	–	–	–
64	–	5	–	0	–	12	–	20	–
36	–	28	–	6	–	7	–	23	–
51	–	17	–	3	–	10	–	20	–
36	–	40	–	4	–	5	–	14	–
–	–	–	–	–	–	–	–	–	–
75	23	6	51	5	3	3	5	12	18
–	–	–	–	–	–	–	–	–	–
51	–	13	–	5	–	3	–	28	–
–	–	–	–	–	–	–	–	–	–
–	–	–	–	–	–	–	–	–	–
36	–	26	–	1	–	6	–	31	–
86	65	0	3	3	0	2	5	8	28
51	48	19	15	2	6	6	7	22	24
–	65	–	1	–	–	–	4	–	30
88	59	6	13	0	2	1	13	6	13
15	14	13	8	17	20	10	11	45	48
39	–	34	–	3	–	5	–	19	–
–	–	–	–	–	–	–	–	–	–
36	–	28	–	5	–	4	–	26	–
–	–	–	–	–	–	–	–	–	–
29	20	18	20	4	4	13	9	36	47
40	–	20	–	2	–	4	–	34	–
38	–	16	–	7	–	10	–	29	–
49	–	9	–	5	–	10	–	27	–
24	35	16	15	9	9	11	10	40	32

Table 9.2: Manufacturing Earnings and Output

| | Earnings per employee | | | | |
| | Growth rate | | Index (1980=100) | | |
	1970–80	1980–88	1986	1987	1988
1. Algeria	−1.0	−	−	−	−
2. Angola	−	−	−	−	−
3. Benin	−	−	−	−	−
4. Botswana	2.6	−5.7	71	−	−
5. Burkina Faso	−	−	−	−	−
6. Burundi	−7.5	−	−	−	−
7. Cameroon	3.2	−	−	−	−
8. Cape Verde	−	−	−	−	−
9. Central African Rep.	−	−	−	−	−
10. Chad	−	−	−	−	−
11. Comoros	−	−	−	−	−
12. Congo, People's Rep.	−	−	−	−	−
13. Côte d'Ivoire	−0.9	−	−	−	−
14. Djibouti	−	−	−	−	−
15. Egypt, Arab Rep.	4.1	0.5	103	−	−
16. Equatorial Guinea	−	−	−	−	−
17. Ethiopia	−4.6	0.2	97	106	100
18. Gabon	−	−	−	−	−
19. The Gambia	−	−	−	−	−
20. Ghana	−	7.8	170	−	−
21. Guinea	−	−	−	−	−
22. Guinea-Bissau	−	−	−	−	−
23. Kenya	−3.4	−0.1	97	102	106
24. Lesotho	−	−	−	−	−
25. Liberia	−	1.7	99	−	−
26. Libya	−	−	−	−	−
27. Madagascar	−0.9	−10.3	−	−	−
28. Malawi	−	1.4	−	−	−
29. Mali	−	−	−	−	−
30. Mauritania	−	−	−	−	−
31. Mauritius	1.8	−1.0	86	93	98
32. Morocco	−	−3.6	76	80	−
33. Mozambique	−	−	−	−	−
34. Namibia	−	−	−	−	−
35. Niger	−	−	61	68	−
36. Nigeria	−0.8	−	−	−	−
37. Rwanda	−	−	−	−	−
38. Senegal	−4.9	−	−	−	−
39. Sierra Leone	−	−	−	−	−
40. Somalia	−5.1	−	−	−	−
41. South Africa	2.7	0.0	101	100	104
42. Sudan	−	−	−	−	−
43. Swaziland	−	−	−	−	−
44. Tanzania	−	−12.7	−	−	−
45. Togo	−	−	−	−	−
46. Tunisia	4.2	−	−	−	−
47. Uganda	−	−	−	−	−
48. Zaire	−	−	−	−	−
49. Zambia	−3.2	−	−	−	−
50. Zimbabwe	1.6	−0.9	100	98	100

Source: Adapted from World Bank, 1991, pp. 216–17.

Table 9.2: (cont.)

Total earnings as a % of value added				Gross output per employee (1980=100)			
1970	1986	1987	1988	1970	1986	1987	1988
45	–	–	–	120	–	–	–
–	–	–	–	–	–	–	–
–	–	–	–	–	–	–	–
–	36	–	–	–	56	–	–
–	–	–	–	–	–	–	–
–	–	–	–	–	–	–	–
30	–	–	–	80	–	–	–
–	–	–	–	–	–	–	–
–	–	–	–	–	85	–	–
–	–	–	–	–	–	–	–
–	–	–	–	–	–	–	–
–	34	–	–	–	–	–	–
27	–	–	–	52	–	–	–
–	–	–	–	–	–	–	–
54	56	–	–	89	191	–	–
–	–	–	–	–	–	–	–
24	19	20	20	61	114	115	118
–	–	–	–	–	–	–	–
–	–	–	–	–	–	–	–
23	14	–	–	193	133	–	–
–	–	–	–	–	–	–	–
–	–	–	–	–	–	–	–
50	44	44	44	42	165	186	182
–	–	–	–	–	–	–	–
–	–	–	–	–	–	–	–
–	–	–	–	–	–	–	–
36	–	–	–	106	–	–	–
37	–	–	–	126	–	–	–
46	–	–	–	–	–	–	–
–	–	–	–	–	–	–	–
34	44	43	44	139	72	69	68
–	–	–	–	–	95	95	–
29	–	–	–	–	–	–	–
–	–	–	–	–	–	–	–
–	7	7	6	–	–	–	–
18	–	–	–	105	–	–	–
22	10	–	–	–	–	–	–
–	44	–	–	–	–	–	–
–	–	–	–	–	–	–	–
28	27	–	–	–	–	–	–
46	49	49	48	–	–	–	–
31	–	–	–	–	–	–	–
–	–	–	–	–	–	–	–
42	–	–	–	122	–	–	–
–	–	–	–	–	–	–	–
44	–	–	–	95	–	–	–
–	–	–	–	–	–	–	–
–	–	–	–	–	–	–	–
34	–	–	–	109	–	–	–
43	36	35	34	98	116	115	116

Table 9.3: Growth of Consumption and Investment

	Average annual growth rate (percent)					
	General govern. consumption		Private consumption, etc.		Gross domestic investment	
	1965–80	1980–89	1965–80	1980–89	1965–80	1980–89
1. Algeria	8.6	4.0	5.0	3.1	15.9	−1.1
2. Angola	−	−	−	−	−	−
3. Benin	0.7	−0.1	1.9	2.7	10.4	−9.3
4. Botswana	12.0	12.5	10.2	6.8	21.0	0.4
5. Burkina Faso	8.7	7.3	2.5	3.3	8.5	6.9
6. Burundi	7.3	5.4	7.5	2.4	9.0	9.3
7. Cameroon	5.0	6.4	4.1	3.0	9.9	1.7
8. Cape Verde	−	−	−	−	−	−
9. Central African Rep.	−1.1	−2.5	4.9	2.1	−5.4	5.7
10. Chad	−	−	−	−	−	−
11. Comoros	−	−	−	−	−	−
12. Congo, People's Rep.	5.5	4.0	1.9	3.7	4.5	−10.7
13. Côte d'Ivoire	13.2	−6.3	6.9	7.3	10.7	−12.1
14. Djibouti	−	−	−	−	−	−
15. Egypt, Arab Rep.	a	3.8	6.7	3.6	11.3	0.6
16. Eq. Guinea	−	−	−	−	−	−
17. Ethiopia	6.4	−	3.0	−	−0.1	−
18. Gabon	10.7	3.3	7.5	−0.2	14.1	−4.9
19. The Gambia	−	−	−	−	−	−
20. Ghana	3.8	−2.3	1.2	2.2	−1.3	6.9
21. Guinea	−	−	−	−	−	−
22. Guinea-Bissau	−	−	−	−	−	−
23. Kenya	10.6	1.7	5.2	5.1	7.2	0.4
24. Lesotho	12.4	−0.4	9.9	0.6	17.8	4.4
25. Liberia	3.4	−	3.2	−	6.4	−
26. Libya	−	−	−	−	−	−
27. Madagascar	2.0	0.6	1.2	−0.6	1.5	0.1
28. Malawi	5.7	3.9	3.6	2.2	9.1	−4.5
29. Mali	1.9	3.0	5.2	2.7	1.8	10.8
30. Mauritania	10.0	−3.5	1.3	3.5	19.2	−5.4
31. Mauritius	7.1	2.8	6.4	4.7	8.3	15.0
32. Morocco	10.9	4.7	5.4	2.8	11.4	4.5
33. Mozambique	−	−2.7	−	0.9	−	0.4
34. Namibia	−	4.3	−	1.1	−	−7.0
35. Niger	2.9	1.8	−1.4	−0.9	6.3	−7.7
36. Nigeria	13.9	−2.6	6.9	−4.8	14.7	−12.9
37. Rwanda	6.2	4.6	4.5	0.3	9.0	8.8
38. Senegal	2.9	1.6	1.7	2.9	3.9	3.9
39. Sierra Leone	a	0.5	3.0	−2.3	−1.0	−3.3
40. Somalia	12.7	7.0	4.5	0.9	12.1	−2.7
41. South Africa	5.3	3.7	3.8	2.2	4.1	−4.5
42. Sudan	0.2	−	4.4	−	6.4	−
43. Swaziland	−	−	−	−	−	−
44. Tanzania	a	8.1	3.5	2.4	6.2	2.1
45. Togo	9.5	1.7	1.2	5.1	9.0	−2.9
46. Tunisia	7.2	3.6	8.8	3.5	4.6	−4.4
47. Uganda	a	−	1.4	−	−5.7	−
48. Zaire	0.7	4.0	1.8	1.9	6.6	3.3
49. Zambia	5.1	−5.4	−0.7	4.1	−3.6	−4.5
50. Zimbabwe	10.6	9.4	5.1	−2.2	0.9	2.7

Source: Adapted from World Bank, 1991, pp. 218–19.

market economy does not favor African countries, drought, and the exponential increase in population. These constraints have hindered technological and industrial development. Africa's difficulty is succinctly articulated by Hyder (1992:24):

> The African giant has woken up in a century when the world around it is in such high gear both scientifically and technologically that, to survive, let alone to prosper, it is absolutely mandatory that Mother Africa too has to run (and to run very, very, hard) to catch up with the rest of the world. The choices are few: go back to sleep and dismiss the whole vision as a bad dream; accept technological servitude as an inevitable corollary to the personal serfdom of the colonial age; "Stop the world. I want to get off!" or, get up and go. Most of us would agree that the first three alternatives are either unfeasible or untenable. We are left with the last choice.
>
> Part of the problem of African development is the lack of proper global and historical perspective on the part of its leadership. It is in the nature of politics worldwide for politicians to be more obsessed with their own survival *now* rather than to be primarily concerned with global historical perspectives, unless the former is inextricably intertwined with the latter. There is therefore nothing uniquely African about the African political leadership's penchant to see its own survival as more important than what judgment history will pronounce upon that leadership.

African governments must incorporate science and technology into their development strategy in order to fully achieve adequate self-sufficiency especially with food supply and environmental planning. In the last fifty years many African countries have not been able to feed their people and have depended heavily on foreign countries for food aid. In today's world any country that is unable to compete scientifically and technologically will be at the periphery of global affairs. Hence, Africa requires rigorous planning for national development of individual countries in order to achieve cohesion of the continent and a global order that does not have room for dependency.

The Future of Africa

If current economic, social, and environmental degradation continue in Africa, future generations will have very little to look forward to. As a result of deteriorating conditions, African leaders, international development agencies, leaders of the industrialized countries, the United Nations agencies such as UNEP, nongovernmental organizations (NGOs), and the Organization of African Unity (OAU) have organized several initiatives to help reverse the downward trend in Africa.

Many of the projects organized by the United States Agency for

International Development now attempt to incorporate the interests and desires of Africans. For instance, the conservation of wildlife resources in Africa embraces not just Western ideas but also African perspectives. The United Nations Development Programme (UNDP) has several projects in Africa which endeavor to reverse the economic decline.

The UNDP recognizes the importance of preserving the African environment and understanding the carrying capacity of areas within particular countries. For example, members of UNDP teams have been visiting African countries and advising both the government officials and local people on how they can preserve their environment by living in harmony with it. One such country is Inhaca, an island off the coast of Africa. Traditional customs have helped in preserving this island for centuries, but population increases, wars, and migration patterns are exacerbating the problems of environmental degradation. Population density is exceeding the capacity of the land to serve its several roles of use for agriculture, housing, conservation of endangered species, transportation, and industrialization. Thus the UNDP's role is to provide technical expertise for conservation, preservation, and development that will give the environment the equilibrium that is necessary for sustainability of agriculture, ecology, and economics.

Another United Nations agency that has attempted to make a dent in the future of Africa is the Economic Commission for Africa (ECA). The Commission has a Natural Resources and Transportation Division which assists African countries in matters concerning energy, minerals, and water resources. The past and present activities of this division include assisting African countries in establishing policy-making mechanisms which will enhance proper use of resources. The ECA provides technical assistance in how to gather data on the natural resources of the continent. The inventory is crucial to the planning of the countries' future.

Research and African Development

The challenge for research in Africa is to make possible the sustainability of agriculture, ecology, and the economy of African countries. In order for sustainability to occur, several steps need to be taken.

With respect to the ecological systems and the wildlife, the following steps need to be researched and incorporated into the planning strategy:

1. Determine the sustained yield capabilities of the exploited species and ecosystems by ascertaining that the utilization never exceeds the ability of the resource to recover to its original stage.
2. Resource administrators must determine ways of adopting conser-

vative management techniques that would enhance the protection of species and ecosystems.

3. Investigative research must ensure that access by road or any other means to a resource does not eventually lead to the unmanageable utilization of the resource.

4. The importance of protected areas has been growing in Africa. Nature reserves have an important role to play.

Efforts of Man and the Biosphere program should be encouraged. Funding from agencies such as the U.S. Agencies for International Development (AID), the World Wildlife Fund for Nature and efforts of colleges such as Yale University (Cameroon, Kenya, Madagascar), University of North Carolina–Charlotte (Botswana), University of California–Berkeley (Cameroon), Syracuse University (Kenya), University of California–San Diego, Washington University (Madagascar), Duke University (Madagascar), University of Michigan–Ann Arbor (several East African countries, Seychelles), University of Minnesota–St. Paul (Tanzania), and Cornell University (East Africa) should be encouraged. The universities maintain research stations which conduct valuable studies on the preservation and conservation of resources.

Funding from U.S. institutions to African countries has made conservation a reality in many countries. Table 9.4 shows a list of countries that have received assistance in terms of funding, technical assistance, and other forms of assistance to help preserve the wildlife and the environment. In 1989, Africa received about $4,202,042 for research assistance and 93 research projects were conducted; it received $3,182,320 for site and species management for 49 projects; for 16 policy planning analysis projects the cost to U.S. institutions was $1,552,778; and 42 educational projects cost U.S. institutions approximately $584,576. Strengthening existing institutions in Africa is very crucial in sustaining development and ensuring the participation of the local citizens in the process of research and development that relates to their own natural resources. The realization of this fact led to the investment of $903,756 by U.S. institutions in such endeavors. International and domestic efforts to sustain development in Africa are necessary and should not be underestimated despite the mistakes that have been made in the past.

Research projects in Africa are very diverse. The following organizations and agencies have done research or are currently involved in research efforts in Africa: Natural Resource Conservation Trust (NRCT), World Wildlife Fund (WWF), Peace Corps, Missouri Botanical Gardens, Wildlife Conservation International, Woods Hole Oceanographic Institute, U.S. Fish and Wildlife Service, Ethiopian Wildlife and Natural History Society, Station d'Etude des Gorillas et Chimpanzees (SEGC), Gabon Wildlife Department, Kenya Wildlife Conservation and Management Department,

Table 9.4: U.S. Biodiversity Investments
per 1000 Hectares in Africa in 1989

	Land Area (000 ha)	1989 Funding ($ US)
Botswana	56,673	106,561
Burundi	2,565	2,263
Cameroon	46,540	380,603
Central African Rep.	62,298	196,264
Congo	34,150	5,000
Côte d'Ivoire	31,800	10,000
Egypt	99,545	66,280
Ethiopia	110,100	121,554
Gabon	25,767	119,700
The Gambia	1,000	5,695
Kenya	56,697	2,101,170
Liberia	9,632	23,456
Madagascar	58,154	2,835,649
Malawi	9,408	900
Mali	122,019	3,700
Mauritania	102,522	837
Morocco	44,630	44,966
Niger	126,670	6,800
Rwanda	2,495	298,991
Senegal	19,253	1,600
Seychelles	27	149,699
Sierra Leone	7,162	54,873
Somalia	62,734	5,000
Swaziland	1,720	897
Tanzania	88,604	742,758
Uganda	19,955	1,020,701
Zaire	226,760	119,750
Zambia	74,072	162,872
Zimbabwe	38,667	105,245

Source: Adapted from Abramovitz, 1991, p. 41.

Museum of Natural Science, Louisiana State University, U.S. Agency for International Development, Jersey Wildlife Preservation Trust, Smithsonian Institute, Madagascar Environmental Research Group, CARE, and National Academy of Sciences.

These agencies are playing significant roles in development through research. For example, the U.S. Agency for International Development in partnership with an American company and the Cameroon government has been able to privatize a seed multiplication project in Garoua

(Cameroon). Such privatization encourages donors and host countries to find permanent solutions to agricultural problems in Africa and offer sustainable development strategies to Africa's agricultural problems. This is not to imply that African agriculture has never been sustained. As a matter of fact Africa used to be self-sufficient with respect to its agricultural needs. Mismanagement and population explosion have made self-sufficiency impossible in Africa in modern times.

Probably the best example of an international agency that has endeavored to increase and improve food production and ensure sustainable food production is the International Institute for Tropical Agriculture (IITA) which is based in Ibadan (Nigeria). Over the past twenty-five years, it has conducted valuable research for the agricultural development of Africa. IITA's research encompasses the soils, ecosystems, and social settings in which African farmers practice their traditional and mechanized agriculture. The institute's studies have provided essential and valuable findings that have been instrumental in limiting soil erosion, improving soil fertility, understanding the sort of appropriate technology that is suitable for African soils, and providing alternative methods to fallow cultivation—such as alley farming which is an agroforestry in which multipurpose trees are planted in rows while food crops are planted in "alleys" between the trees (Ajayi 1991:26).

Conclusion

The future development of Africa lies predominantly in the hands of Africans who have to be innovative in their approaches to economic development, industrial development, and environmental management. However, international efforts and assistance are already integral parts of Africa's future and should be understood. The efforts of the World Bank, African Development Bank, and the NGOs are essential in bringing about a framework that will enable African nations to participate fully in the global economy without destroying the environment. Development objectives should embrace conservation goals established by environmental departments (ministries) of each nation, and foreign assistance granted to countries must require environmental and social sensitivity so that political stability can be attained.

Industrialization will enable Africa to participate fully in global economic systems. The United Nations Industrial Development Organization has been instrumental in bringing some industrial activities to Africa. It should re-invigorate its efforts in coordination with the donor countries that are interested in investing in Africa. Efforts of organizations such as the International Labor Organization (ILO), International Tropical

Timber Organization (ITTO), United Nations Development Program (UNDP), World Commission on the Environment and Development (WCED), World Resources Institute (WRI), and Convention on International Trade in Endangered Species (CITES) must be continued in Africa in order to bring about a balanced development that takes the interests of Africans seriously and incorporates the participation of Africans in development agendas and projects.

Since development is evolutionary, one must ensure that sustainability of development is maintained so that the use of Africa's natural resources enhances economic investment in the continent and that institutional and technological change do not jeopardize the ecological, social, and political systems of the continent.

10. Women's Contribution to the Preservation of Africa's Resources

Introduction

The previous chapters have detailed human impact on the African environment. The historical interaction between man and the environment in Africa has been examined from theoretical and applied standpoints. African development threatens its environment. The recognition of the appropriateness of the development in Africa is the underlying theme of many of the chapters. The development of an agronomically, economically, and ecologically sound society in Africa must incorporate the significant contribution of women in all facets of planning.

In supporting the inclusion of women's role in the planning of phases of the utilization of Africa's resources one only needs to examine the work of women in African societies in order to come to the same conclusion as the author's. Women produce food and are engaged in many facets of African life, under sometimes impossible circumstances. On the farms and in the homes, it is the women who are responsible for the bulk of the work that is performed in order to meet the family's basic needs (Figures 10.1 through 10.6).

Women's potential is hindered by several factors which make it impossible for Africa to benefit fully from their contributions. The hindrances are as follows:

1. Maternal mortality continues to be a leading cause of death for African women, about 650 deaths per 100,000 live births. African women have an average of about 6.2 births per woman, the highest fertility rate in the world.

2. The illiteracy rate of African women is one of the highest in the world. Two-thirds of the women who are 25 years and older are illiterate. Education is the key to full utilization of African women's potential. Figure

235

Figure 10.1: Young girls returning home with buckets of water, Uyo, Nigeria, 1991.

Figure 10.2: Woman farmer going to her farm, Ikot-Ekpene, Nigeria, 1991.

Figure 10.3: Young mother and child, Eket, Nigeria, 1991.

Figure 10.4: Women traders, Lagos, Nigeria, 1991.

Figure 10.5: Young hawker of goods, Orile, Nigeria, 1991.

Figure 10.6: Club manager with "middle-class" friends, Eket, Nigeria, 1991.

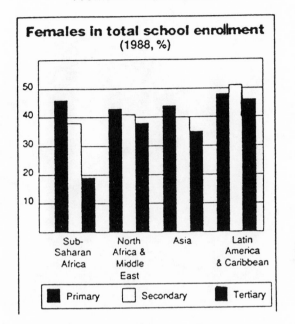

Source: *Africa Recovery,* September 1991, Vol. 5, nos. 2–3, p. 47.

Figure 10.7: Females in total school enrollment (1988, %).

10.7 shows that although Sub-Saharan Africa is doing well in primary education when compared to the other areas of the world, it is not doing well in the secondary and tertiary education of women. Some African governments such as Nigeria and Ghana are attempting new educational strategies to increase the education of women in post-primary school levels. Figure 10.8 shows the enthusiasm of secondary school girls of Uyo, Nigeria. State governments of Nigeria are playing active roles in education.

3. The third and probably the most devastating is the problem of Acquired Immune Deficiency Syndrome (AIDS). In some countries more than 40 percent of women between the ages of 30 and 39 have the disease, and many more are carriers of HIV disease. The repercussions of the disease are enormous for Africa's future. Agricultural production could reach the lowest levels in Africa by the year 2020 if the AIDS crisis is not dealt with through education and medical means.

Figure 10.9 shows the role of women in agriculture. Their role is economically, socially, and environmentally important to Africa's future.

African historical literature is replete with documentation of how women have contributed enormously to sustaining early societies. Alongside men and sometimes alone, women plough and cultivate the

Figure 10.8: Young Nigerian secondary-school students, Uyo, Nigeria, 1991.

agricultural savanna and forest lands of Africa. They are directly and indirectly involved in activities that affect the vegetation, soil, water, plant, and animal life forms, and other smaller ecological systems (subsystems) of Africa. Hence, to continue to perpetuate the marginalization of women in developmental strategies and policies is inappropriate, nonprogressive, and counterproductive.

History of Domination

The full potential of the African woman's contribution has not been realized due to several reasons. One of the reasons has been the historical domination of women by forces which seem to make their contribution secondary to the man's role in key decisions and in roles of implementation of planning ideas. This phenomenon of domination, although worldwide, seems to be more rigid in Africa than in the industrialized countries where women have succeeded in achieving some political equities. The achievements have been translated into visibility in many spheres of life such as industry, government, education, commerce, and business.

On the other hand, the African woman's place in African societies has been determined by the culture and later by slavery and colonialism. In pre-colonial Africa, before the slavery period, women played the role of

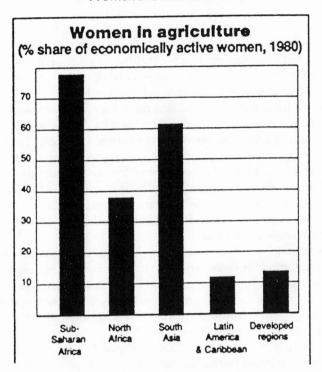

Women in agriculture
(% share of economically active women, 1980)

Source: *Africa Recovery*, September 1991, Vol. 5, nos. 2-3, p. 47.

Figure 10.9: Women in agriculture (% share of economically active women, 1980).

raising the family and engaging in subsistence agriculture. This period was the beginning of the sedentary African societies (after the hunter-gatherer age). The men ran the societies and conducted petty trading with other villages. The Yoruba, Ibo, Efik, Annang, Housa, and Ebibio of Nigeria represent groups that practiced this type of lifestyle.

Women and young girls fetched water and engaged in other household chores that exposed them to interaction with the natural systems of Africa. They were found at streams, lakes, rivers, forests, savannas, and deserts attempting to make nature produce the basic necessities for their existence.

In agriculture, the African woman with the assistance of her children plowed the land and produced the food necessary for the family. She also raised domesticated animals such as chickens and goats in the family compounds. The men provided assistance by clearing the land, and occasionally assisting in chores related to the domesticated animals.

This division of labor or the stratification of duties in African societies was denied the opportunity of gradual evolution into a more equitable society for men and women upon the arrival of the trans–Atlantic and trans–Saharan slave-trade. The emphasis of European and Arab slave trade was to take away the young, healthy, productive Africans, and as a result many societies in Africa were set back in their natural development. The African woman's place was further reduced to a secondary role by the slave-trade institution, making her subservient to the slave-traders.

Colonial rulers exacerbated this problem by dealing only with men in affairs of government and exploiting the natural resources. The establishment of large agricultural plantations for the production of cash crops in Africa initially involved able-bodied men for the difficult tasks, but eventually the women had to accompany their husbands to the plantations. The families became part of the "plantation cultures." They left the cultivation of their staple food crops for the work on the plantations which produced cash crops for Europe.

The African woman's role in development of African societies was heightened during the early periods of the discovery of minerals in Africa by the colonialists. Men were employed by the companies, and the women did not only have to take care of the homes but were responsible for agriculture and the future direction of the exploitation of the natural resources in their communities.

Upon independence in the 1950s, 1960s, and 1970s, African men continued the established institutions left by the colonialists. Today, it is not surprising that about 80 percent of the staple food (subsistence agriculture) is produced by women. Hence, the involvement of women's role is paramount to the conservation and preservation of Africa's natural resources.

Sustainable Development and the Role of Women

Before examining exactly how, why, when, and where women's efforts should be applied in the conservation and development of Africa's resources, it is important to reiterate that development strategies without a sound sustainability methodology are meaningless. Past efforts and development projects funded by national governments of Africa, international organizations, foreign governments, and donor agencies failed precisely because these projects lacked the necessary sustainable components of development. Essentially, sustainable development must have the following characteristics:

> 1. It should entail living on the country's income without destroying the country's natural resource capital.
> 2. It should ensure future generations' ability to meet their needs while allowing today's generation the opportunity to have a progressive existence.

3. The long-range development goals and objectives of a country must be met by blending a set of management techniques that would enhance balancing human needs with the ecological equilibrium.

These characteristics are important aspects of sustainability, which is defined by the World Commission on Environment and Development (1987) as "a process of change in which the exploitation of resources, the direction of investments, the orientation of technological development, and the institutional change are all in harmony and enhance both current and future potential to meet human needs and aspirations."

African women have demonstrated their ability as good custodians of the African environment. African history supports this argument. Their ability to raise their children and to provide the urban and rural communities of Africa with most of the necessary food are proofs of their capability. However, in light of the exponential population increase in Africa, women and men must recognize the significance of family planning. The challenge in searching for sustainable development paths includes limiting the number of individuals making demands on the limited resources of Africa. Certainly family planning must be part of the process for sustainable development. It is the conviction of this author, based on conversations with African women and men (in Africa and abroad), that there is a resistance to the use of contraception in Africa. The affordability of contraceptive devices coupled with religion (Islam and Catholicism) makes family planning efforts very difficult. Nonetheless, the path for sustaining Africa's future is clear — population must be controlled.

Education of both rural and urban women on the necessity of small families, the depletion of natural resources, widespread desertification, species loss, deforestation, malnutrition, and hunger in Africa is very important. But it is also imperative that the education of men be emphasized in all sectors of life. The old belief in the large number of progeny in Africa has to be cast away because the new era in Africa does not demand such large numbers of offspring. If the quality of life is to be improved in Africa, then emphasis must be placed on limiting the population by making men understand that large numbers of children do not translate into or equal wealth as was believed in the past. Rather, such a condition perpetuates poverty, misery, and the degradation of the environment. Educating women will also empower them to engage in activities which could engender sustainable development. For instance, educated women could ensure that existing institutions facilitate sustainable projects and that institutions that are not indicating profit or progress in addressing human needs are made more responsible or eliminated.

Mrs. Maryam Babangida (first lady of Nigeria) and Professor Wangari Maathai are excellent examples of women who are attempting to improve the position of women in African societies and by so doing improving the environmental conditions of Africa. Professor Maathai is an environmentalist who founded the Green Belt Movement in Kenya and galvanized grassroots efforts to stop haphazard development in Kenya. Such development would have destroyed the Uhuru Park which is considered Nairobi's most popular park (*West Africa* 1991a).

Mrs. Babangida has been attempting to empower women to play significant roles in the development of their communities. She has been responsible for several seminars which involved the wives of other African heads of state to investigate avenues for eradicating hunger and poverty from Africa. Mrs. Babangida's and Professor Maathai's efforts earned them the 1991 Africa Prize for Leadership for Sustainable End of Hunger. If Africa is to recover, women must play significant roles in the environmental conservation movement.

Table 10.1 shows the statistics on African women and men with respect to mortality rate, life expectancy, and education. Although the life expectancy for women is greater than that of men in virtually all African countries, fewer women receive primary and secondary education. Although Table 10.1 does not show data for post-secondary education, it is statistically safe to claim that there are fewer women receiving university educations in Africa. The woman's role is predominantly relegated to having children and in the rural areas of Africa engaging in some form of agricultural practice.

Akakpo (1992:412–13) argues that some cultural practices have worked against women's advancement in some African countries. But she makes the point of indicating that the traditions and customs are influenced and reenforced by religious practices, government policies, and domestic and international economic dynamics. Poor economic conditions usually affect women the most since their interests are lower on the priority scale of the government. Ayisi (1991:60–63) bemoans the African women's plight when she claims that besides the obstacles of war and poverty which limit women's advancement, chauvinistic attitudes exacerbate the problem of nonadvancement of women in African societies. Ayisi describes the development situation in Mozambique and Zambia as geared toward excluding women in planning meetings or workshops. This type of behavior is discouraging and demoralizing to the women. She describes women's obstacles in the following way:

> Marriage is one option open to young women. In the predominantly Muslim Nampula province, many girls marry and have children in their early teens. Polygamy is common. A man can find it difficult or impossible to support one wife and his children in Mozambique, one of the poorest countries in the world, not to mention two or more wives. Sometimes, a woman can be left alone to fend for herself and the children.

An indicator of women's status in Mozambique is the maternal mortality rate — one of the highest in the world. Some estimates of mothers dying from infections and other preventable illnesses are as high as 250 per 100,000 live births.

The need for a women's program within the union became apparent when at one of the meetings two years ago called by Rhoda Leceister, a Zambian agriculturalist, 45 men and no women turned out. "I was the only woman," said Leceister. "I had been noticing before that the women weren't seen equally."

To find out why women were not present at the meeting and to understand the lives of the women, Leceister conducted interviews with both men and women. The men's views differed a little but most seemed unsure about women's role in the cooperatives. "Some felt women should be farming only the family plot and working at home, looking after the children," said Leceister. "Others said that women should not talk directly to men."

The position or status of women is changing very slowly. They must be partners in the developmental process; they are at the center of the African crisis. They are at the beginning of the crisis and are the recipients of the worst situations and through it all, they have been responsible for many of Africa's successes.

Tables 10.2a and 10.2b show the amount of forest and water resources in some African countries. They indicate the annual deforestation between 1981 and 1985. In order to reverse the trend of forest destruction in Africa, women must play significant roles in the sustainable use of the natural resources. At the current rate of use, it is most likely that environmental degradation will continue to occur at an alarming rate. Agriculturally, cash-crop production has exacerbated the poor welfare of women. By today's world economic standards, cash crop production has not solved Africa's economic problems. The living standards of Africans have not improved for the majority of the people. In many instances, as was previously alluded to in an earlier chapter, the establishment of plantations resulted in the displacement of many women from their small farms, while others had to follow their husbands. Displacement of women from their former farmlands often resulted in the clearing of new forest lands for agriculture, and, ultimately, environmental degradation ensued.

The Environment and Women

Images of famine in Africa often portray the suffering of children and women. In the midst of the suffering, images indicate the warmth and affection between the children and their mothers. The burden of African women is enormous because with the ever-deteriorating economic condi-

Table 10.1: African Women in Development

	Under 5 mortality rate (per 1,000 live births)		Health and Welfare Life expectancy at birth (years)				Maternal mortality (per 100,000 live births)
	Female 1989	Male 1989	Female 1965	1989	Male 1965	1989	1980
1. Algeria	87	95	51	66	49	64	129
2. Angola	211	234	37	47	34	44	—
3. Benin	154	173	43	53	41	49	1,680
4. Botswana	42	55	49	69	46	65	300
5. Burkina Faso	190	210	40	49	37	46	600
6. Burundi	102	118	45	51	42	48	—
7. Cameroon	119	136	47	59	44	55	303
8. Cape Verde	—	—	—	—	—	—	—
9. Central Afr. Rep.	154	173	41	52	40	49	600
10. Chad	203	225	38	48	35	45	700
11. Comoros	—	—	—	—	—	—	—
12. Congo, People's R.	170	183	47	57	41	51	—
13. Côte d'Ivoire	141	159	44	55	40	51	—
14. Djibouti	—	—	—	—	—	—	—
15. Egypt, A.R.	99	114	50	61	48	59	500
16. Equatorial Guinea	—	—	—	—	—	—	—
17. Ethiopia	188	208	43	49	42	46	2,000
18. Gabon	151	171	44	55	41	51	124
19. The Gambia	—	—	—	—	—	—	—
20. Ghana	130	148	49	56	46	53	1,070
21. Guinea	224	249	36	44	34	43	—
22. Guinea-Bissau	—	—	—	—	—	—	—
23. Kenya	98	114	50	61	46	57	510
24. Lesotho	128	146	50	58	47	54	—
25. Liberia	170	195	46	55	43	53	173
26. Libya	88	104	51	64	48	60	—
27. Madagascar	162	180	45	52	42	50	300
28. Malawi	237	251	40	48	38	47	250
29. Mali	210	239	39	49	37	46	—
30. Mauritania	196	218	39	48	36	45	119
31. Mauritius	21	30	63	72	59	67	99
32. Morocco	87	103	51	63	48	60	327
33. Mozambique	193	214	39	50	36	47	479
34. Namibia	121	141	47	59	44	56	—
35. Niger	208	231	38	47	35	43	420
36. Nigeria	155	174	43	54	40	49	1,500
37. Rwanda	188	209	45	51	42	47	210
38. Senegal	123	140	42	50	40	47	530
39. Sierra Leone	239	264	34	44	31	40	450
40. Somalia	204	227	40	49	37	46	1,100
41. South Africa	85	100	54	65	49	58	550
42. Sudan	161	181	41	52	39	49	607
43. Swaziland	—	—	—	—	—	—	—
44. Tanzania	176	197	45	51	41	47	370
45. Togo	136	154	44	55	40	52	476
46. Tunisia	53	66	52	67	51	66	1,000
47. Uganda	151	171	47	50	44	47	300
48. Zaire	143	161	45	54	42	51	800
49. Zambia	112	128	46	56	43	52	110
50. Zimbabwe	60	72	50	66	46	62	150

Source: Adapted from World Bank, 1991, pp. 266–67.

Table 10.1: (cont.)

Education

% of cohort persisting to grade 4				Females per 100 males			
Female		Male		Primary		Secondary	
1970	1984	1970	1984	1965	1988	1965	1988
90	—	95	—	62	80	45	76
—	—	—	—	—	—	89	—
59	64	67	63	44	51	44	39
97	95	90	95	129	107	77	103
71	84	68	82	48	59	27	46
47	84	45	84	42	75	10	52
59	85	58	86	66	85	28	64
—	—	—	—	—	—	—	—
67	67	67	74	34	62	19	40
—	—	—	—	23	40	6	18
—	—	—	—	—	—	—	—
86	82	89	89	71	95	29	76
77	82	83	83	51	—	19	44
—	—	—	—	—	—	—	—
85	—	93	—	64	75	41	68
—	—	—	—	—	—	—	—
57	45	56	50	38	64	28	67
73	80	78	78	84	98	39	81
—	—	—	—	—	—	—	—
77	—	82	—	71	80	34	66
—	62	—	67	—	45	19	31
—	—	—	—	—	—	—	—
84	75	84	73	57	94	38	70
87	86	70	75	157	125	100	153
—	—	—	—	—	—	33	—
92	—	95	—	39	—	13	—
65	—	63	—	83	95	64	94
55	64	60	65	—	80	40	60
52	68	89	75	49	59	30	42
—	91	—	96	31	70	11	44
97	99	97	99	90	88	53	97
78	77	83	79	42	63	31	66
—	—	—	—	—	78	85	54
—	—	—	—	—	—	—	—
75	76	74	88	46	56	19	42
64	—	66	—	63	—	43	—
63	82	65	81	69	97	37	35
—	88	—	92	57	69	35	51
—	—	—	—	55	—	37	—
46	59	51	65	27	—	11	—
—	—	—	—	—	—	—	—
—	81	—	80	55	—	30	—
—	—	—	—	—	—	—	—
82	88	88	89	60	99	33	54
85	77	88	70	42	63	26	32
—	90	—	94	52	82	37	74
—	—	—	—	—	82	30	54
56	—	65	—	48	78	15	—
93	97	99	—	78	90	39	—
74	87	80	87	—	95	—	88

Table 10.2a: Forests, Protected Areas, and Water

	Forest area (1,000s of square kms)		Protected land areas			
	Total area 1980 Total:Closed		Annual deforestation 1981–85 Total:Closed		Area (thousands of square kms)	As a percentage of total land area
					Number	
1. Algeria	18	15	0.40	–	4.97	17	0.2
2. Angola	536	29	0.94	0.44	8.90	3	0.7
3. Benin	39	0	0.67	0.01	8.44	2	7.6
4. Botswana	326	0	0.20	–	100.25	9	17.7
5. Burkina Faso	47	3	0.08	0.03	7.39	7	2.7
6. Burundi	0	0	0.01	0.01	0.00	0	0.0
7. Cameroon	233	165	1.90	1.00	17.02	12	3.6
8. Cape Verde	–	–	–	–	–	–	–
9. Central Afr. R.	359	36	0.55	0.05	39.04	7	6.3
10. Chad	135	5	0.80	–	1.14	1	0.1
11. Comoros	–	–	–	–	–	–	–
12. Congo, Peo. Rep.	213	213	0.22	0.22	13.53	10	4.0
13. Côte d'Ivoire	98	45	5.10	2.90	19.58	10	6.2
14. Djibouti	–	–	–	–	–	–	–
15. Egypt, Arab Rep.	0	0	–	–	6.85	9	0.7
16. Eq. Guinea	–	–	–	–	–	–	–
17. Ethiopia	272	44	0.88	0.08	68.73	25	6.2
18. Gabon	206	205	0.15	0.15	17.53	6	6.8
19. The Gambia	–	–	–	–	–	–	–
20. Ghana	87	17	0.72	0.22	11.75	8	5.1
21. Guinea	107	21	0.86	0.36	0.13	1	0.1
22. Guinea-Bissau	–	–	–	–	–	–	–
23. Kenya	24	11	0.39	0.19	30.95	30	5.4
24. Lesotho	0	0	–	–	0.07	1	0.2
25. Liberia	20	20	0.46	0.46	1.31	1	1.4
26. Libya	2	1	–	–	1.55	3	0.1
27. Madagascar	132	103	1.56	1.50	10.31	31	1.8
28. Malawi	43	2	1.50	–	10.67	9	11.3
29. Mali	73	5	0.36	–	8.76	6	0.7
30. Mauritania	6	0	0.13	0.01	14.83	2	1.4
31. Mauritius	0	0	0.00	0.00	0.04	1	2.0
32. Morocco	32	15	0.13	–	2.98	10	0.7
33. Mozambique	154	9	1.20	0.10	0.00	0	0.0
34. Namibia	184	–	0.30	–	–	–	–
35. Niger	26	1	0.67	0.03	16.54	4	1.3
36. Nigeria	148	60	4.00	3.00	9.60	4	1.1
37. Rwanda	2	1	0.05	0.03	2.62	2	10.5
38. Senegal	110	2	0.50	–	21.77	9	11.3
39. Sierra Leone	21	7	0.60	0.06	1.01	3	1.4
40. Somalia	91	15	0.14	0.04	0.00	0	0.0
41. South Africa	3	3	–	–	58.02	152	4.8
42. Sudan	477	7	5.04	0.04	81.16	13	3.4
43. Swaziland	–	–	–	–	–	–	–
44. Tanzania	420	14	1.30	0.40	119.13	20	13.4
45. Togo	17	3	0.12	0.02	4.63	6	8.5
46. Tunisia	3	2	0.05	–	0.45	6	0.3
47. Uganda	60	8	0.50	0.10	13.32	18	6.7
48. Zaire	1,776	1,058	3.70	1.82	88.27	9	3.9
49. Zambia	295	30	0.70	0.40	63.59	19	8.6
50. Zimbabwe	198	2	0.80	0.00	27.60	19	7.1

Source: Adapted from World Bank, 1991, pp. 268–69.

Table 10.2b: Forests, Protected Areas, and Water

	Total (cubic kms)	Internal renewable water resources annual withdrawal (1970-87)			
		As a percentage of total water resources	Per capita (cubic meters)		Industrial and agricultural
			Total	Domestic	
1. Algeria	3.00	16	161	35	125
2. Angola	0.48	0	43	6	37
3. Benin	0.11	0	26	7	19
4. Botswana	0.09	1	98	5	93
5. Burkina Faso	0.15	1	20	6	14
6. Burundi	0.10	3	20	7	13
7. Cameroon	0.40	0	30	14	16
8. Cape Verde	—	—	—	—	—
9. Central African Rep.	0.07	0	27	6	21
10. Chad	0.18	0	35	6	29
11. Comoros	—	—	—	—	—
12. Congo, People's Rep.	0.04	0	20	12	8
13. Côte d'Ivoire	0.71	1	68	15	53
14. Djibouti	—	—	—	—	—
15. Egypt, Arab Rep.	56.40	97	1,202	84	1,118
16. Eq. Guinea	—	—	—	—	—
17. Ethiopia	2.21	2	48	5	43
18. Gabon	0.06	0	51	37	14
19. The Gambia	—	—	—	—	—
20. Ghana	0.30	1	35	12	23
21. Guinea	0.74	0	115	12	104
22. Guinea-Bissau	—	—	—	—	—
23. Kenya	1.09	7	48	13	35
24. Lesotho	0.05	1	34	7	27
25. Liberia	0.13	0	54	15	39
26. Libya	2.62	374	262	39	222
27. Madagascar	16.30	41	1,675	17	1,658
28. Malawi	0.16	2	22	7	15
29. Mali	1.36	2	159	3	156
30. Mauritania	0.73	10	473	57	417
31. Mauritius	0.36	16	415	66	348
32. Morocco	11.00	37	501	30	471
33. Mozambique	0.76	1	53	13	40
34. Namibia	0.14	2	77	5	72
35. Niger	0.29	1	44	9	35
36. Nigeria	3.63	1	4	14	30
37. Rwanda	0.15	2	23	6	17
38. Senegal	1.36	4	201	10	191
39. Sierra Leone	0.37	0	99	7	92
40. Somalia	0.81	7	167	5	162
41. South Africa	9.20	18	404	65	340
42. Sudan	18.60	14	1,089	11	1,079
43. Swaziland	—	—	—	—	—
44. Tanzania	0.48	1	36	7	28
45. Togo	0.09	1	40	25	15
46. Tunisia	2.30	53	325	42	283
47. Uganda	0.20	0	20	7	14
48. Zaire	0.70	0	22	13	9
49. Zambia	0.36	0	86	54	32
50. Zimbabwe	1.22	5	129	18	111

Source: Adapted from World Bank, 1991, pp. 268-69.

tions, they continue to bear more and more responsibilities in taking care of the children and farming.

As the major providers for the family, rural women are in charge of securing food, firewood, and water. As a large number of women continue to cultivate the land for subsistence purposes by utilizing agricultural practices that leave little time for the land to rejuvenate, environmental degradation sets in. The collecting of firewood, which is the major source of energy for domestic cooking, by rural women adds to environmental problems. In obtaining the firewood, trees are cut down with the help of men. In many urban settings the energy source is still firewood, and as a result, there is a tremendous decline in the savanna and forest trees. The destruction of the savannas and forests sets up a chain of environmental degradation which has already been discussed in an earlier chapter. But it should be pointed out that the poor people of Africa who depend on the natural system for their sustenance are the ones who are most affected. Women and children form a majority of this group. They are the victims of environmental degradation. There is no doubt that the depletion of African forests, the impact of mechanized agriculture, and water pollution have increased the African woman's burden.

Women and Aid

Sustainable development would be possible in Africa if and when governments and organizations put emphasis on assisting all segments of the African population in the development strategy. It behooves everyone to recognize the importance of the role of African women in conservation and preservation. Women are responsible for gathering firewood which often demands travelling long distances to carry heavy loads of firewood. In some parts of Africa, such as the Sahel region, women carry approximately 30 to 38 kilograms of firewood from three to six miles. Not only does cutting the branches of trees and in some cases the trees destroy the ecological system, but the burden of long distances and heavy loads is much too taxing on the women. Hence, aid to African countries for sustainable development must target rural women. Alternative sources of energy would help these women tremendously, but they must be able to engage in other activities which can diversify and strengthen their capabilities. They must be executives, educators, nurses, doctors, and resource managers walking side by side with men (Figures 10.10 and 10.11).

The first step would be for donor agencies to require full participation of women at the grassroots of projects. The United States Agency for International Development has already begun this by requiring local participation in development programs. Another aspect which will assist women

Figure 10.10: Nigerian women, educator and nurse, with a male engineer, Benin City, Nigeria, 1991.

Figure 10.11: Nigerian woman enjoys the calmness of Lekki Beach, Nigeria, 1991.

to undertake full participation in Africa's development and thus assist in conservation is to remove the barriers which have restricted women from obtaining credit or gaining access to credit. The United Nations Economic Commission for Africa and African Training and Research Center for Women UNECA/ATRCW (1990:6) claims the impediments confronting African women in their efforts to fully participate in development areas such as agriculture extension services and technology are as follows:

1. Social customs that restrict women's ability to deal with credit officials.
2. The nature and type of credit programs whose size and repayment schedules are not suitable to women's activities, and outlook.
3. The westernized nature of formal credit institutions which, as a function of their origin, conceptualization, and method of operation, render almost all rural and urban poor women ineligible for credit.
4. The non-availability to many women of the time and skills necessary for loan negotiations.
5. The lack of collateral, as the majority of women do not have title to land or other property.
6. Legal restrictions which in some cases require that the husband must co-sign for the loan.
7. Bureaucracy on the part of the lending officers who are usually prejudiced.

These hurdles need to be overcome and dealt with swiftly for there to be true progress for sustainability. Loans could enable women to step up the progress in domestic technology in order to process the agricultural produce they have in their farms. The processing of staple foods will relieve women of the burden of having to process the food by hand. Research should then focus on improving rural technology and methods of assisting women to become more efficient in their production techniques. Above all, biases must be eradicated in terms of what emphasis research attention should be focused on. Traditionally, research has been focused on cash crops, and food crops, which are the main responsibility of women, have not received enough attention. The International Institute of Tropical Agriculture in Nigeria and other similar research agencies have made some attempt to improve the variety of subsistence crops.

Abramovitz and Nichols (1992:86), in examining the role of women in preserving biodiversity, posed some interesting questions which seem appropriate to this chapter:

1. How do women interact with their surroundings?
2. What unique knowledge about local species and ecosystems do they gain from these interactions?
3. And how can this knowledge be tapped to better effect?
4. What structures and policies restrict and undervalue women, and

how can these be changed so that sustainable development efforts will have a better chance of succeeding?

5. How do these realities alter the way in which conservation and sustainable development should be pursued?

As the author has already pointed out in another section of this chapter, the history of African women shows how they have worked with men and in other cases alone in using their immediate environment. Hence they are a wealth of resource with regard to the knowledge of the environment. They have a unique understanding of species endemic to their environment and how to use them for medicinal purposes. However, policies established by governments dominated by men make it impossible to make their knowledge available to a large majority of the society. Thus effort should be made to include rural women in the planning and conservation endeavors conducted at local levels in rural areas. This point has already been made, but it must be reiterated here because of the significance of women in conservation and sustainable development in Africa.

Women influence all aspects of African life, and their work traverses all spheres of economic development. In the agricultural sector, their tremendous efforts in providing more than 85 percent of the labor necessary are noteworthy. Women are involved in providing assistance in all the phases of farming operations. In commenting about the women's role in the traditional system of the Segou Region of Mali, Thiam (1985:73) makes the following observations:

1. *Gathering.* The women gather leaves and fruits (sorrel, *gombo* (okra), *dah* fibers, bean leaves, baobab leaves, karite nuts, wild grapes, vines, monkey bread, *nere*, etc.).

2. *Processing.* They process the agricultural products and the plants they have gathered into beer *(dolo)*, doughnuts, flatcakes, dried gombo, *soumbala* (a condiment which is used as a powder in sauces, and is similar to curry), karite butter, and native soap.

3. *Cotton processing.* They spin cotton to make clothing for the entire family.

4. *Market gardening.* They farm small kitchen gardens which produce onions, tomatoes, sweet potatoes, manioc, pepper, beans gombo, and other condiments. At Bambougou, they also farm tobacco along the riverbank.

5. *Livestock.* The women raise poultry and small grazing animals always for the purpose of meeting family expenses if the need arises.

6. *Crafts.* The wives of blacksmiths are potters. Natural and indigo dyeing processes are practiced by low castes. Basket weaving is a feminine art, whereas cloth weaving, tool making, sewing, and embroidery are done by men.

7. *Commerce.* The women work in small-scale commercial activities: the sale of surplus food (grain, processed food, fresh garden products, drinks, and cotton goods — from cotton which they have spun themselves).

It is obvious that because of the significant position of women in the development of Africa, they should and must be given access, incentives, and encouragement to continue to assist in the sustainability of Africa's natural, economic, and social systems.

Women and Biodiversity

The subject of aid to Africa represents a trajectory of complex concepts because of experiences and differing opinions surrounding the subject. But it is noteworthy to mention that since colonial structures reenforced the downgrading of women's status in Africa, foreign assistance in terms of technical training, education, opportunity, and research must help to improve the status of women in all spheres of human endeavors. Aid must encourage technical expertise for women so that they can play significant roles in the conservation of Africa's resources. By so doing, the aid that is given to African countries by foreign governments and agencies and nongovernmental organizations must have as a "line item" a designated amount for women's assistance. The assistance should enable rural women to acquire land by buying the acreage necessary for cultivation. African governments can assist in this regard by having land reforms that would make it possible for women to acquire land. Another area where African governments can use international aid to assist women is in settlement projects. The establishment of settlement schemes can enable African countries to diversify the economic base and strengthen institutions. Such a scheme was established in Nigeria in 1959. The Ilora farm settlement project was established in the former western Nigeria which comprises a number of states. Due to the fact that the government of Nigeria has been creating new states in the last decade, the names of the states may change given the political nature of the country. Suffice it to say that there are at least five states involved. The goals of the settlement were to:

1. Attract educated young people into viable farming units as an alternative to urban living.
2. Demonstrate that carefully planned farming systems can be satisfying and lucrative.
3. Raise agricultural production to supply the growing population of the country as well as to maintain exportable products (Spiro 1985:XI).

This type of project can help to focus and train young women alongside men so that they can be equal partners in agricultural practices and have technical skills and education necessary to sustain Africa's environment. Since this type of project is usually multipurpose, not only can young girls acquire skills as productive farmers but their participation in settlement projects will also enable them to obtain modern production skills, such as the use of equipment and fertilizers, processing, and marketing of crops. Trained women will enhance the sustainability of the surrounding environment and discourage haphazard agricultural development. The ecological balance of the community is not disturbed by the planned, self-contained community.

Impacts of Structural Adjustment Programs on Women

The Structural Adjustment Program (SAP) is a recent development which was supposed to bring African countries' economies into a competitive platform with the Western industrialized countries, stimulate investment, allocate Africa's resources more equitably between the urban and rural areas, and make development more sustainable. The SAP's major thrust was meant to stimulate agricultural production in the rural communities and enhance the substitution of goods manufactured in Africa for goods produced in industrialized countries. Hence those in Africa who produce export goods were to profit from their efforts while those who were major importers were to be discouraged since their endeavors would not be profitable. Unfortunately, this was not the result. SAPs have not helped either the urban dwellers or the rural farmers (the majority of which are women). Rural women farmers have had difficulties making ends meet because of the devaluation of local currencies brought about as a result of the implementation of SAPs. The escalating cost of living has made agricultural practice difficult. Although the produce from the farms costs more, women farmers have not benefited at all. The SAP was supposed to redistribute wealth from the urban to the rural parts of Africa. Unfortunately discussions with people in urban and rural parts of Nigeria, Ghana, Sierra Leone, and Liberia seem to indicate that the majority of people in both the urban and rural parts of these countries are having great economic problems. The SAP was supposed to encourage production of food crops at affordable prices, but it appears that this is not the case in Africa. The price of food commodities has been escalating, and the environmental decline has been increasing at a rapid pace. Women farmers in Africa, as well as men, are not producing as much as they should be due to the bad economic climate.

Conservation and Women

When one examines the literature on the conservation of wildlife in Africa, very little is discussed about the role of women. It is often forgotten that the conservation of wildlife is possible because women play important supporting roles which are usually not given enough credit. Conservation cannot succeed in Africa without the support and full participation of women who are closest to the natural resources in rural areas. They understand the ecological system because they have always used it to sustain their families. The sustainability of the diversity of Africa's environment and ecological systems is dependent upon women's tender care. Women are the caretakers of nature.

African civil wars have been devastating to the wildlife population and have had a negative impact on the tourism industry. Decades of civil strife often leave their impact by destroying the wildlife species and the habitats upon which they exist. For example, prior to its independence, Zimbabwe (formerly Rhodesia) had decades of unrest and seven years of actual fighting. The war had an impact on the parks (which encompass one-eighth of the country), which are the habitats for hundreds of elephants, impalas, lions, and giraffes. Park rangers (wardens) were attacked, and several were killed. Research stations in the parks of Zimbabwe were completely destroyed, and the results of years of intensive research for wildlife management were lost. Poaching practices increased, and tourism to the parks declined sharply, causing the country to lose millions of dollars in revenue. At the peak of tourism in 1972, it was reported that the number of tourists that visited Zimbabwean parks was 500,000 (Pitman 1983). After the war, government efforts have led to the gradual increase in the number of wildlife. Since the potential annual income from wildlife recreation is estimated to be about $US80 million per year, it behooves all Zimbabweans and the government to protect the wildlife and have good management practices that would ensure the existence of the wildlife in perpetuity.

The wars of Africa have always been very devastating to women. Young women fight in the wars, and older women still have to support their families while their husbands are in the battlefields. What is needed during the stable periods in African countries is full participation of women in the conservation strategies and plans. This is important because in Western industrialized societies, the success of the conservation and preservation movement is in part due to the participation of women, although some may argue that women's participation is token. Nonetheless, women of industrialized societies have the skills and education necessary to demand full participation. It is argued here that African women can adapt to new situations to engage in the management of wildlife. If Jane Goodall could work with gorillas, Alison Jolly with lemurs, and Kes Hillman with rhinos, African women could do the same. They have proven their ability by providing most of the labor needed for agriculture in Africa south of the Sahara.

Table 10.3: Elephant Numbers: Regions and Selected Countries

	1981a/Total	1989b/Total
Central Africa:		
Chad	NA	2,100
Central Afr. Rep.	31,000	23,000
Congo	10,800	42,000
Equatorial Guinea	NA	500
Gabon	13,400	74,000
Zaire	376,000	112,000
Central Africa Total	436,200	277,000
East Africa:		
Ethiopia	NA	8,000
Kenya	65,000	16,000
Rwanda	150	50
Somalia	24,300	2,000
Sudan	133,000	22,000
Tanzania	203,900	61,000
Uganda	2,300	1,600
East Africa Total	429,500	110,000
Southern Africa:		
Angola	12,400	18,000
Botswana	20,000	68,000
Malawi	4,500	2,800
Mozambique	54,800	17,000
Namibia	2,300	32,000
South Africa	8,000	7,800
Zambia	160,000	32,000
Zimbabwe	47,000	52,000
Southern Africa Total	309,000	204,000
West Africa:		
Benin	1,250	2,100
Burkina Faso	NA	4,500
Ghana	970	2,800
Guinea	800	560
Guinea Bissau	NA	40
Ivory Coast	4,800	3,600
Liberia	2,000	1,300
Mali	780	840
Mauritania	40	100
Niger	800	440
Nigeria	1,820	1,300
Senegal	200	140
Sierra Leone	500	380
Togo	150	380
West Africa Total	17,600	15,700
Africa Total	1,192,300	622,700

NA = not available
a) UNEP/IUCN/WWF, *Elephants and Rhinos in Africa — A Time for Decision,* 1982. Based on findings and recommendations of the African Elephant and Rhino Specialist Group. b) Recent estimates (October 1989) from Ian Douglas-Hamilton of the African Elephant and Rhino Specialist Group.
Source: Adapted from Barbier et al., 1990, p. 2.

Estimates indicate that there are about 13,500 to 19,000 rhinos remaining in Africa. The number of elephants has been declining in many African countries due to poaching. Only South Africa, Zimbabwe, and one or two other countries in Southern Africa have shown significant increases in the last year. Table 10.3 shows the population of elephants in African countries for 1981 and 1989.

Women, as they have done for centuries, can continue to assist men in the governments' objectives to manage the natural resources properly. Past traditions and customs that have not fully utilized women in decision making and key conservation positions must not be allowed to persist. The wildlife of Africa would prosper and Africa would prosper from women's impact. After all, the central issue in conservation is economics.

Conclusion

Involving women in the conservation of wildlife in Africa will be nothing new. The education of large numbers of rural women with conservation techniques will strengthen already established institutions and will open up new avenues for the creation of new institutions that will incorporate technological and scientific methods with the enormous traditional knowledge which a large majority of the rural indigenous people already possess.

The conservation of fauna would be of tremendous significance to African people, and in this regard, women have a great deal of knowledge. With successful programs, traditional and modern pharmaceutical benefits can be derived. It should be emphasized that African women need the incentives and encouragement of both their own governments and international communities. The assistance must target rural and urban communities and should be long-range and comprehensive. Only then can sustainability in its true meaning be realized.

11. Conclusions and Recommendations for Planning and Management

> The maintenance and development of the human habitat requires that some areas be retained in their wild state. The quality of water, the maintenance of genetic materials, the protection of scenic and aesthetic areas and the opportunity to enjoy and appreciate natural heritage, all depend upon the conservation of natural areas [IUCN 1985:4].

This book is about the sustainability of Africa's ecological systems. The reader by now is quite aware of the threat to the forests, savannas, rivers, estuaries, wetlands, soil, and the air in Africa. The demand and industrialization threaten these resources. It thus behooves all concerned about the interest of Africa and Africans to work together to achieve a future for Africa that removes dependency on the rest of the world.

There are several key issues that must be adequately addressed in order for progress to be achieved in Africa. The main problem confronting many African countries in the last three decades is the problem of debt repayment to foreign banks and industrialized countries. This has always led to the devaluation of local currency and an unnecessary exploitation of natural resources. More recently, structural adjustment programs have been taking place in many African countries such as Nigeria, Ghana, and a host of others. The aim is to bring the African economies more in line with the economies of the rest of the world. Some African leaders and scholars have argued that structural adjustment programs have brought a great deal of hardship to their people. It is the opinion of this author that better and effective policies are critically needed.

Objectives and Policies for Development

Many of Africa's environmental problems are spreading from the rural areas into the urban setting, and so it is argued in this section that in order to foster an orderly expansion of urban centers throughout the intensive growth corridors of many of Africa's regions, two basic policies need to be incorporated into the development plan:

> 1. Intensive urban development should only occur within intensive growth corridors where adequate services and facilities can be supplied. This strategy will eliminate unnecessary destruction of the forest and savanna areas that ought to be preserved.
> 2. A high level of community facilities and services should be provided within intensive growth corridors, consistent with the patterns, trends, and needs of development of the particular African country.

As was mentioned in an earlier chapter, housing is a major issue in Africa. Homelessness is a growing phenomenon in the continent. This problem is especially exacerbated by the burgeoning refugee situation in some African countries. The forest is being cleared for shelter, and squatter settlements are growing in large proportion. Hence one of the objectives of African countries must be to encourage patterns of residential development which allow necessary public and community services to be provided as efficiently as possible. In order to achieve this objective new residential development should not contribute to shanty development, urban sprawl, or a scattered pattern of urban development (Figures 11.1, 11.2, 11.3, and 11.4). New residential development should be designed and located where the provision of adequate public and community services is feasible and where such development will not overload water and other services.

High-density residential development to help curb the housing shortage must be within intensive growth corridors (Figure 11.5). Large new residential developments and high-density dwelling types should be located only within intensive growth corridors with good accessibility to major highways or public transportation service. One of the important aspects of planning is to guide growth in an orderly fashion. It is thus suggested that major public services in Africa should be constructed to encourage development within defined growth corridors.

Commercial and industrial development should also be concentrated in intensive growth corridors of countries. Such developments will foster the development that is bound to be in equilibrium with the environment.

In several places in this book, the significance of parks, reserves, and forests to the people of Africa and the world at large has been stressed. It is imperative in many African countries blessed with wildlife and forests to promote the public provision and protection of large areas of permanent open space and forests between regions of intensive growth corridors. Such protected areas are important, because during the past 160 years the African lands have been plowed, marshes have been drained, and forests

Figure 11.1: Shanty development, Lagos suburb, Nigeria, 1989.

Figure 11.2: Shanty housing and business establishments, Lagos suburb, Nigeria, 1989.

Figure 11.3: Scattered public housing, Lagos, Nigeria, 1991.

Figure 11.4: Poorly planned housing development, Lagos, Nigeria, 1991.

Figure 11.5: Modern public high-rise building, Victoria Island, Nigeria, 1991.

cut for homes, factories, and highways. With increases in population and advances in technology, the pace of human activities in Africa has changed the landscape. Only a few natural communities of wild plants and animals still remain as they have existed, undisturbed through the ages. Public open space should be utilized to protect those areas adjacent to intensive growth corridors which are most in danger of encroachment of urban development. The public open spaces should be located where they will enhance the scenic qualities of the region and contribute to an aesthetically pleasing pattern of urban development.

One of the problems confronting Africa is the loss of prime agricultural land, and policies to encourage preservation should be put in place. Land outside the intensive growth corridors with soils most suited for intensive cropping use should be protected and preserved for agricultural use. Incompatible urban intrusions must be discouraged, and urbanization of lands currently in agricultural use should be allowed only in a progressive and orderly manner. All attempts should be made to preserve agricultural land.

One of the issues raised in Chapter 9 of this book is the lack of, or poor, industrial development in Africa (excluding the Republic of South Africa). In an attempt to industrialize, haphazard development must be avoided at all costs. Each country should ensure that an adequate number of locations suitable for industry should be provided, and such sites should be preserved for future industrial needs. Moreover, new and planned industrial developments should be of a scale and intensity which permits for an orderly expansion of services and utilities. Local, state, and national governments must give incentives to existing industrial developments which are efficient in the use of necessary services and do not cause serious, irreversible environmental problems. The incentives could be in the form of loans, expansion opportunities, tax benefits, and other suitable encouragement.

In this book, the discussions have elaborated on how human activities have affected African resources. The land and water of Africa have experienced a great deal of changes. The land forms have changed with respect to slope stability, sediment yield, and weathering. Man through his activities has changed these characteristics of the land form and the quantity and quality of water in Africa. Construction of dams, irrigation, agricultural practices, and a host of other development processes impact the rivers, streams, lakes, and other water bodies in Africa. Hence, it is important for African countries to have all levels of government establish objectives to encourage the conservation and preservation of significant land and water resources. To achieve these objectives, attempts must be made to ensure that significant sand, gravel, and limestone deposits are protected from urban development and that extractive activities are screened so that reclamation of land is undertaken after extraction is completed. Wooded areas, the natural beauty of the African landscape, and unique wildlife habitats should be preserved. Natural groundwater recharge areas and surface water resources must be protected from pollution and the encroachment from urban development. This is especially important since a high percentage of health problems in Africa are caused by contaminated water.

African governments such as that of Nigeria realize the importance of acquiring regional areas where the benefits of conserving topographical, soil, geological, water, vegetation, cultural, historic, and wildlife resources can be achieved systematically. This country is organizing programs to safeguard the environment. Intensive development must take into consideration the constraints presented by the soil. One very common problem with development projects in Africa is that they are not always long-range and comprehensive in outlook, so distortion and degradation of the environment usually emanate after the conclusion of projects. It stands to reason that there should be an objective to encourage future development which does not exceed the capacities of the land's soil and drainage characteristics. Soil structure and texture should be fully studied before construction commences, and intensive development should not occur where soil conditions present severe constraints for that development. Development that would result in erosion should be discouraged until plans to limit the erosion have been fully implemented.

Other policies germane to guiding growth and development in Africa include the following:

1. *Preserving unusual ecological, geological, and scientifically significant areas in their natural state.*

Africa is blessed with many natural areas which are important because of their endemism. Places such as the Ngorongoro National Park in Tanzania, Amboseli National Park in Kenya, and many places in Madagascar need to be preserved for their scientific, recreational, and unique characteristics.

These natural areas are sources of beauty and inspiration, both as scenery and in the more intimate sense of the form and beauty of individual living things. Private, public, national, and international entities must attempt to preserve and conserve these natural areas by making sure that there are programs and tools available to protect them.

The natural areas could serve the African public and the world at large as living museums, examples of a rich and diverse natural world from which the great African societies were built. As has been discussed in an earlier chapter, there are many of these natural areas which are being managed by national governments with assistance from international organizations and agencies, private individuals, and foundations and universities. These natural areas could be the historic memorials that serve as living links with man's primitive past in such a way as to enhance human understanding and perception of the world in which we live. This natural heritage, the very roots of our existence, should be protected, nurtured, and embraced with reverence.

Another reason for the preservation of Africa's natural areas is that they serve as outdoor classrooms for students (African and foreign) of all ages. The Serengeti, for instance, provides an important teaching resource.

Natural areas of Africa are gaining momentum as wonderful vacation and safari spots. As was shown in Chapter 9, tourism to Africa has increased tremendously in the last decade and will probably continue for decades to come if political and social stability remain in the countries that receive significant revenue from tourism. With the increase in leisure time in industrialized (mainly Western) countries, tourism to Africa will continue to fill the void for people wanting to visit exotic places. These natural places will offer gratifyingly wide opportunities for social and environmental understanding of cultures while serving as wonderful emotional and psychological uplifts for visitors.

2. *It is crucial not to allow intensive urban development to disturb natural drainage patterns.* Another policy germane to development is to

ensure that development does not occur within flood plains or flood prone areas so that all development can provide a retention capacity equal to the capacity displaced by that development. Intensive development should not occur in areas adjoining streams and other waterways. It is advisable for government and private interest groups to acquire open space close to waterways for protection and preservation purposes.

Population and Dependency

The rate of population increase in Africa is much higher than in the rest of the world. However, there are differences in the annual rate of population increase among African countries. It is generally agreed that the population explosion has resulted in many of the economic and environmental problems of Africa. For many Africans the population problem is a contentious issue because it portrays Africa as a continent that has not been able to handle its population problems. Unchecked population explosion will inevitably lead to exceeding the carrying capacity of the resources. It will not be a mistake to argue that in some African regions, the carrying capacity has been exceeded and that in many other places we are approaching a point where the land will be unable to maintain itself in a "productive" way. It appears then that one area that needs immediate attention is population control.

One way of controlling population is through education. This issue needs to be raised at all levels of education — primary, secondary, and college. It must also transcend all religious and cultural norms which prevent people from critically analyzing the dilemma they and their countries face as a result of unchecked population. Each country in Africa must spend the time and money on reproduction education and population awareness in schools. Education will also enhance the chances of controlling the deadly disease AIDS which has devastated some African rural villages and is spreading in the heterogeneous population in urban settings. Moreover, unwanted pregnancies and the number of teenage pregnancies will decrease, thereby decreasing the population and the demand on the environment and natural resources. Education is perhaps the most important tool for controlling population because it reaches people at the critical time when decisions about their futures and their contributions to their countries are being made.

One country that is making tremendous efforts of educating its urban and rural population on the impact of large families is Nigeria. It has not only tried reaching young people in their classrooms, but it has a media campaign about population. The television networks and radio stations that are government operated have regular advertisements on the importance of small family size. Rural inhabitants understand the economic and environmental ramifications of large families. It now behooves the government to assist its people on proper contraception.

Stabilization of population growth will enable development projects to be sustained. Stabilization of population growth will also enhance sustainability of the agriculture, economy, and ecology of Africa. In many parts of Africa in this decade of the 1990s, drought has brought great difficulties. It is argued that the worst drought of the twentieth century is going on in Botswana, Zimbabwe, Mozambique, and South Africa. Drought compounds the problem of population explosion. Meldrum (1992:26) describes the current 1992 drought as devastating and enormous in magnitude. She claims:

> Southern Africa's drought is a natural disaster of biblical proportions. It is the worst this century. Scorching crops right across the continent from Angola on the west coast to Mozambique and Tanzania on the east.
> The drought respects no boundaries. At a time when southern Africa is caught up in a tenuous peace process and difficult democratization efforts, the drought has weighed in heavily on political balances throughout the region.
> In some cases, the effects of the drought are tipping the political scales in favor of change, such as in Malawi. In other countries, the drought is hindering the process of democratic reform, as in Zambia. The drought is threatening Angola's hard-won peace and is troubling Namibia's stability.

It is almost impossible to discuss sustaining Africa's biological and environmental diversity without discussing the importance of foreign and international aid. The literature on African development is inundated with topics on how aid does not help Africa, but it should be pointed out that the plight of Africans due to drought, famine, and wars will continue without international assistance. Private voluntary organizations (PVOs) such as the Academy for Educational Development, International Division (AED), and Adventist Development and Relief Agency International (ADRA) have played important roles in Africa's development and in sustaining its environmental diversity. There is an extensive list of PVOs that are involved in assisting African countries in the publication by InterAction entitled *Diversity in Development: U.S. Voluntary Assistance to Africa* (1986). This volume provides a synopsis on the projects that PVOs are engaged in. Suffice it to mention that although PVOs have received a lot of criticism in the past, their presence is very critical at this point in African history because of all the turmoil that the continent is facing. They will be instrumental in keeping Africa's presence in the center of global agendas, especially in light of the fact that Africa's ecology demands immediate and continuous monitoring because there is so very much at stake.

The purposes and goals of PVOs are many and can be designed to specifically address the needs of specific countries. But the broad areas these organizations tend to apply themselves to in Africa, as well as other developing nations, as stated by InterAction (1985:6) include:

1. Improving the quality of life in rural Africa through the development of water resources, increased food production, and the delivery of health services (e.g., Africare).
2. Address family planning needs of communities in Africa.
3. Educate rural communities on basic economic and social significance of their environment.
4. Address agricultural issues such as livestock, poultry, and other related agricultural services (e.g., Heifer Project International).
5. Assisting African societies in placing development programs (e.g., Private Agencies Collaborating Together, PACT).

The involvement of PVOs in Africa has been growing since its establishment. The demand on the organizations is also growing because of the enormity of the ecological, economic, social, and political problems in many African countries. Table 11.1 shows the countries in Africa where the activities of PVOs have helped in lessening some of the problems faced by these countries.

The importance of nongovernmental organizations in the sustainability efforts in Africa is made clear when one examines the situation in Mozambique. There are 180 nongovernmental organizations (NGOs) working in that country, and the drought problem in that country would have been even more devastating without the assistance of these organizations. However, the drawback of aid is that countries such as Mozambique sooner or later become dependent upon the foreign aid. A more serious and better strategy would be comprehensive self-reliance of Africans learning how to help themselves on a long-term basis. Aid is important initially, but eventually Africans must work to sustain their development and the biological and environmental diversity of their countries. Funds could come from NGOs to operate community outreach programs to enable local citizen participation in governmental processes that are essential to safeguarding the environment.

Attempts must be made to change cultural taboos which make birth control impossible, and more important, population control should be combined with conservation programs. Methods such as waste reduction, recycling, and reuse of material should be encouraged in Africa. Some countries are doing better than others in this area. But before elaborating on specific conservation strategies, it should be stressed that in some African countries corruption has made it impossible to achieve goals that are crucial in saving the environment. It is worse in some countries where corruption is thought to have become institutionalized. In order to make progress such barriers must be removed. Otherwise, it is a vicious circle that jeopardizes the future of Africa.

Conservation

The United Nations Conference on Environment and Development (UNCED), held in June of 1992 in Rio de Janeiro, Brazil, raised a number of very important issues in terms of what is happening to the natural systems of the world. Attention has turned to the environment in a manner that has never before been achieved. The idea is to discuss the root causes of environmental degradation, the environmental impact of destroying thousands of tracts of forests. In Madagascar the problem is enormous for this island nation off the southeastern coast of Africa. Its wealth cannot and must not be lost. The flora and fauna offer natives and the world medicinal and pharmaceutical opportunities that assist with problems of malaria fever, leukemia, and a host of other health-related problems.

The World Health Organization and other international organizations are very interested in the indigenous knowledge of traditional medicine. The tropics of Africa as well as South America and Asia are sources of plants used for medicinal purposes. The United States National Institutes of Health (NIH) has been collecting for study approximately 4,500 higher plant species per year since 1991 from the tropics of Africa, South America, and Asia. It is hoped that there will be a document describing the utilization of the plants for purposes such as folk medicine, traditional healers, pharmaceutical use, and food industries. The documentation could also include the importance of the plants in local use, internal trade, and export. There could also be a description of how the plants are prepared for traditional remedies, their chemical properties and constituents, and their therapeutic importance.

The projected continental and international use of African plants for medicinal purposes would enhance their conservation. The essence of the identification of the endangered species will be made known to millions of people around the world who might assist through financial donations or voluntary assistance. The governments of the world could then set up higher priorities for monitoring the conservation of African plants.

The deforestation of African countries is responsible for the loss of rich soil, flooding, and drought. Conserving the forest will enable the well-forested watershed of Africa to regulate its natural water supply.

The Earth Conference has put the environmental agenda in the forefront of global issues to be addressed by world leaders. What is needed in Africa is strong leadership in this race against time. The rate at which

Table 11.1: African Countries by Region

Country	Pop.	GNP per cap	Emergency Conditions	# of PVOs	# of Projs.	% of Total Projs.	% of Funding
Northeast Africa							
Djibouti	0.3	n.a.	Drought/Civil Strife	4	26		
Ethiopia	36.0	140	Drought/Civil Strife/Floods	37	267		
Somalia	6.5	250	Drought/Cholera	26	43		
Sudan	21.8	400	Drought/Civil Strife	32	103	17	40
East							
Burundi	4.6	240	Soil Erosion/ Cholera	11	37		
Kenya	20.2	340	Cholera	61	322		
Rwanda	6.3	270	Deforestation	17	48		
Tanzania	21.7	240	Erratic Rain	34	100		
Uganda	14.7	220	Civil Strife	35	86	22	13
Southeast Central							
Madagascar	10.0	290		10	25		
Malawi	7.1	210		20	69		
Mozambique	13.9	n.a.	Drought/Civil Strife/Cyclone	12	22		
Zambia	6.8	580	Drought	29	107		
Zimbabwe	8.6	740		32	166	15	6
Southern							
Botswana	1.1	920	Drought	18	33		
Lesotho	1.5	470	Drought	14	28		
Namibia	1.1	1,760		2	4		
South Africa	32.5	2,450	Cholera	13	26		
Swaziland	0.6	890		15	16	4	4
West Central							
Angola	7.9	n.a.	Displaced Persons/ Civil Strife	11	18		
Central Afr. R.	2.7	280		6	11		
Chad	5.2	n.a.	Drought/Civil Strife	11	18		
Congo	1.7	1,230		1	4		
Gabon	1.0	4,250		5	5		
Zaire	33.1	160		26	90	7	10
West							
Benin	4.0	290	Transiting Returnees	10	24		
Burkina Faso	6.9	180	Drought/Cholera	19	82		
Cameroon	9.7	800	Cholera	21	39		
Cape Verde	0.3	360	Drought/Floods	3	12		
E. Guinea	0.3	n.a.	Cholera	5	10		

Table 11.1: (cont.)

Country	Pop.	GNP per cap	Emergency Conditions	# of PVOs	# of Projs.	% of Total Projs.	% of Funding
Gambia	0.8	290		5	10		
Ghana	14.3	320		32	162		
Guinea	6.1	300		3	3		
Guinea-Bissau	0.9	180		8	10		
Ivory Coast	10.1	720		8	11		
Liberia	2.2	470		23	38		
Mali	7.7	150	Drought/Cholera	22	84		
Mauritania	1.9	440	Drought/Cholera	11	34		
Niger	6.5	240	Drought	13	46		
Nigeria	91.2	760		27	70		
Senegal	6.7	440	Drought in the North	24	100		
Sierra Leone	3.6	380		24	63		
Togo	3.0	280		15	38	32	22
North Africa							
Algeria	22.2	2,400		4	4		
Egypt	48.3			19	84		
Libya	4.0	7,500		0	0		
Morocco	24.3	750	Drought	9	21		
Tunisia	7.2	1,290		4	10	4	3

Notes: Not included with 21 projects among them are the following: Comoros, Mauritius, Reunion, Sao Tome, and Principe Seychelles. Population figures are for mid-1985 in millions. GNP per capita is for 1982.

Source: Adapted from InterAction (American Council for Voluntary International Action), 1985, pp. 22–23.

the environment is being destroyed is alarming, and immediate conservation efforts (both African and international) are needed to help combat the problem. Efforts of individual countries; regional cooperative efforts, such as the involvement of the Economic Community of West African Society; and international collaborative efforts are essential for ensuring the future of the African environment.

Former U.S. President George Bush pledged several hundred million dollars for saving the world's forests. This is just a drop in the bucket in terms of reversing the deforestation problem. What are really needed are global policies on environmental damage, population control, and climate change due to global warming.

Conservation is essential in Africa because the continent is endowed with the largest reserves of unharnessed natural resources in the world.

The wildlife, minerals, water, and forests present the richest diversity in the world. Their protection is crucial to human existence. It is generally agreed that if Zaire, Zambia, and Zimbabwe, which are located in the south-central part of the continent are properly developed agriculturally they could provide enough food for the whole of Africa. Africa has the potential for other development in areas such as solar energy and the rivers (with the appropriate technology) which could provide water for some areas that lack water for domestic consumption.

The conservation that is needed in Africa should be based on rural development. Trained personnel are needed to implement conservation strategies, and efforts must be made to educate local citizens to be involved in the management of natural resources. Information on the natural resources must be kept and updated in order to understand the trend of decline or increase in the number of wildlife and plants. The participation of local universities and research institutions is paramount to the success of the protection of natural resources. Programs such as UNESCO's Man and the Biosphere (MAB) provide opportunities for systematic research on the ecosystems and the ecological processes that keep the African environment in equilibrium. Their efforts must continue and should endeavor to involve African scientists at all levels of research and management of programs. Other programs offered by the Scientific Committee on Problems of the Environment (SCOPE) of the International Council of Scientific Unions (ICSU) are also necessary.

It is envisaged that with all these long-range strategies, Africa will be a nonmarginalized continent, and the issue of its dependency will be resolved. The countries of Africa will collaborate on an equal basis with other countries of the world to make the world habitable for all humankind.

Appendix: Survey Instrument

Question: How serious do you consider the following issues in your area?

Rank response as follows: (Circle response)	Very Serious [VS]	Somewhat Serious [SS]	Hardly Serious [HS]	Not Sure [NS]	Refrain/ No Answer [NA]
1. The loss of good farmlands.	VS	SS	HS	NS	NA
2. The misuse of soil and water re-sources.	VS	SS	HS	NS	NA
3. The destruction of the forest.	VS	SS	HS	NS	NA
4. The scarcity of firewood.	VS	SS	HS	NS	NA
5. The disappearance of wildlife.	VS	SS	HS	NS	NA
6. The loss of natural places.	VS	SS	HS	NS	NA
7. Water pollution.	VS	SS	HS	NS	NA
8. The shortage of fresh water.	VS	SS	HS	NS	NA
9. The impact of road construction.	VS	SS	HS	NS	NA
10. The impact of agri-cultural intensifica-tion (explain).	VS	SS	HS	NS	NA
11. The impact of agri-cultural extensifica-tion (explain).	VS	SS	HS	NS	NA

273

Rank response as follows: (Circle response)	Very Serious [VS]	Somewhat Serious [SS]	Hardly Serious [HS]	Not Sure [NS]	Refrain/ No Answer [NA]
12. The impact of housing and infra-structure construc-tion.	VS	SS	HS	NS	NA
13. Local government involvement in land-use issues.	VS	SS	HS	NS	NA

Rank response as follows: (Circle response)	Very Adequate [VA]	Somewhat Adequate [SA]	Hardly Adequate [HA]	Not Sure [NS]	Refrain/ No Answer [NA]
14. Federal government involvement in land-use issues.	VA	SA	HA	NS	NA
15. Local government involvement in land-use issues.	VA	SA	HA	NS	NA
16. Federal government involvement in land-use issues.	VA	SA	HA	NS	NA

Rank response as follows: (Circle response)	Strongly Agree [SA]	Agree [A]	Don't Know or No Opinion [DK/NO]	Disagree [D]	Strongly Disagree [SD]
17. Conservation and preservation poli-cies are clearly outlined by local government.	SA	A	DK/NO	D	SD
18. Conservation and preservation poli-cies are clearly outlined by state government.	SA	A	DK/NO	D	SD
19. Conservation and preservation poli-cies are clearly outlined by federal government.	SA	A	DK/NO	D	SD

20. Would you support government strategies to conserve/ preserve natural resources such as the forest, land, air, soil, and water?   SA   A   DK/NO   D   SD

Surface Water Quantity

21. Information available on present and future demands on water resources.   SA   A   DK/NO   D   SD

22. Drainage and run-off conditions.   SA   A   DK/NO   D   SD

Surface Water Quality

23. Information on surface water quality.   SA   A   DK/NO   D   SD

24. Additional natural or man-made discharges into surface water.   SA   A   DK/NO   D   SD

Ground Water Quality

25. Impact of manmade discharges on ground water.   SA   A   DK/NO   D   SD

26. Impact of natural discharges on ground water.   SA   A   DK/NO   D   SD

Air Quality

27. Particulates in the air.   SA   A   DK/NO   D   SD

28. Dust in the air.   SA   A   DK/NO   D   SD

29. Open burning operational.   SA   A   DK/NO   D   SD

30. Traffic and industrialization activities.   SA   A   DK/NO   D   SD

Aquatic Ecosystems

31. Human activity impact on flora and fauna.   SA   A   DK/NO   D   SD

32. Quality of aquatic ecosystem affected by industrialization.   SA   A   DK/NO   D   SD

Rank response as follows: (Circle response)	Strongly Agree [SA]	Agree [A]	Don't Know or No Opinion [DK/NO]	Disagree [D]	Strongly Disagree [SD]
33. Quality of aquatic ecosystem affected by agriculture.	SA	A	DK/NO	D	SD

Agricultural Lands

34. Cultivated land is diminishing.	SA	A	DK/NO	D	SD
35. Cultivated lands are damaged.	SA	A	DK/NO	D	SD

Soil Erosion

36. Increase in soil erosion.	SA	A	DK/NO	D	SD
37. Increase in topsoil loss.	SA	A	DK/NO	D	SD
38. Poor agricultural practices lead to soil degradation.	SA	A	DK/NO	D	SD
39. Lack of scientific knowledge.	SA	A	DK/NO	D	SD

Slope Stability

40. Infrastructure construction destabilizes slopes.	SA	A	DK/NO	D	SD
41. Slope destabilization is hazardous to people and livestock.	SA	A	DK/NO	D	SD

Energy/Mineral Resources

42. The extraction of energy/mineral resources is perceived as...	SA	A	DK/NO	D	SD
43. The handling of waste generated by the extraction is a(n)...	SA	A	DK/NO	D	SD
44. The extraction de-	SA	A	DK/NO	D	SD

grades the quality
of the environ-
ment.

45. Extraction displaces   SA   A   DK/NO   D   SD
    the indigenous
    population/culture.

Bibliography

Abramovitz, N. Janet. *Investing in Biological Diversity: U.S. Research and Conservation Efforts in Developing Countries.* World Resources Institute: Washington, D.C., 1991.

_____, and Roberta Nichols. "Women and Biodiversity: Ancient Reality, Modern Imperatives." *Development: Journal of the Society for International Development,* 1992, 2:85–90.

Adams, Alexander B. *First World Conference on National Parks.* Washington, D.C.: National Park Service, United States Department of the Interior, 1962.

Adedibu, Afolabi A. "The Impact of Government Policy on Indigenous Housing in Ilorin, Nigeria." *Ekistics,* 1981, 48 (287):133–37.

Africa Recovery. "Environment." *Africa Recovery* (September 1991), nos. 2–3.

Ajayi, Ferri. "Food for Thought." *Africa Report* (September–October 1991): 25–28.

Akakpo, Barbara. "Women, Poverty, and Right: Oxfam Project Aims to Create Fairer World for Women." *West Africa* (March 9–15, 1992): 412–13.

Alexander, M. William. "Human Resources Utilization: Increasing Food Demand." In V.U. James (ed.), *Urban and Rural Development in Third World Countries.* Jefferson, N.C.: McFarland, 1991.

Allen, Robert. "The World Conservation Strategy: What It Is and What It Means for Parks." *Parks* 5, no. 2 (July–September 1980): 1–5.

Anderson, Dennis, and Robert Fishwick. *Fuelwood Consumption and Deforestation in African Countries.* World Bank: Working Papers, No. 704, The World Bank: Washington, D.C., 1984.

Ayeni, Olugbenga. "Rectifying the Damage." *West Africa* (May 13–19, 1991): 750.

Ayensu, S. Edward. *Medicinal Plants of West Africa.* Reference Publications, Inc.: Algonac, Michigan, 1979.

Ayisi, Ansah Ruth. "Battling the Odds." *Africa Report* (July–August 1991): 60–63.

Bale, John, and David Drakakis-Smith. *Tourism and Development in the Third World.* London: Routledge, 1988.

Bannister, Anthony, and Rene Gordon. *The National Parks of South Africa.* South Africa: C. Struik Publishers in Cooperation with the National Parks Board of Trustees, 1984.

Barbier, B. Edward, Joane C. Burgess, Timothy M. Swanson, and David W. Pearce. *Elephants, Economics and Ivory.* London: Earthscan Publications Ltd., 1990.

Barnes, Sandra T. "Public and Private Housing in Urban West Africa: The Social Implications." In K.C. Minion and Peter C.W. Gutkind (eds.), *Housing the Urban Poor in Africa.* Syracuse, N.Y.: Syracuse University Press, 1982.

Borota, Jan. *Tropical Forests: Some African and Asian Case Studies of Composition and Structure.* Amsterdam: Elsevier, 1991.

279

Boza, Mario Andres L., and Gilles H. Leniux. "Les Parcs Nationaux du Costa Rica." In J.G. Nelson, R.D. Needham, D.L. Mann, 1978, pp. 295–332.

Breen, C.M., F.H. Chutter, B. de Merona, and M.A.H. Saad. "Rivers." In J.J. Symoens, Mary Burgin, and John J. Gaudet (eds.), *The Ecology and Utilization of African Inland Waters.* Nairobi, Kenya: United Nations Environment Programme, 1981.

Briscoe, John, and David de Ferranti. *Water for Rural Communities: Helping People Help Themselves.* Washington, D.C.: The World Bank, 1988.

Bunting, A.H., and E. Bunting (eds.). "The Future of Shifting Cultivation in Africa and the Tasks of Universities." *Proceedings of the International Workshop on Shifting Cultivation: Teaching and Research at University Level* (July 4–9, 1982). Ibadan, Nigeria, and Rome: FAO, 1984.

Burgess, J.S., and J. Woomington. "Threat and Stress in the Clarence River Estuary of Northern South Wales." *Human Ecology,* 9(4) 1981: 419–31.

Carpenter, Richard A., ed. *Assessing Tropical Forest Lands: Their Suitability for Sustainable Uses.* Dublin: Tycooly International Publishing Ltd., 1981.

Cater, E. "Tourism in the Least Developed Countries." *Annals of Tourism Research,* 14, 1987, 202–25.

Churchill, A. Anthony, David de Ferranti, Robert Roche, Carolyn Tager, A. Alanj Walter, and Anthony Yager. *Rural Water Supply and Sanitation: Time for Change.* World Bank Discussion Papers No. 18. Washington, D.C.: World Bank, 1987.

Cohen, E. "Authenticity and Commoditization in Tourism." *Annals of Tourism Research,* 15, 1988, 371–85.

Commentary. "The Nigerian Population." Radio Nigeria. May 28, 1991.

Connally, Euginia Horstman. "Wildlife Parks in Kenya." *National Parks* (May/June 1983): 28–32.

Curtin, D. Phillips. *The Atlantic Slave Trade: A Census.* Madison: University of Wisconsin Press, 1969.

Daily Times (Nigeria). "Environmental Problems" (June 13, 1991): 32.

Deerr, Noel. *The History of Sugar.* 2 vols. London, 1949–50.

Drake, H. Max. "Research Method or Culture-bound Technique? Pitfalls of Survey Research in Africa." In William M. O'Barr, David Spain, and Mark A. Tessler (eds.), *Survey Research in Africa: Its Applications and Limits.* Evanston: Northwestern University Press, 1973.

Dumont, René, and Marie-France Mottin. *Stranglehold on Africa.* London: Andre Deutsch, 1983.

Dzisah, Melvis. "Tourism Prospects: Stemming the Decline." *West Africa* (November 18–24, 1991): 1927.

Eddy, William. "Rhythms of Survival." *National Parks* (September/October 1987): 21–23.

Eden, M.J. "Palaeoclimatic Influences and the Development of Savanna in Southern Venezuela." *Journal of Biogeography,* 1974, 1:95–109.

Editorial. "Agriculture WFC Meeting." *West Africa* (May 13–19, 1991).

———. "Bank Gives Environment High Profile." *West Africa* (September 23–29, 1991b): 1602.

———. "Commodities: $50 bn in Lost Revenue." *West Africa* (September 2–8, 1991a): 1462.

———. "Elephants Kill Too." *West Africa,* 29 (July/August 1991c), 4:1255.

———. "Environment: Deforestation Plagues Africa." *West Africa* (September 2–8, 1991): 1462.

_____ (C.S.). "FAO Warns Again." *West Africa* (June 24–30, 1991): 1029.

_____. "Environmental Problems in Developing Countries." *West Africa* (February 3–9, 1992): 210.

El-Affendi, Abdelwahab. "Out of Africa's Troubles." *Africa Events* (August 1991, 36–37).

Ephson, Ben. "Ghana's Potential: Rich Cultural Heritage." *West Africa* (April 22–29, 1991): 661.

_____. "Tourism in Ghana: Harnessing the Potential." *West Africa* (June 8–14, 1992): 971–75.

Federal Government of Nigeria. *Nigerian Population Census Figures.* Lagos, Nigeria: Government Printer, 1992.

Fromm, Michael. "World Parks." *National Parks* (May/June 1983): 22.

Giess, W. "A Preliminary Vegetation Map (1:3,000,000, colored) of South West Africa." *Dinteria,* 1971, 4: 5–114.

_____. "A Short Report on the Vegetation of the Namib Coastal Area from Swakopmund to Cape Frio." *Dinteria,* 1968, 1:13–29.

Goldschmidt, Walter. *Man's Way.* New York: Holt, 1959.

Goudie, Andrew. *The Human Impact: Man's Role in Environmental Change.* Cambridge, Mass.: MIT Press, 1982.

Greenwood, D.J. "Culture by the Pound: An Anthropological Perspective on Tourism as Cultural Commoditization." In V.L. Smith (ed.), *Hosts and Guests.* Philadelphia: University of Pennsylvania Press, 1977.

Harcourt, Kelly, and Sandy Harcourt. "Silverback Calls the Shots." *International Wildlife,* 10, no. 1 (January/February 1980): 20–24.

Hills, T.L. "Savannas: A Review of a Major Research Problem in Tropical Geography." *Canadian Geographer,* 1965, 9:216–28.

Husbands, Winston. "Social Status and Perception of Tourism in Zambia." *Annals of Tourism Research,* 1989, 16:237–53.

Huxley, Julian (Sir). "Timeless Thoughts of World Renowed Biologist and Humanist." *International Wildlife,* 2, no. 6 (November/December 1972).

Hyder, Mohamed. "Stern Realities." *Africa Events,* 1992, pp. 24–25.

Idowu, Paxton. "Developing Water Resources." (Excerpts from an interview with Allhaji Abubakar Hashidu) in *West Africa* (January 20–26, 1992): 100.

InterAction. *Diversity in Development: U.S. Voluntary Assistance to Africa, Project Descriptions by Country and Sector.* New York: American Council for Voluntary International Action, 1985.

_____. *Diversity of Development: U.S. Voluntary Assistance to Africa, Summary of Findings.* New York: American Council for Voluntary International Action, 1985.

International Union for Conservation of Nature and Natural Resources (IUCN). *1985 United Nations List of National Parks and Protected Areas.* Gland, Switzerland: IUCN, 1985.

_____. *World Conservation Strategy: Living Resource Conservation for Sustainable Development.* Gland, Switzerland: IUCN, 1980.

_____/UNEP. *IUCN Directory of Afrotropical Protected Areas.* Gland, Switzerland: IUCN, 1987.

James, Valentine. "Housing Conditions in Rural Africa: The Case of Rural Nigeria." *Proceedings of the 15th Annual Conference of Third World Foundations.* Chicago. April, 1989.

_____. *Resource Management in Developing Countries: Africa's Ecological and Economic Problems.* New York: Praeger (Bergin & Garvey), 1991a.

_____. *Urban and Rural Development in Third World Countries: Problems of Population in Developing Countries*. Jefferson, N.C.: McFarland, 1991b.

Karue, C.N. "Problems of Animal Production in Shifting Farming Communities." In A.H. Bunting and Edward Bunting (eds.), *The Future of Shifting Cultivation in Africa and the Tasks of Universities*. Rome: FAO, 1984.

Kaul, R.N. *Dynamics of Tourism: A Trilogy, The Phenomenon* 1. New Delhi: Sterling Publishers Private Limited, 1985.

Kromm, David E. "Management of the Proposed Tallgrass Prairie National Park, U.S.A." In J.G. Nelson, R.D. Needham, and D.L. Mann (eds.), *International Experiences with National Parks and Related Reserves*. Waterloo, Ontario: University of Waterloo, 1987.

Kucznski, Robert R. *Population Movements*. Oxford, 1936.

La Bastille, Anne. "Advocate for Rhinos: Up Against Poachers." *International Wildlife*, 13, no. 1 (January/February 1983): 40.

_____. "Eight Women in the Wild." *International Wildlife*, 13, no. 1 (January/February 1983): 36–42.

Laishley, Roy. "Commodity Price Down." *Africa Recovery*, 6, no. 1 (April).

Lal, R., P.A. Sanchez, and R.W. Cummings, Jr. *Land Clearing and Development in the Tropics*. Rotterdam, Netherlands: A.A. Balkema, 1986.

Lamin, Dominic. "Declining Fortunes." *West Africa*, 30 (October–November 5, 1989): 1800.

Lenski, Gerhard. *Power and Privilege: A Theory of Social Stratification*. New York: McGraw-Hill, 1966.

Levin, A.C. *Housing Co-operatives in Developing Countries: A Manual for Self-Help in Low-Cost Housing Schemes*. New York: John Wiley & Sons, 1981.

Lowes, P. "Half Time in the Decade." In J. Pickford (ed.), *Developing World Water*. London: Grosvenor Press International, pp. 16–17.

Lugo, Ariel E., J.R. Clark, and R.D. Child. *Ecological Development in the Humid Tropics: Guidelines for Planners*. Morrilton, Ark.: Winrock International, 1987.

Lundberg, D.E. *The Tourist Business*. 5th ed. New York: Van Nostrand Reinhold Company, 1985.

MacGregor, Jenny. "The Paradoxes of Wildlife Conservation in Africa." *Africa Insight*, 1989, 19, no. 4.

Machlis, Gary E., and David L. Tichnell. *The State of the World's Parks: An International Assessment for Resource Management, Policy and Research*. Westview, Colo.: Westview Press, 1985.

McIntosh, R.W. *Tourism Principles, Practices, Philosophies*. 2nd ed. Columbus, Ohio: Grid, Inc., 1972.

McNeely, Jeffrey A., Kenton R. Miller, Walter V. Reid, Russell A. Mittermeir, and Timothy B. Werner. *Conserving the World's Biological Diversity*. Gland, Switzerland: IUCN, 1990.

Maier, Karl. "Biting the Bullet." *Africa Report* (May/June 1992): 43–46.

Mason, Herbert L. "Economic Values in Parks and Preserves." In *First World Conference on National Parks*. Washington, D.C.: National Park Service, United States Department of the Interior, 1962, pp. 107–12.

Mathews, D.O. "The Strict Nature Reserve and Its Role." In *First World Conference on National Parks*. Washington, D.C.: National Park Service, United States Department of the Interior, 1962, pp. 259–68.

Mathieson, A., and G. Wall. *Tourism: Economic, Physical and Social Impacts*. London: Longman, 1986.

Meldrum, Andrew. "The Big Scorcher." *Africa Report*, 1992, pp. 25-27.
Miller, S. Richard. "Why Should Africa Be Different?" *International Wildlife*, 7, no. 2 (March/April 1977): 19.
Morell, Virginia. "Masai: A Proud People in Kenya Is on a Collision Course with Wildlife." *International Wildlife*, 15, no. 3 (May/June 1985).
Morgan, W.B., and R.P. Moss. "Savanna and the Forest in Western Nigeria." *Africa*, 1965, 35:286-93.
Myers, Norman. "Good Gnus, Bad Gnus." *International Wildlife*, 11, no. 2 (March/April 1981): 5-13.
_____. "Should We Exploit Africa's Wildlife to Save It? Postscript from Norman Myers." *International Wildlife*, 12, no. 2 (March-April 1982).
_____. "The Small Cats of Africa." *International Wildlife*, 6, no. 2 (March-April 1976).
_____. "Witch Doctors Are Good Guys Again." *International Wildlife*, 11, no. 1 (January/February 1981): 25-26.
Nomachi, Kazuyoshi. "Scorched Islands of the Sahara." *International Wildlife*, 10, no. 6 (November/December 1980): 56-61.
Nwade, Augustine. "Water Shortage in Awka." *Daily Champion* (May 22, 1991): 5.
O'Barr, M. William, David Spain, and A. Mark Tessler (eds.). *Survey Research in Africa: Its Applications and Limits*. Evanston: Northwestern University Press, 1973.
Obeng, L., and J. Gaudet. "Ecological Implications of Hydrodevelopment." In J.J. Symoens, et al. (eds.), *The Ecology and Utilization of African Inland Waters*. Nairobi, Kenya: The United Nations Environment Programme, 1981.
Oguntola, Akin B. "A Proposal for Recreation in Nigeria's Sapoba Forest Reserve." *Parks*, 1980, 5, no. 1: 15-17.
Ojo, G.J. Afolabi. "Nigerian National Parks, and Related Reserves." In J.G. Nelson, R.D. Needham, and D.L. Mann (eds.), *International Experiences with National Parks and Related Reserves*. Waterloo, Ontario: University of Waterloo, 1978, pp. 271-93.
Okereke, Uzo. "Local Council and Rural Development." *Daily Times* (Nigeria) (June 13, 1991): 32.
Okigbo, B.N. "Shifting Cultivation in Tropical Africa: Definition and Description." In A.H. Bunting and Edward Bunting (eds.), *The Future of Shifting Cultivation in Africa: And the Tasks of Universities*. Proceedings of the International Workshop on Shifting Cultivation: Teaching and Research at University Level. July 4-9, 1982 (Ibadan, Nigeria). Rome: FAO, 1984.
Okpala, D.C.I. *Institutional Problems in the Management of Nigerian Urban Environment*. Ibadan: Nigerian Institute of Social and Economic Research, 1986.
Olembo, R.J. "Keynote Speech." In J.J. Symoens et al. (eds.), *The Ecology and Utilization of African Inland Waters*. Nairobi, Kenya: The United Nations Environment Programme, 1981.
Omaar, Rakiya, and Janet Fleischman. "Arab vs. African." *African Report* (July-August 1991): 36-38.
Owen, John S. "The National Parks of Tanganyika." In *First World Conference on National Parks*. Washington, D.C.: National Park Service, United States Department of the Interior. New York, 1962, pp. 51-59.
Peters, M. *International Tourism*. London: Hutchinson, 1979.
Phillips, John. *Agriculture and Ecology in Africa: A Study of Actual and Potential Development South of the Sahara*. New York: Frederick A. Praeger, 1960.

Pitman, Dick. "Zimbabwe: Wildlife and Independence." *International Wildlife*, 1, no. 1 (January/February 1983): 32–35.

Price, Sandra. "I Didn't Know My Country Was So Beautiful." *International Wildlife*, 9, no. 1 (January/February 1979).

Quézel, P. "Analysis of the Flora of Mediterranean and Saharan Africa." *Annals of the Missouri Botanical Gardens*, 1978, 65:479–534.

_____. *La Végétation du Sahara, du Tchad à la Mauritanie.* Stuttgart: Gustav Fischer; Paris, Masson. 333 pp. (Geogot. sel., 2), 1965.

Radio Nigeria. "Evening News Broadcast." May 21, 1991. Nigerian Broadcasting Service.

Robbins, Charles, and Janice Robins. "Sahara: Ocean of Fire." *International Wildlife*, 3, no. 3 (November-December 1973): 56–62.

Sayer, Jeffrey A. "Tourism or Conservation in the National Parks of Benin." *Parks*, 1980, 5, no. 4: 13–15.

Shantz, H.L., and C.F. Marbut. *The Vegetation and Soils of Africa.* New York: AMS Press, Inc., 1971.

Shaw, M. Timothy, ed. *Alternative Futures for Africa.* Boulder, Colo.: Westview Press, 1982.

_____. "Introduction: The Political Economy of Africa's Futures." *Alternative Futures for Africa.* Boulder, Colo.: Westview Press, 1982.

Shelton, Napier. "Parks and Sustainable Development." *National Parks* (May/June 1983): 16–20.

Shepherd, Ann. "The Lost Decade." *Africa Report*, 1992.

Shubomi, Rasheed. "Problems of Food Shortage and Preservation." *Daily Times* (Nigeria) (June 11, 1991): 13.

Smith, Gayle. "The Hunter." *Mother Jones* (September/October 1991): 36–37.

Smith, Stephen J. *The Atlas of Africa's Principal Mammals.* Sandton, South Africa: Natural History Books, 1985.

Spiro, Heather. *Women's Roles and Gender Difference in Development: The Ilora Farm Settlement in Nigeria.* West Hartford, Conn.: Kumarian Press, 1985.

Stewart, Julian. *Theory of Culture Change.* Urbana: University of Illinois Press, 1963.

Symoens, J.J., Mary Burgis, and John J. Gaudet, eds. *The Ecology and Utilization of African Inland Waters.* Nairobi, Kenya: United Nations Environment Programme (UNEP), 1981.

Talbot, Amaury Perry. *In the Shadow of the Bush.* London: William Heinemann, 1912.

Thiam, Mariam. "The Role of Women in Rural Development in the Segou Region of Mali." In Lucy E. Creevey (ed.), *Women Farmers in Africa: Rural Development in Mali and the Sahel.* Syracuse, N.Y.: Syracuse University Press, 1986.

Timberlake, Lloyd. *Africa in Crisis: The Causes, the Cures of Environmental Bankruptcy.* Washington, D.C.: International Institute for Environment and Development, 1985.

Todaro, Michael P. *Economic Development in the Third World.* New York: Longman, 1985.

Travis, John. "Third World: S(ave) O(ur) S(heep)!" *Science*, 255 (February 1992): 678.

Turner, L., and J. Ash. *The Golden Hordes: International Tourism and the Pleasure Periphery.* London: Constable, 1975.

UN Economic Commission for Africa/African Training and Research Center for

Women. *Increasing the Access of African Women to Credit: An Integrated Approach.* Addis Ababa, Ethiopia: ECA/ATRCW, 1990.

UNESCO/AETFAT/UNSO. *Vegetation Map of Africa.* Paris: UNESCO, 1983.

van den Berghe, P. "Colonialism, Culture nd Nature in African Game Reserves: Comment on Almagor." *Annals of Tourism Reserach,* 1986, 13:101–5.

Wabara, Ebere. "Ideato's Huge Erosion Burden." *Daily Times* (Nigeria) (June 13, 1991): 32.

Wallace, P. Charles. "Waging War on Kenya's Poachers." *International Wildlife,* 11, no. 5 (September/October 1981).

Wannenburg, Alf. "Africa's Bushmen: All Their Prey Are Brothers." *International Wildlife,* 12, no. 2 (March-April 1982): 44–54.

Washington, D.C. International Union for Conservation of Nature and Natural Resources, World Resources Institute, Conservation International, World Wildlife Fund-US and The World Bank.

Watt, Mitchell John, and Maria Gerdina Breyer-Brandwijk. *The Medicinal and Poisonous Plants of Southern and Eastern Africa.* London: E. & S. Livingstone, Ltd., 1962.

Werner, Timothy B. *Conserving the World's Biological Diversity.* Washington, D.C.: Island Press, 1990.

West Africa. "Commodities: Cocoa, Sugar Prices Plunge" (July 8–14, 1991): 1130.

_____. "Development Linked to Environment" (July 29/August 4, 1991a): 1250.

_____. "Empowering the Voiceless" (September 20/October 6, 1991b): 1631.

_____. "IFAD Pledges Aid" (June 10–16, 1991c): 957.

_____. "In the Mire of Starvation" (June 24–30, 1991d): 1027. [Food Aid Requirements, 1991d.]

_____. "Profits Illegally Siphoned to European Banks: Ghana Timber Scandal." Economy & Business (March 23–29, 1992): 508.

_____. "UK Food Aid for Africa" (June 10–16, 1991e): 957.

White, F. *The Vegetation of Africa: A Descriptive Memoir to Accompany UNESCO/AETFAT/UNSO Vegetation Map of Africa.* Paris: UNESCO, 1983.

Wickins, L. Peter. *Africa 1880–1980 An Economic History.* Cape Town, South Africa: Oxford University Press, 1986.

Wilkinson, Paul F. "The Global Distribution of National Parks and Equivalent Reserves." In J.G. Nelson, R.D. Needham, and D.L. Mann (eds.), *International Experiences with National Parks and Related Reserves.* Waterloo, Ontario: University of Waterloo, 1978.

Williams, J.G. *A Field Guide to National Parks of East Africa.* London: Harper-Collins, 1985.

World Bank. *Tourism: Sector Working Paper.* New York: World Bank, 1972.

_____. *The World Bank and the Environment.* Washington, D.C.: World Bank, 1990a.

_____. *World Development Report 1991: The Challenge of Development.* Oxford, England: Oxford University Press, 1991.

World Commission on Environment and Development. *Our Common Future.* Oxford, England: Oxford University Press, 1987.

World Health Organization (WHO). *Technology for Water Supply and Sanitation in Developing Countries.* World Health Organization Technical Report Series 742. Geneva, Switzerland: WHO, 1987.

World Resources Institute, The World Bank, and the United Nations Development Programme. *Tropical Forests: A Call for Action.* Part I. New York: World Resources Institute, 1985a.

_____. *Tropical Forests: A Call for Action.* Part 2. New York: World Resources Institute, 1985b.

World Tourism Organization. *Current Travel and Tourism Indicators.* Madrid, Spain: World Tourism Organization, 1990.

Yansane, Aguibou Y. "Decolonization, Dependency and Development in Africa: The Theory Revisited." In Aguibou Y. Yansane (ed.), *Decolonization and Dependency: Problems of Development of African Societies.* Westport, Conn.: Greenwood Press, 1980.

Index

Aardvark 158
Aberdere 162
Abiakpo Ikot Essien 54
Abramovitz, N. J. 232
Acacia suma Kurz 157
Accra 12
Acquired Immune Deficiency Syn-
    drome (AIDS) 164
Addo Elephant 26
Adedibu, A. A. 64
Africa: development 220; food sup-
    ply 95; present position in global
    affairs 222
Africa Prize (1991) 244
Ajayi, F. 233
Akagera 24
Akakpo, B. 244
Akwa Ibom state 9, 54
Alexander, M. W. 129
Algeria 95
Alkaloids in plant families 126
Amboseli National Park 265
American Minor Breeds Conservancy
    121
Amphibians 36
Anambra state 202
Ananukwa 106
Anderson, D. 135
Andropogon plants 156
Angiosperms 36
Angola 95, 99
Animal rights 34
Annona 157
Antelope, roan 158
Arabo-Berbers 122
Arugungu festival 90
Atlantic Ocean 173
Augrabies Falls 26

Awka 202
Ayeni, O. 9
Ayensu, S. E. 126
Ayisi, A. R. 244

Baare 40
Babangida, Maryam 243
Baboon 158
Bamboo 59
Bantu 122
Barbaig pastoralist 37
Barbier, B. E. 257
Barnes, S. T. 67, 68
Barter tradition 118
Basse-Lobaye 21
Bauhinia reticulata DC 157
Bauxite 95
Belgium 117
Bermuda 85
Beydanes 216
Bia 21
Biological diversity 11, 21, 22, 143,
    196
Biosphere reserve 22
Birds 36
Bixby, Don 121
Blesbok 158
Bontebok 26
Borassus 157
Borota, J. 133
Boshe-Okawango National Park 24
Botswana 88
Brachystegia laurentii LOUIS 134
Braun 117
Brazil 14
Breen, C. M. 207

Briscoe, J. 192
Bromelain 126
Brong Ahafo region 164
Bunting, A. H. 111
Bunting, E. 111
Burkina Faso 99
Bushmen of the Kalahari 180
Butyrospermum parkii Kotschy 157

Calabar 73
Cameroon 51
Caribbean nations 85
Carrying capacity 7, 11
Cats, small 165
Cattle: African N'Dama 121; American Holstein 120, 121; European Friesian 120
Celtis L. genera 133
Center for Applied Studies in International Negotiations (CASIN) 116
Chad 95, 99
Cheetahs 165
Chimpanzees 34
Chirisa Safari Area 31
Chotts 176
Churchill, A. A. 193
Cocaine 126
Cocoa 118
Colonialism 35
Conservation 255, 269
Cornulaca mocantha 173
Côte d'Ivoire (Ivory Coast) 36, 99
Cultural diversity 37, 196
Curtin 216
Cussonia djalonensis Cheval 157

Daily Times 146
Date palm 173
Deerr, N. 216
de Ferranti, D. 192
Deforestation 8
Dependency 87
Depopulation 98
Desert: absolute 172, 176; and its habitat 175; plant and animal adaptation 174; and semi-desert environment 172

Desertification 10
Development 259
Diamonds 95
Dimonika 21
Diversity 11, 21, 22, 36, 99, 143, 196
Dja 21
Drake, H. M. 148
Drobo Herbal Treatment Center 164
Drought 267
Dumont, R. 219
Dzisah, M. 36

Earth Charter 14
Ecological systems 1, 11; disasters 37
Economic Commission for Africa (ECA) 230
Economic Community of West African Society 271
ECOWAS (Economic Community of West African States) 40
Eden, M. J. 155
Eket 48
El-Affendi, A. 222
Eland 158
Encroachment 21
Endangered species 21
Entada sudanica Schwein f. 157
Entandrophragma C. DC. 133
Entropy 37, 172
Environmental diversity 17
Ephson, B. 40, 80, 86, 90
Erythrina 157
Ethiopia 93, 99, 116
Europe 11
European influence 214
Ezenwoke 106

Fallow periods 142
Family planning 243
FAO (United Nations Food and Agricultural Organization 98, 117, 121
Farming systems 8, 9, 111, 118, 142
Fleischman, J. 216
Folk healers 163
Folk medicine 163
Food shortage 116
Forests 134, 135

Fossey's Karisoke Research Center 163
France 117
Fromm, M. 26
Fuelwood 134
Fulani nomads 219
Future of Africa 229

Gabon 10
"Garden of Eden" xxi
Gardenia 157
Garoua 232
Gaudet, J. J. 196
Ghana 10, 36, 99
Giess, W. 179
Gilbertiodendron dewevrei J.
 LEONARD 134
Giraffes 161
Global recession 1
Gnu 165
Gold 95
Golden Gate Highlands 26
Goldschmidt, W. 147
Goodall, Jane 256
Greenbelt movement in Kenya 244
Greenwood, D. J. 88
Grysbok 158
Guinea 95

Habitat deterioration 31
Hahidu, Alhaji Abubakar 199
Halogypsophilous vegetation 176;
 types of 177
Hamadas 176
Hanang Plains 37
Haratines 216
Harcourt, K. 163
Harcourt, S. 163
Herbaceous plants 152
Herbalist 126
High density residential development
 260
Hillman, Kex 256
Hills, T. L. 152
Homelessness 260
Hottentot 122
Houses: modern 64; traditional 59
Housing 68, 71, 260

Human interests vs. environmental
 conservation interests 31
Hunter-gatherer groups 120
Husbands, W. 89, 90
Hydroelectric power plants 199
Hyena 158
Hyphaene 157

ICSU (International Council of
 Scientific Unions) 272
Ideota 103
Idowu, P. 199
Ifuho 54
Ikeja 49
Ikot-Ekpene 7, 54; local government
 67
Ikot-Obong 47
Ikot Obong Edong 54
Ikure (compound land) 58
ILO (International Labor Organiza-
 tion) 233
Ilora farm settlement project 254
Imo state 103
Impact assessment 196–201
Impacts of structural adjustment 254
Impassa-Makokou 21
Indigenous people 51
Institutional capability 8
InterAction 267, 268
International Drinking Water Supply
 and Sanitation Decade 183, 187
International Fund for Agricultural
 Development (IFAD) 117, 184
International legislation 21
International tourism 73
Islam 217
ITTO (International Tropical Timber
 Organization) 234
Itu 48, 73
IUCN (International Union for Con-
 servation of Nature and Natural
 Resources) 25

Jackal 158
Jamaica 85
James, V. 5, 172
Jazairy, Idriss 184

Jolly, Alison 256
Jonglei diversion canal 196

Kakum Nature Reserve 90, 93
Kalahari 10, 158, 173; desert 120,
    180; game reserve 180
Kalahari Gemsbok 26
Karoo 26
Karoo-Namib 158
Karue, C. N. 120
Kente apparel 90
Kenya 10, 12, 88
Kerosene 134
Khaya A. Juss. 133
Kigelia 157
Klipspringer 158
Kruger 26
Kucznski 216
Kuwait 117

Lagos 12
Lagos Island Business Center 50
Lagos Port 49
Lake Chad 90
Lake Menaka 164
Lake Turkana 164
Lamin, D. 119
Land-reform decree 68
Langebaan 26
Lenski, G. 147
Leopards 165
Lesotho 88
Levin, A. C. 63
Leukemia, childhood 164
Liberia 99
Lions 165
Lophira alata BANK ex GAERTN, f. 133
Lophira alata Banks 157
Lowes, P. 183
Luangwa Valley of Zambia 33
Lugo, A. E. 113
Luki 21

Maathai, Professor Nangari 243
MAB (Man and the Biosphere) 272;
    program 231

MacGregor, J. xxi
Machlis 31
McNeely, J. A. 21
Madagascar 99
Malawi 34, 99
Mammals 36
Maternal mortality 235
Mathews, D. O. 36
Mathieson, A. 88
Mauritania 99, 217
Mauritius 10
Mediterranean 87
Meldrum, A. 267
Metropolitan Hotel 80
Miller, S. R. 160
Monts Nimba 21
Moor 122
Morell, V. 51
Morgan, W. B. 155
Morphine 126
Moss, R. P. 155
Mottin, M. F. 219
Mount Kenya 164
Mountain zebra 26
Mozambique 99, 244
Multinationals 6, 10
Murtala Mohammed Airport 49
Muslim Nampula 244
Myers, Norman 162, 163, 165

Naiguran, John 52
Nairobi 12
Namib Desert 10, 179
Nana Kofi Drobo 164
National parks 25; of East Africa 27
Natural resource depletion 5
Netherlands 117
NGOs (Nongovernmental Organiza-
    tions) 35, 229
Ngorongoro National Park 162, 265
Nichols, R. 252
Nicotine 126
Niger 99
Niger delta of Nigeria 73
Nigeria 31, 36
NIH (National Institutes of
    Health) 269
Nilo-Hamites 122
Nilotics 122

Nimba 21
NITEL cables 106
Nkap 54
Nomachi, K. 175
Nomadic and seminomadic pastor-
   alists 120
Nomadic Fulani 122
Nomadic Masai 52
North America 11
Nwade, A. 202
Nwoase 164
Nwosu, O. 106

Oasis 175
Oban 34, 73
Obeng, L. 196
Odzala 21
Ogun 118
Oguntola, A. B. 33
Ojo, G. J. A. 26, 31
Okereke, U. 98
Okpala, D. C. I. 146
Olembo, R. J. 196
Omaar, R. 216
Omo 21
Ondo 118
Onitsha 39
Organization of African Unity
   (OAU) 216, 229
Oribi 158
Osun 118
Otuli 106
Outer Namib fog desert 179

Palaeoclimatic influences 155
Palm fronds 1, 59
Parc National Volcans 163
Park systems 23, 25, 27, 51
Parkia africana R. Br. 157
Pastoral and agropastoral commu-
   nities 120
Pennisetum plants 156
Periwinkles of Madagascar 164
Peru 163
Peters, M. 88
Phillips, J. 155
Phyto-geographic regions 174

Pitman, D. 256
Poaching 21
Polygamy 244
Population 31, 51, 98, 120, 243, 260,
   266
Price, Sandra 161
Project Impact Matrix 197
Protected lands 33, 35
Pulaar 217
PVOs (Private voluntary organiza-
   tions) 267, 270

Quézel 173, 174
Quinine 126
Qwa River 81

Radio Nigeria 8, 203
Red Sea coastal deserts 173
Reedbuck, mountain 158
Regs 176
Reparations to Africa 216
Reptiles 36
Rhinoceros 164
Rivers state 9
Roofing: thatched 59; zinc 59
Rome 98
Rural depopulation 98
Rwanda 163

Sahara 158
Saharan vegetation 174
Saharomontane vegetation 176
Saint Thomas Anglican Church 40, 41
Salt pans 176
Samburu 162
San Joaquin Valley 200
Sanitary programs 71
Sauma, Edouard 98
Savanna: fauna and flora of 156;
   origins 152
SCOPE (Scientific Committee on
   Problems of the Environment) 272
Scrub hare 158
Sebkhas 176
Segou Region of Mali 253

Selenium 200
Serengeti 165
Shanty development 260
Shantz, H. L. 156
Shaw, M. T. 222
Sheet erosion 109
Shelton, N. 31
Sheraton 87
Sierra Leone 10, 99
Slash and burn 142; practices 8, 9
Slave trade (transatlantic) 214
Slessor, Mary 47, 48
Smith, G. 158, 217, 220
Soil formation 107; A horizon 109; B horizon 109; C horizon 109
Somalia 10, 95, 99
Soninke 217
South Africa (Republic of) 26
South America 21
Southern Venezuela 155
Species diversity 11
Springbok 158
Stewart, J. 147
Stipa tenacissima 173
Strychnine 126
Strychnos 157
Sudan (the) 95
Sudan-Sahelian office 110
Survey research 147
Sustainable development 243, 243; and water supply 201
Swallowtail (butterflies) 36
Synthetic pesticides 6

Tsetse flies 33
Tsitsikama Coastal 26
Tsitsikama Forest 26
Tuareg 122, 175
Tubu 122
Tunisia 10
Turraeanthus africana PELLEGR. 133

Uapaca BAILL. 133
Uganda 10, 99, 163
Umuago-Urualla 106
Umueze 106
UNCED (United Nations Conference on Environment and Development) 14
UNDP (United Nations Development Programme) 230
UNEP (United Nations Environmental Programme) 229
United Nations 8
UNPAAERD (United Nations Program of Action for African Economic Recovery and Development) 11, 102
Urban growth 98
Uruk Uso 54
USAID (United States Agency for International Development) 229–30, 231
Utu Ikpe 54
Uyo 54

Tai 21
Tanzania 24, 88
Tarrietia utilis SPRAGUE 133
Taylor, Charles 221
Terminalia superba ENGL. et DIELS. 134
Thermodynamics, second law of 172
Thiam, M. 253
Timberlake, L. 35, 37
Tourism 73, 85, 88, 89
Tourism Development Scheme for the Central Region of Ghana (TODSCER) 90
Travis 120
Tsessebe 158

Vaal rhebok 158
Victoria Island 263
Virgin Beach of Bremu Akyinim 93
Volcano 24
Volcans 21
Vultures 47, 48

Wabara, E. 103
Wadis 176
Wall, G. 88
Wallace, P. C. 164
Warthog 158
Water borne diseases 184

Water diversion 12
Water sources and population dis-
    tribution 194
West Africa 40, 106, 220, 244
Western industrialized nations xxi
Western land use practices 24
White, F. 173
Wickins, L. P. 213, 217
Wildebeest 158
Wildlife 21; in Africa 72, 159
Wilkinson, P. F. 26
Witch doctor 163
Wolof 217
Women: and biodiversity 254; and
    conservation/environment 242,
    245, 255; historical domination of
    240; literacy rate 235
Woody plant 152
World Bank 8, 10, 12, 14
World Commission on Environment
    and Development 243
World Food Council (WFC) 116

World Health Organization (WHO)
    163, 269
World health statistics 190, 191, 192
World Resources Institute 135, 147
World Tourism Organization 167, 168

Xeromorphic plants 152

Yangambi 21
Yansane, A. Y. 87

Zaire 34, 163
Zambia 34, 89
Zebra 158
Ziama 21
Zimbabwe 31